Silent Films/Loud Music

Silent Films/Loud Music

New Ways of Listening to and Thinking about Silent Film Music

Phillip Johnston

BLOOMSBURY ACADEMIC
NEW YORK • LONDON • OXFORD • NEW DELHI • SYDNEY

BLOOMSBURY ACADEMIC
Bloomsbury Publishing Inc
1385 Broadway, New York, NY 10018, USA
50 Bedford Square, London, WC1B 3DP, UK
29 Earlsfort Terrace, Dublin 2, Ireland

BLOOMSBURY, BLOOMSBURY ACADEMIC and the Diana logo are trademarks of
Bloomsbury Publishing Plc

First published in the United States of America 2021
This paperback edition published 2023

Copyright © Phillip Johnston, 2021

For legal purposes the Acknowledgments on p. xii constitute an extension of
this copyright page.

Cover design: Louise Dugdale
Cover image © *Trip to the Moon* (1997) by Richard Merkin.
Courtesy of Carrie Haddad Gallery.

All rights reserved. No part of this publication may be reproduced or transmitted
in any form or by any means, electronic or mechanical, including photocopying,
recording, or any information storage or retrieval system, without prior
permission in writing from the publishers.

Bloomsbury Publishing Inc does not have any control over, or responsibility for, any
third-party websites referred to or in this book. All internet addresses given in this
book were correct at the time of going to press. The author and publisher regret
any inconvenience caused if addresses have changed or sites have ceased
to exist, but can accept no responsibility for any such changes.

Whilst every effort has been made to locate copyright holders the publishers
would be grateful to hear from any person(s) not here acknowledged.

Library of Congress Cataloging-in-Publication Data
Names: Johnston, Phillip, author.
Title: Silent films/loud music: new ways of listening to and thinking about silent
film music / Phillip Johnston.
Description: New York: Bloomsbury Academic, 2021. | Includes bibliographical
references and index. |
Summary: "Silent Films/Loud Music discusses contemporary scores for silent film as a
rich vehicle for experimentation in the relationship between music, image, and narrative.
Johnston offers an overview of the early history of music for silent film paired with his
own first-hand view of the craft of creating new original scores for historical silent films:
a unique form crossing musical boundaries of classical, jazz, rock, electronic, and folk.
As the first book completely devoted to the study of contemporary scores for silent film,
it tells the story of the historical and creative evolution of this art form and features an
extended discussion and analysis of some of the most creative works of contemporary
silent film scoring. Johnston draws upon his own career in both contemporary film
music (working with directors Paul Mazursky, Henry Bean, Philip Haas and Doris Dörrie,
among others) and in creating new scores for silent films by Browning, Méliès, Kinugasa,
Murnau & Reiniger. Through this book, Johnston presents a discussion of music for silent
films that contradicts long-held assumptions about what silent film music is and must be,

with thought-provoking implications for both historical and contemporary film music"–Provided by publisher.
Identifiers: LCCN 2021013248 (print) | LCCN 2021013249 (ebook) | ISBN 9781501366406 (hardback) | ISBN 9781501366413 (epub) | ISBN 9781501366420 (pdf) | ISBN 9781501366437
Subjects: LCSH: Silent film music–History and criticism. | Silent film music–Analysis, appreciation.
Classification: LCC ML2075 .J65 2021 (print) | LCC ML2075 (ebook) | DDC 781.5/42–dc23
LC record available at https://lccn.loc.gov/2021013248
LC ebook record available at https://lccn.loc.gov/2021013249

ISBN: HB: 978-1-5013-6640-6
PB: 978-1-5013-6958-2
ePDF: 978-1-5013-6642-0
eBook: 978-1-5013-6641-3

Typeset by Deanta Global Publishing Services, Chennai, India

To find out more about our authors and books visit www.bloomsbury.com and sign up for our newsletters.

To Hilary Bell and Ivy and Moss Johnston.

Contents

List of Illustrations x
Acknowledgments xii
Prelude xiv

1 Music for Silent Films: From Synchronicity to Polysynchronicity 1
2 Scores for Silent Film: Then and Now 27
3 Opportunities in Contemporary Scores for Silent Film 51
4 Contemporary Scores for Silent Film: Four Case Studies 69
5 The Application of Polysynchronicity: Five Case Studies 105
6 Jazzin' the Silents: Jazz and Improvised Music in Contemporary Scores for Silent Film 123
7 Imaginary Authenticity: Scores for Modern Silent Films 139
8 *Wordless!*: Music for Comics and Graphic Novels Turns Time into Space (and Back Again) 161
9 Silent Film Composers Speak! 173

Appendix 1: Scores 187
Appendix 2: Contemporary Composer for Silent Film Interview 198
References 202
Index 211

Illustrations

Figures

4.1–4.2	*Sherlock Jr.* (Keaton/Bruckman, 1924)	70
4.3–4.11	*Sherlock Jr.* (Keaton/Bruckman, 1924)	73
4.12	*The Golem: How He Came into the World* (Wegener/Boese, 1920)	75
4.13	*The Golem DVD* (Black Francis)	79
4.14	*The Golem DVD* (Gary Lucas)	82
4.15	*The General* drum motif (Alloy Orchestra)	86
4.16	*The General* (Keaton/Bruckman, 1926)	88
4.17	*The Passion of Joan of Arc* (Dreyer, 1928)	96
A	Phillip Johnston. *The Unknown* Boston Museum of Fine Arts 1993	101
B	Richard Einhorn, *The Passion of Joan of Arc*	101
C	The Club Foot Orchestra, (L to R) Matt Brubeck, Sheldon Brown, Myles Boisen, Steve Kirk, Chris Grady, Deirdre McClure (back to camera), Catharine Clune, Elliot Kavee, Nik Phelps, Beth Custer, Richard Marriott	102
D	Alloy Orchestra (L to R): Roger Miller, Terry Donahue, Ken Winokur	102
E	Blue Grassy Knoll. (L to R) Gus Macmillan, Phil McLeod, Simon Barfoot, Mark Elton, Steph O'Hara	103
F	Gary Lucas, performing his score for *The Golem*	103
5.1	*Money Man* (Haas, 1992)	106
5.2	*Money Man* (Haas, 1992)	107
5.3	*The Unknown* (Browning, 1927)	109
5.4	*The Unknown* (Browning, 1927)	110
5.5	*La danse au feu* (Méliès, 1899)	111
5.6	*La mélomane* (Méliès, 1903)	111
5.7	*Hydrothérapie fantastique* (*The Doctor's Secret*) (Méliès, 1909)	112
5.8	*Page of Madness* (*Kinugasa*, 1926)	114
5.9	*Faust* (Murnau, 1926)	119
5.10	*Faust* (Murnau, 1926)	119

8.1	*Crime Does Not Pay* #42 (PD)	162
8.2	Comic book collage for concert version of *Drawn to Death* (2000)	163
8.3	Poster image for *Wordless!* (2013)	164
8.4	Excerpt from bass part for *The Parade* (Lewin, 1957)	165
8.5	*Plastic Man* #18 (PD)	170

Tables

3.1	*Marvelous Méliès* Analysis	58
3.2	*Ballerinas from Hell* Analysis	59
3.3	*Méliès the Magician* Analysis	60
3.4	*First Wizard of Cinema* Analysis	61
3.5	*Wild and Weird* Analysis	61
3.6	*Air* Analysis	62
4.1	Club Foot Orchestra, Scene Change Sequence (*Sherlock Jr.*)	72
4.2	Blue Grassy Knoll, Scene Change Sequence (*Sherlock Jr.*)	74
4.3	Uses of "The Miriam and Florian Theme" (*The Golem*)	78
4.4	Use of Motivic Material and Application of Tempo Changes (*The General*)	88
4.5	Interaction Between Visuals, Text, Music, and Song Lyrics (*The Passion of Joan of Arc*)	93
4.6	Tracking Parallel Narratives (*The Passion of Joan of Arc*)	94
8.1	Interactions of Genre and Film Scoring Techniques (*Wordless!*)	169

Acknowledgments

I extend my thanks to Rick Altman, Gillian B. Anderson, Emilio Audissino, Australian Institute of Music, Black Francis, Andy Caploe, Julian Curwin, K. J. Donnelly, Michael Dorf, Film Society of Lincoln Center, Hannah Fink, Joel Forrester, Krin Gabbard, Claudia Gorbman, Tom Gunning, Richard Hermitage, Roberto Illiano, Gary Lucas, Tim Kennedy, Guy Maddin, Nadia Margolis, Ben Marshall, Philip Matthias, Sayre Maxfield, Elizabeth McMahon, Kathryn Millard, Museum of Modern Art, Music and the Moving Image, Newcastle Conservatorium, Lena Petersen and The Carrie Hadad Gallery, Mark Ribot, Ron Sadoff, David Schwartz, Art Spiegelman, Colin Spiers, Lloyd Swanton, Sydney Conservatorium, Richard Vella, Jordan Verzar, Jason Weiss, Emile Wennekes, Greg White, James Wierzbicki, Christian Zabala, John Zorn, and all of the great musicians who have performed music for silent films with me.

Thanks to Hilary and Ivy for proofreading, editing, patience and encouragement, warding off despair.

Permissions

Interviews

Heartfelt thanks to the silent film score composers interviewed in Chapter 9 (and their thoughts are scattered elsewhere throughout the book): Richard Einhorn, Gus Macmillan, Richard Marriott, and Ken Winokur, and all the members of the bands Blue Grassy Knoll, the Club Foot Orchestra, and the Alloy Orchestra.

And only love to all film music composers everywhere, silent or otherwise.

Text

Lyrics (songs from *The Golem*), by kind permission of Black Francis and Songs Of Universal, Inc. on behalf of Lone Child Music, Universal Music Publishing.

Lyrics (songs from *Faust*) by Hilary Bell, by kind permission of APRA.

Latin lyrics (from *Passion of Joan of Arc*) translated by Latin scholar Peter Marshall, used by generous permission of Nadia Margolis.

Previous Publication

Parts of Chapter 5 were previously published in altered form in *Screen Sound Journal* n3, 2012, as "The Polysynchronous Film Score: Songs for a Contemporary Score for F.W. Murnau's *Faust* (1926)," used by permission.

Chapter 6 was published in altered form as "Jazzin' The Silents: Jazz and Improvised Music in Contemporary Scores for Silent Film" in *Cinema Changes: Incorporations of Jazz in the Film Soundtrack*, edited by Emile Wennekes and Emilio Audissino, Turnhout, Brepols, 2019 (Speculum Musicae, 34). Used by permission.

Chapter 8 was originally published (in altered form) in *Southerly* Number 76.1, 2016, as "*Wordless*! Music for Comics and Graphic Novels Turns Time into Space (and Back Again)," used by permission.

Prelude

In 1991, a friend[1] told me that a band that I had known when I lived in San Francisco in the 1970s, the Club Foot Orchestra, had performed new original music for Robert Wiene's 1920 silent[2] film *The Cabinet of Dr Caligari*. He said, "That would be a good job for you." He was right.

I had always loved silent films, from watching them on daytime television as a child to going to repertory houses, like San Francisco's Intersection Theater (which featured readings by Beat poets when they weren't showing silent films) and New York's Elgin Theater (where the Hells Angels would come into daytime shows and clear out two rows so they could watch Buster Keaton films). Listening to film music soundtrack recordings had been one of my biggest influences as a composer; because my instrumental music was as much influenced by composers like Bernard Herrmann, Ennio Morricone, and Nino Rota as Thelonious Monk, Kurt Weill, and Don van Vliet, people would often comment that my music sounded like film music, long before I scored my first film. By the early 1990s, I had been working as a composer for contemporary films since Lynne Tillman and Shelia McLaughlin's *Committed* (1984) and had recently scored films including Doris Dörrie's *Geld* (1989) and Philip Haas's film of Paul Auster's novel *The Music of Chance* (1993). Having one foot in the world of film scoring and one foot in the world of jazz and New Music,[3] I had found an area where these two worlds could collide.

We approached the American Museum of the Moving Image about a commission, and Head of Film and Video David Schwartz decided to make it a festival, bringing in other artists associated with the Knitting Factory, curated by artistic director Michael Dorf. This became the 1993 festival called Silent Movies/Loud Music,[4] featuring scores for silent films performed live by Samm Bennett, Tom Cora, Christine Baczewska, Amy Denio, Don Byron, and myself. I chose Tod Browning's 1927 film *The Unknown*, starring Lon Chaney and Joan Crawford.[5] That concert was a success, showcasing a fascinating variety of approaches to music and film, and while it wasn't the first to combine contemporary music and silent film, it was part of the early years of an art form that has been developing, expanding, and growing ever since. Today, film, music, and arts festivals around the world show early films with new scores composed or improvised for them, and there are a number of silent film festivals that routinely feature live performances of music and film. The styles vary from historical recreations to classical, jazz, folk, electronic, and freely improvised scores and vary from solo performers to full orchestras.

However, serious discussion and analysis of this vital art form are still relatively rare. Critical writing about these performances consists mostly of a few reviews of performances, with a couple of notable exceptions.[6] And this discussion has rich possibilities, as it inherently has implications for a number of areas—not only issues around contemporary silent film music but for contemporary sound film music, and for the relationship between music and image/narrative more broadly. The existing discussion of these performances usually focuses on two issues. The first is their relationship to what many filmgoers think of as traditional/historical silent film music. That is to say, both audiences and critics have certain ideas about what musical accompaniment for films was like in the early era of film, and they tend to react to any contemporary score, positively or negatively, in terms of how it compares to their conceptions of these early scores. That many of these conceptions vary quite a bit from what researchers now know about the practice of historical silent film accompaniment (and much is unknown) explains the truism of the out-of-tune spinet playing selections of solo ragtime piano to accompany sped-up figures in shadowy black-and-white. The discussion often focuses principally on the impact that certain stylistic choices, such as the juxtaposition of rock or electronic music, have on a 100-plus-year-old film. The second issue is that film music, whether for silent or sound films, is often assessed primarily on the basis of how well it "supports" the narrative. Virtually all instructional texts on film scoring repeat this mantra that the music's primary, even exclusive, duty is to "tell the story." Film composer Hans Zimmer emphatically asserts that "At the end of the day I can tell you everything you need to know in one word: Story. Stick with the story. Figure out the story. Stick with the story like glue."[7] This is not to say that the history of film music is not rife with the brilliant, the imaginative, and the obscure when it comes to musical storytelling: the art form continues to evolve in conception, technique, and execution. And as the study of film music has produced a rich literature of interpretation of film music practices and philosophy, there is language both literary and musicological for a nuanced discussion of the role of music in film. However, film music scholarship is a niche pursuit, and I would suggest that assumptions are still deeply rooted and that the contemporary music for silent film is a rich area for investigation of this relationship. As Marco Bellano writes, "notwithstanding the relevant differences in the way silent cinema is today received and understood by audiences" that composers still "develop audiovisual devices which seem identical to the ones used by historical composers, on a theoretical level."[8] Tim Anderson, in evoking Tom Gunning's concept of "the cinema of attractions," writes that "cinema before 1908 presented diverse terrain where style and aesthetics were employed not only to deliver stories but also to *display* attractions that escaped the demands of formal narrative structures."[9] If one accepts the idea that the early history of film alternatively contains both spectacle *and* narrative, then the consensus is that narrative won the war, as spectacle faded into more specialized types of genre films. However, the distinction between these two approaches never made the leap into the discussion of the role of music in film. Film music became more and more firmly linked to its responsibility for conveying narrative.

But is this the only relationship that music can have with film? I'd like to suggest that the pre-synch-sound era of film can be viewed, not as the early training-wheels prelude to a more sophisticated and highly evolved version of itself which is the sound era, but rather as a distinct art form, which even in its most narrative form retained a certain degree of spectacle. And that in the same way that other senses sharpen when one of them is taken away at birth or by accident, silent films can sometimes be more lush, more voluptuous, more abstract, more expressive than sound films, and the music that is paired with them automatically takes on a more intimate and transformative role. What we do surmise about the early history of silent film music is that the earliest accompaniments for silent film were improvised.[10] But there is virtually no documentation of these early scores, which were improvised based on diverse traditions and techniques. The desire of critics, producers, and audiences for greater control over the relationship between film and music led first to the creation of cue books, and then to compiled scores[11] and finally to original scores composed completely or in part for a particular film. The relationship between music and film went from a virtual Wild West of infinite possibilities, through increasing degrees of formalization, ultimately to, in the sound era, one score for one film. Regardless of quality, it was the same, unchanging, forever: complete control.

In the time since "music for film" became "music for narrative film," the conversation about the relationship between music and film has often centered on the dichotomy between *synchronous* and *asynchronous* film scoring. *Synchronous* film scoring refers to music which closely follows the narrative and the dramatic beats of the film, in other words, what we hear most often. *Asynchronous* film scoring is music that provides subtext, music that tells us something different than what we see on the screen at first glance, and/or provides significant additional information. Clearly, this description of synchronicity is both a generalization and an oversimplification, and composers for film have written scores containing brilliant and subtle reinventions of the music/narrative relationship and continue to do so. And academic writers about film music have posited diverse frameworks for interpretation, which I will discuss further in Chapter 1 and beyond. However, like Elmer Fudd stretching a giant rubber band, the discourse, theoretical or practical, has a tendency to keep snapping back to this synchronous/asynchronous duality, generally in fealty to "story." However, interpreting the "original meaning" of a 100-year-old film is not an easy task. We can never see a historical film through the eyes of a contemporaneous audience, or of the creator for that matter. Using known scores as models is unreliable, because as anyone who has worked in the contemporary film industry knows all too well, the road from conception to what ends up on the screen—not just in music, but also in screenwriting, acting, editing, even color correction—is one that contains as many potholes as it does yellow bricks. In a sense, any discussion of musical synchronicity is moot: synchronous to what? What do we see literally on screen at any one moment? The speed at which objects are moving? The moral, political, philosophical, or professional point of view that we feel is being expressed, and its similarity or dissimilarity to our own? What we feel is "the story"? What we imagine was the director's original intent? In a sound film, where the picture/narrative is eternally locked to one score, it is questionable to talk of the film's meaning and the music separately: the music is part of a fabric of elements that create meaning in "the film" as a whole.[12] However, in the case of the silent film, with even the possibility of separating the music and the picture, the entire equation changes, and the film's meaning remains eternally fluid, to be made new with the introduction of different music and sound.

In so many contemporary film scores, silent or sound, despite the substitution of rock music or electronic music or indie-rock songs for a traditional symphony orchestra, for the most part, the *relationship* between music and film usually remains essentially the same. For a chase scene, instead of fast and frantic ragtime, we hear fast and frantic electronic dance music: the music's genre has changed, but its function hasn't. It is easy to understand why not, because the commercial and practical pressures on composers remain the same: to tell the story. And there are numerous issues which conspire to make the current commercial or independent film a less likely locale for music/film experimentation. However, there are works that investigate possibilities for alternative relationships between music and film image/narrative. In order to discuss some of these possibilities, I will introduce the term "polysynchronous," which will be discussed in more detail toward the end of Chapter 1. The use of this neologism is not only to suggest an alternative to the dichotomy of the terms synchronous and asynchronous but also to create a category that includes a wider variety of more unorthodox film music practices. In defining polysynchronicity, my intent is to emphasize the "poly," not the "synchronicity." It is not intended to mark off the borders of polysynchronicity as a separate country but, rather, to suggest the investigation of places *outside* of synchronous/asynchronous, places which just don't quite fit the usual terms of analysis or expectation. Some of the scores I write about here could be called nonsynchronous, or hyper-synchronous, or simply "odd." But I will suggest the use of the term "polysynchronicity" here not as a lock but as a key.

The wide-open spaces of silent film—ironically, that is to say, a film which has music throughout, rather than the short cues of most contemporary sound films—are hospitable to extended improvisation and composition. These spaces are further expanded by the elimination of the need to avoid competition with dialogue and other film sound (sound effects/sound design). In a contemporary score for silent film, the entire sound field is left to the music. Music, being the only inhabitant of the audio field experienced by the audience, assumes an outsized role and is not only supplying narrative and semiotic information but also "is the communicating link between the screen and the audience, reaching out and developing all into one single experience."[13] The absence of a living director also gives the composer/musician an element of freedom that is rarely present in the contemporary commercial film production environment. Of course, filmmaking is collaboration across many fields: the contemporary score for silent film is not *better* or necessarily freer or more original, but it *is* different. Since the beginning of film scoring, composers have sometimes grumbled about decisions made by directors, though usually ruefully conceding the gospel of film music: that its fundamental obligation is to support one narrative. Yet scoring a film that is circa 100 years old situates the project squarely in the realm of art music, and even more so, in the realm of multimedia/happenings. The contemporary score for silent film is no longer a film with the "background music" performed live, but rather a living kinetic dialogue between artists and across centuries. Composer Ed Hughes writes of one project that "the intervention of the music . . . seemed to open out the possibility of a different kind of counterpoint and mode of appreciation, akin to reflective points in an opera."[14] This art form contains multitudes.

Sometime during the mid-1970s, I attended a concert of a solo pianist accompanying silent films. The pianist was Joel Forrester, and the concert took place in a fourth-floor loft on the Bowery in New York City, where Forrester lived with his wife. On a rickety screen, the films were shown on a projector in the large open space, and the audience was made up of musicians, friends, and neighbors. It was just the kind of "potentially disruptive and heterogeneous space of spectacle and distraction"[15] like the early nickelodeons that Anderson describes as the home of "jackass music."[16] That night, Forrester (who has made a substantial side-career of silent film accompaniment to his main occupation as a performing jazz pianist and band-leader) made Murnau's *Nosferatu* (1922) into a comedy, and a Laurel and Hardy film into a horror movie, with the music he created from a combination of spontaneous improvisation and the improvised application of his own compositions. While I had hitherto been aware of the power of screen music to shape an audience's perception of a film's narrative and the meaning of its images, this performance brought home to me two ideas in a visceral way: that the composer of music for a silent film is able to reinvent the film, and a historical silent film is not a static relic but rather a fluid set of meanings that can continue to have a new life with the addition of new musical collaborators.

Today we are still at the beginning of a fascinating new art form: contemporary scores for silent film. This form is distinct from a film-with-background-music: it brings film back to its original heritage as spectacle, allows every film to have many scores, and also helps the first thirty years of thrilling, terrifying, and heartbreaking films to continue to live, to be fresh, and to evolve. It doesn't *replace* the art form of more conventional soundtracks for silent films, historical or otherwise, nor does it draw a solid line between these scores and more unorthodox ones. Each score is beautiful in its own way. But the contemporary score for silent film, both recorded, and, at its best, in live performance, is a distinct art form which must be assessed on its own merits, independent of previous conceptions of the relationship between music and film. This form offers rich opportunities on multiple levels for explorations of polysynchronicity in film music. And these explorations can contribute to the overall body of work that is contemporary film music.

This book does not give an all-inclusive portrait of the state of contemporary music for silent film today, nor does it give a complete summary of contemporary film music scholarship. Rather, it represents an investigation of *some* of the possibilities inherent in a reexamination of some widely held beliefs about what film music is and can be, and a suggestion that the art form of contemporary scores for silent film represents a rich opportunity for experiments and alternatives. However, in order to contextualize what is to some degree a series of case studies, it is necessary to acquaint the reader with a foundation which gives an overview of a series of topics, which have been treated in greater detail by others. These include a history of both silent and sound film music theory and practice, as well as analytical frameworks, professional techniques and music theory, and some historical storytelling. After laying down this foundation in this introduction and the first two chapters, the next three chapters show the application of these ideas in a series of case studies of work by both myself and others. This is followed by three slightly more obliquely related chapters that relate to my own interests and practice: the application of jazz and improvised music to silent film scores, scores for new silent films created over the last twenty-five years or so, and music for comics/comix. The relevance of this last will become apparent, but here I will just say that I think music for comics and graphic novels will be, in different forms, an exciting new area of multimedia that has literally just begun. Finally, the book ends by allowing contemporary composers for silent film, who have been silent until now, to speak for themselves.

Ultimately, this is a book by a practitioner suggesting that, for analysts of both film and music (both critical and academic), and for practitioners and audiences (of both film and film music), there is value in examining the relationship between film and music without taking all of the widely held assumptions at face value. Its primary purpose is simple: to describe a different way of experiencing and assessing film music and to demonstrate why the contemporary score for silent film is a particularly rich environment for the exploration of new relationships between film and music. I suggest that this diverse collection of film scores can be loosely gathered under the umbrella term "polysynchronicity," and I try to illustrate the ways in which composers and musicians are already exploring this relationship in both sound and silent films. I also hope that it can act as an invitation to composers who are looking for "perennial sources of inspiration."[17] This approach does have pertinence to both historical and contemporary films, but, as I hope to persuade you, a contemporary score for a silent film can be more than background music for a historical curiosity; rather, it can be a partner in a new combined performative spectacle that reinvents the most basic assumptions regarding the relationship between music and image/narrative.

One final caveat: while I refer throughout the book to both the pleasures and challenges of live performance in the presentation of contemporary scores for silent film and have happily been a frequent practitioner of this craft for over twenty-five years,[18] I don't examine the issue of performativity and stagecraft in depth here. The reason is that, by necessity, I have examined almost all of the scores discussed here on DVD, and, for that reason, I focus here for the most part on composition rather than performance. While silent film music performance is a fascinating topic worthy of deeper discussion, I will have to save in-depth discussion of it mostly for a future time; however, for some discussion of it by practitioners, see Chapter 9.

Notes

1 It was Andy Caploe, who was my manager, booking agent, and friend at the time.
2 The usefulness of the term "silent film" is questioned by some, and one can see the statement "silent films were never silent" used to mean a variety of different things throughout the literature. (The same can be said of the term "sound film.") However, as a shorthand to indicate films with no synchronized soundtrack, both historical and contemporary, I have been unable to find any alternative that doesn't feel cumbersome or artificial. So this is a trigger warning that I will be using the term "silent film" throughout this book, with the full acknowledgment of its limitations.
3 Among others, with my bands the Microscopic Septet and the Public Servants.
4 From which I drew the title of this book: thank you, Michael.
5 Thanks to filmmaker Tim Kennedy, who drew my attention to the collaborations of Tod Browning and Lon Chaney: *The Unknown* (1927), *London After Midnight* (1927), *West of Zanzibar* (1928), and *The Unholy Three* (1925/1930), his final film.
6 Claus Tieber and Anna Windisch, *The Sounds of Silent Films: New Perspectives on History, Theory and Practice* (New York and Hampshire: Palgrave Macmillan, 2014) and *Today's Sounds for Yesterday's Films: Making Music for Silent Cinema*, ed. K.J. Donnely and Ann-Kristin Wallengren (UK: Palgrave Macmillan, 2016).
7 Hans Zimmer, "Hans Zimmer Teaches Film Scoring," Masterclass.com, accessed May 5, 2019, https://www.masterclass.com/classes/hans-zimmer-teaches-film-scoring.com.
8 Marco Bellano, "Silent Strategies: Audiovisual Functions of the Music for Silent Cinema," *Kieler Beiträge zur Filmmusikforschung* 9 (2013), 48–9.

9. Tim Anderson, "Reforming 'Jackass Music': The Problematic Aesthetics of Early American Film Music Accompaniment," in *The Movie Music Reader*, ed. Kay Dickinson (London: Routledge, 2003).
10. Also, "from theater to theater, many different musicians worked on the same single silent picture. As a result, each film could have many different 'scores.'" Marco Bellano, "The Tradition of Novelty—Comparative Studies of Silent Film Scores: Perspectives, Challenges, Proposals," in *The Sounds of Silent Films: New Perspectives on History, Theory and Practice,* ed. Claus Tieber and Anna Katharina Windisch (New York and Hampshire: Palgrave Macmillan, 2014), 208–20.
11. *Cue books* are collections of suggested music, organized by use, for film musicians and music directors, often collected and/or composed by well-known silent film musicians/composers. *Compiled scores* are specific lists of precomposed music that give a musician or theater music director a guide to specific pieces of music to play along with each scene of the film. See Chapter 2 for further discussion of these and other silent film era techniques.
12. See Audissino's discussion of Neo-formalism and the "form/content split" in Emilio Audissino, *Film Music Analysis: A Film Studies Approach* (Southampton, UK: Palgrave, 2017), 46–7, 69.
13. Bernard Hermann, "Music in Films—A Rebuttal," in *The Routledge Film Music Sourcebook*, ed. James Wierzbicki, Nathan Platte and Colin Roust (New York and London: Routledge, 2012), 117–19.
14. Ed Hughes, "Silent Film, Live Music and Contemporary Composition," in *Today's Sounds for Yesterday's Films*, 189.
15. Anderson, "Reforming Jackass Music," 49.
16. Louis Reeves Harrison, "Jackass Music," *Moving Picture World* 8, no. 3 (January 21, 1911), 124–5, reprinted in *The Routledge Film Music Sourcebook*, ed. James Wierzbicki, Nathan Platte, and Colin Roust (New York and London: Routledge, 2012), 11–16.
17. Bellano, "The Tradition of Novelty," 213.
18. In fact, for copyright reasons, as of this writing, none of my scores have been released with the film, though many of them have been recorded professionally and released on CD: in synchronization with the films, they have been, and can still *only* be, heard live.

1

Music for Silent Films

From Synchronicity to Polysynchronicity

Of the music of the silent film era overall, more is known about general practices than about specific musical performances. The few complete notated scores that survive, mostly from the later years of that period, present only a partial record of the music for films, both notated and non-notated, composed and improvised, that would have been performed. The exact content of the vast body of work of improvised scores for historical silent films created by both professionals and inspired amateurs is lost forever.[1]

Silent film music scholar Rick Altman writes,

> Not only are the performances themselves forever lost, but even their traces. . . . Many original performances were improvised and thus from the start lacked a written record. Where sheet music was used, it has by and large gone the way of other cheaply produced century-old paper documents. Even when the printed music remains, we rarely know when it was used, how it was performed and what its relationship was to which film(s).[2]

The foundational assumptions of these scores regarding the relationship between music and narrative/image were established in the pre-film era of melodrama, magic shows, opera, and dance. They were further developed in the specific context of silent film and then evolved in a related form in the era of synchronized sound that is generally regarded as beginning with *The Jazz Singer* (1927). Many film music practices, such as the use of leitmotif and the mirroring of narrative, have continued largely intact since the late nineteenth century.

Over the last thirty years, the practice of contemporary composers of all genres creating new scores for early films has grown into a rich and diverse new art form, ranging from the historical to the avant-garde. However, the vast majority of these scores adhere, in differing degrees, to century-old tropes in terms of the relationship between film and music. While composers for contemporary sound film have a variety of concerns, contemporary composers for silent film inherently have greater freedom to experiment with this music/film relationship at its most basic level. There is a palpable excitement being generated in the art form by these possibilities, and later in this chapter, I will introduce the term "polysynchronicity" in order to discuss the possibilities and the wider opportunities that lie therein. While the polymorphous perversity of these investigations questions some of these tropes on multiple levels, one must begin with the Romulus and Remus of academic and critical film discourse, synchronicity, and asynchronicity.

Synchronicity and Asynchronicity

The term "synchronous" film score, which still describes the most common model in both commercial Hollywood and independent films, refers to a relationship between the music and the image/narrative whereby that which is on the screen is being reinforced or echoed by the music. This approach has also been referred to as *parallelism*.[3] When the scene is a "sad" scene in narrative terms, the music will have qualities that have become popularly associated with sadness: slow tempo, minor key, and wide vibrato.[4] The *asynchronous* model involves music that provides information that is in one way or another different from what is apparent in the image/narrative, appearing to function in a contradictory manner, or at the very least to add additional subtext. One oft-cited example of this approach is Oliver Stone's use of Samuel Barber's "Adagio for Strings" in the opening of *Platoon* (1986), in which a slow minor-key string quartet accompanies a scene of men going off to the war in Vietnam. The melancholy mood of the music contradicts the convention of martial snare drums and brass that had historically accompanied such scenes in "classical film scoring" (cf. Gorbman, to follow) that imply that war is a glorious affair (at least at the beginning of a film). The unexpected music creates a mood that would not have been there without it (until we see the body bags anyway). Another example of asynchronicity, in which additional information is added, is Francis Ford Coppola's use of Pietro Mascagni's "Cavalleria Rusticana" in the final murder scenes of *The Godfather, Part III* (1990). On the most basic level, the "high culture" implication of the Corleone family sitting at the opera in beautiful clothing is contrasted to the low culture being intercut of their enemies being slaughtered in the streets by thugs, though this is a more complex use of *licensed music*.[5] But although the asynchronous approach opens a rich field of new associations, it nevertheless adopts the same *perspective* as the synchronous as the choice of music expresses the director's intent of a primary narrative, and that the music is defined strictly in terms of its relationship to that narrative.

Gregg Redner's *Deleuze and Film Music* cites the development, concurrent with the development of synchronized sound, of two "concurrent, but aesthetically- and theoretically-divergent"[6] courses: parallelism and counterpoint, which roughly coincide with the terms "synchronous" and "asynchronous," as explained earlier. However, Nicholas Cook, in *Analysing Musical Multimedia*, sees them as two sides of the same coin, the second being a mere inversion of the first as long as the second is still dependent on the image.[7] He posits a third relationship, that of being *complementary*, which I interpret to mean juxtaposition ("the two media are complementary but the film is primary").[8] But the description is not definitive, and he moves on to Kathryn Kalinak's argument that the problem with classical theory is that music and film are considered separately: "the assumption that meaning is contained in the visual image and music either reinforces or alters what is already there."[9] For them, the idea of film itself is unitary, music being only a component of the whole. Herrmann's music for *Psycho* (1960) doesn't amplify tension, it creates it. However, in the case of silent film, the music is not inextricably part the silent film; even when music is written to be performed live, it is inherently separate.[10]

Foundations of Film Music Analysis

It is worth recounting here Claudia Gorbman's influential "Principals of Composition: Classical Film Music: Principles of Composition, Mixing and Editing" (1987): (i) *invisibility*: the technical apparatus of non-diegetic[11] music must not be visible; (ii) *inaudibility*: music is not meant to be heard consciously. As such it should subordinate itself to dialogue, to visuals—that is, to the primary vehicles of the narrative; (iii) *signifier of emotion*: soundtrack music may set specific moods and emphasize particular emotions suggested in the narrative (cf. #IV), but first and foremost, it is a signifier of emotion itself; (iv) *narrative cueing/referential narrative*: music gives referential and narrative cues, for example, indicating point of view, supplying formal demarcations, and establishing setting and characters, and *connotative*: music "interprets" and "illustrates" narrative events; (v) *continuity*: music provides formal and rhythmic continuity—between shots, in transitions between scenes, by filling "gaps," (vi) *unity*: via repetition and variation of musical material and instrumentation, music aids in the construction of formal and narrative unity; and (vii) a given film score may violate any of the aforementioned principles, providing the violation is at the service of the other principles.[12] Later she writes:

> The danger of dwelling on the "classical Hollywood model" of film scoring is that it might give the erroneous impression of uniformity and sameness in studio era film music. The model must not prevent us from seeing the enormous variety of musical discourses and figures it was able to encompass. However unconventional or avant-garde a Hollywood musical score might be, *the film always motivates it in conventional ways.* [my italics] Thus, there is little that's progressive or subversive about jazz in the milieu of drug addiction in *The Man With The Golden Arm*, the electronic sounds that waft over the strange *Forbidden Planet*, or the electronically generated music complicit with the alcoholic dementia of Ray Milland in *The Lost Weekend*. David Bordwell in fact cites *Hangover Square*'s score to argue for Hollywood's capacity for "non-disruptive differentiation," as the film's discordant music is narratively motivated by its connection to a deranged character.[13]

Writers who approach film music more from a psychological vantage point, rather than a historical/procedural one, offer comparable analyses.[14] Annabel J. Cohen gives what she calls the congruence-associationist framework for understanding film music communications in her *Music as a Source of Emotion in Film*:

1. Music masks extraneous noises.
2. It provides continuity between shots.
3. It directs attention to important features of the screen through structural or associationist congruence.
4. When unassociated with a particular focus, it induces mood, as often occurs during the opening credits of a film.
5. It communicates meaning and furthers the narrative, especially in ambiguous situations.
6. Through association in memory, music becomes integrated with the film and enables the symbolization of past and future events through the technique of *leitmotif*.

7. Music heightens the sense of reality of or absorption in a film, perhaps by augmenting arousal, and increasing attention to the entire film context and inattention to everything else.
8. Music as an art form adds to the aesthetic effect of the film [my paraphrase].[15]

These rules function as psychological corollary to Gorbman's "Classical Principles," but, taken together, they illustrate a foundational overview of the "classical" model of the functional role of film music, from both a critical and a psychological viewpoint.

In *Hearing Film: Tracking Identifications in Contemporary Hollywood Film Music*, Anahid Kassabian acknowledges the dichotomy of synchronicity versus asynchronicity: "Since the early history of film, film scholars have attempted to describe the possible relationships between music and visuals. Historically, film theorists generally relegated the music to one of two possibilities: parallelism or counterpoint."[16] These rules-after-the-fact affirm not only the synchronous/asynchronous dichotomy but also many of the other foundational assumptions about the relationship between music and film that have been carried from the silent film era into the sound film era, such as "inaudibility," the audience's "absorption in the film," and the priority of narrative. David Neumeyer and James Buhler affirm,

> [The basic assumption is that] music runs parallel to the image track, which, on a theoretical level, can be conceived as a sort of "super-libretto" to the music. Thus, we can focus on music while acknowledging that it (like all of film sound) remains subordinate to the image.[17]

Film music is thus left with three essential tenets:

1. The relationship between music and film most often adheres to basic formulas that have continued more or less unquestioned since the silent film era.
2. Both critical analysis and professional practice still continue to default to dividing the music-film relationship into two categories: synchronous and asynchronous.
3. There is both a tacit and an explicit belief that the exclusive function of music in *all* films is to support the director's expression of a narrative.

Redner[18] gives a very succinct summation of the historical development of critical writing about film music. He begins by positing three overall approaches, which he characterizes as: the commodification of music (Marxist), musical analysis, and film theory. He goes on to describe four phases in the evolution of critical writing about film music:

1. Early film music literature (1909–26)—practical issues of performance and arrangement
2. The age of monaural sound (1927–56)—parallel versus counterpoint
3. The age of stereo sound (1957–86)—technical (compositional techniques, scoring, recording, and mixing), a branch of parallelism
4. Theory comes to film music literature (1987–98) (Gorbman/Chion/Cook)[19]

Describing the history of film style, Davison says, "Although the specific devices of film style have changed over time (through technological development, for example), the more abstract systems governing the use of these devices (in particular narrative causality, the representation of space, and time) and the interrelations between these systems endured."[20] I'd like to suggest that film music practices have followed a similar pattern. However, experimental or avant-garde filmmakers have long experimented with the relationship between music and film in unexpected ways. Beginning with early European avant-garde films such as Clair's *Entr'acte* (1924, music by Erik Satie) and Léger's *Ballet Mécanique* (1923–4, music by George Antheil), through the 1960s experimental filmmakers (Stan Brakhage, Jack Smith, Kenneth Anger, Hollis Frampton, Tony Conrad, and Michael Snow, among others), and into the digital age, filmmakers and composers have investigated approaches to the music-image relationship ranging from no music to minimalism to maximalism and beyond.[21] In fact, Michael Snow's comments about the music in his film *New York Eye and Ear Control* (1964) (by free jazz saxophonist Albert Ayler and others) reflect some of the ideas discussed here.

> It's like the music is a particular kind of experience, and the film is something quite different that you see simultaneously. That's why the title, *New York Eye and Ear Control*: it was actually being able to hear the music and being able to see the picture without the music saying, This image is sad, or this image is happy—which is a way that movie music is always used. I really wanted it to be possible that you could hear them. So, they're very, very different. It's as if the image part of it is very classical and static. In fact, most of the motion is in the music, actually. So, they're kind of counterpointing and being in their own worlds, but happening simultaneously.[22]

This book focuses on the relationship between music and *narrative* film. But some of the experiments that have been introduced in the world of avant-garde film provide useful material to be applied to the exploration of narrative film music, and particularly to contemporary scores for silent film. This is not to say that there has been no critical writing suggesting contradictions to this dualistic view and questioning Gorbman's "Principles." Jeff Smith's "Unheard melodies? A Critique of Psychoanalytic Theories of Film Music" begins by challenging the *unheard* thread of Gorbman's thesis, although as soon as he begins his argument, he begins by categorizing examples into what are clearly parallelism and counterpoint.[23] In the more recent *Film/Music Analysis*, Emilio Audissino confronts the duality head on:

> First of all, counterpoint in music does not mean a struggle between two melodies that have nothing to do with each other. Counterpoint is the interweaving of two melodic lines having two distinct characters but being in a harmonic and rhythmic fusion. Using "counterpoint" to say that music and visuals are in sharp contrast is not quite right correct.[24]

He quotes Kalinak, attributing this to a "visual bias" of film studies: "Sound was divided according to its function in relation to the image: either parallelism or in counterpoint to the visual image."[25] He attributes this same limitation to "comment"/parallelism: assuming that music is "subsidiary to the visuals," where "in both cases, no real interaction and mutual influence is implied."[26] He goes on to attribute the psychoanalytic theory of film music as an innate prejudice against parallelism, preferencing music that "adds" to the film as superior.

The arguments against the terms "synchronous" and "asynchronous" first recognize them as an accepted trope and second affirm their inadequacy, with which I wholeheartedly agree.

In advocating the "neo-formalist" approach to film/music analysis, Audissino invokes Ben Winters's terminology of "intra-diegetic"[27] to replace the older term "non-diegetic" or underscore, claiming that underscore music cannot be separated from the film, and that to discuss the music and the film as separate elements is an essentially flawed paradigm. His argument posits music as one essential element of the "film" as whole, like camerawork, editing, screenwriting, etc. and to discuss it as being synchronous or asynchronous is akin to saying the screenplay is in contradiction to the film.

However, this point of view only confirms the idea that a live performance (or even a recorded/documented one) of a contemporary score with a silent film is inherently a new event. The score is now "separate" from the film and can be analyzed as such, because it was composed long after the original film was completed and is part of a distinct performance event, differing in nature from the original, because the experience of the film, with this score, is a separate work—the film itself cannot be described as "containing" the score. Whether the "original" historic score can be discussed in these terms is in doubt as well, because even films with a commissioned score that was performed live with it in its own time were often performed with multiple scores. (*Birth of a Nation* is a perfect example, having premiered with a different score on the East and West coasts.) Thus, a new score can only be judged on its own terms, not on the original film's (as conceived by an individual viewer), because the event in question is not the film, but, rather, a new event combining both film and score for that particular moment. Ultimately, synchronous sound/music is only what it says: sound that "appears" to be synchronized and asynchronous music vice versa. Once music is juxtaposed with film, whether permanently or only for a brief instant in time, then it is *synchronized* with it. And, as K.J. Donnelly points out, "matching or not matching sound and image (so-called parallel and counterpoint) might be construed as different ways of thinking."[28] Guitarist Marc Ribot says, "(I recall one of the Lurie brothers saying) 'the truth of film composing is that every piece of music works with every piece of film....' But the other half of that truth is that every piece of music *changes* every piece of film. And that's a big responsibility."[29]

Alternative Film Music Thought in Early Film

From the early era of film, Russian filmmaker Sergei Eisenstein was questioning its most fundamental tenets and practices. "Eisenstein believed in the necessity to establish a genre of 'sound-film' in which the music and the images were governed by an interdependent audio-visual structure far more sophisticated than the formulaic approach to scoring already prevalent in the popular film industry."[30] In his book *The Film Sense*,[31] Eisenstein refers to the equivalences of music and emotion described in the Russian novel *Red Planes Fly East* (Pavlenko, 1938), that largely resemble headings in early silent film "cue books" (see Chapter 2) as "patently absurd definitions," which represent a "narrowly representational comprehension of music."³² Despite his advocacy for counterpoint, much of Eisenstein's description of "hidden" inner synchronization often sounds like a more obscure version of parallelism/synchronicity. However, Eisenstein's application of his montage theory to music implied that music should be treated as a freely functioning collaborator with other elements of film in order to create "an intricate polyphony, and a perception of the pieces (of both music and picture) *as a whole*"³³ (his italics).

His colleague V.I. Pudovkin, who, with Eisenstein and G.V. Alexandrov, coauthored the 1928 "Statement on Sound," wrote persuasively on counterpoint in scoring in his *Film Technique* (1929). In *Film Acting* (1937), he describes his collaboration with composer Yuri Shaporin on his film *Deserter* (1933), by first describing the "usual way": a waltz, a cheery march tune, a danger and disquiet theme, an enemy theme, rousing fanfares, etc., each connected with the dramatic beats of the film, which involve the complete defeat of a workers' revolt by the police. But he and the composer chose another path: "a workers' march tune with constantly running through it the note of stern and confident victory, firmly and uninterruptedly rising in strength from beginning to end."³⁴ The purpose of this non-parallel approach is propaganda.³⁵ He sums up by saying, "Only then when, for each given event, we have found the independent rhythmic lines of sound and image appropriate to it, and thereby endowed its expression with the dual nature that opens the path to its dialectical understanding, shall we obtain the realistic and exceptionally forceful impression that the so numerous technical means of the cinema make possible."³⁶ Edmund Meisel's score for Eisenstein's *Battleship Potemkin* (1925), created in collaboration with the director, with its mixture of synchronous and asynchronous cues, and use of dissonance and unexpected silences, is an example of an early modernist score that sits at the outer edge of the film-scoring conventions of the silent film era, as does Shostakovich's score for Eisenstein's *The New Babylon* (1929).

Hanns Eisler and Theodore Adorno's *Composing for the Films* (1947) was an attack on conventional notions of film music up to that point. Their "rigorous, consistent, global critique of the classical model [of film music]"³⁷ was the first (and arguably the last) serious polemic against conventional assumptions about film music, at least for the next few decades. Their objections, launched like a Molotov cocktail toward polite critical discourse, were solidly rooted in Marxist ideology (as were Eisenstein's and Pudovkin's, whom they also criticized) and twelve-tone dogma, included "the leitmotif, melody and euphony, unobtrusiveness, visual justification, illustration, geography and history, stock music, clichés, and standardised interpretation."[38] Yet despite Eisler's railing against a conventional relationship between music and film, his objections seem to hinge largely on the lack of dodecaphonic music in film scoring, and he maintains a strict adherence to "precise temporal synchronization."[39] Eisler identifies the fundamental task of the film composer as "to compose music that 'fits' precisely into the given picture; intrinsic unrelatedness is here the cardinal sin."[40] The principal objections that this polemic has elicited over the years (other than the obvious ones that audiences are paying to hear more conventional film music) are that, while they are quite articulate about what they are against, they don't have as much to say about what they are for. And the film-scoring career of Hanns Eisler focused primarily on left-wing documentaries and films with more experimental directors. As Claudia Gorbman asks, "What would Eisler have done with *Mildred Pierce*?"[41]

This closely correlates with Brecht's description of the "alienation effect" in theater. Like Pudovkin and Adorno, Brecht was an avowed Marxist who saw his work's primary value in terms of its contribution to the class struggle and its effort to wake audiences up rather than to lull them to sleep. In essays reprinted in *Brecht on Theatre* (1957), he writes, "the efforts in question were directed to playing in such a way that the audience was hindered from simply identifying itself with the characters in the play. Acceptance or rejection of their actions and utterances was meant to take place on a conscious plane, instead of, as hitherto, in the audience's subconscious."[42] And, later,

> The performer's self-observation, an artful and artistic act of self-alienation stopped the spectator from losing himself in the character completely, i.e. to the point of giving up his own identity and lent a splendid remoteness to the events. Yet the spectator's empathy was not entirely rejected. The audience identifies itself with the actor as being an observer, and accordingly develops his attitude of observing or looking on. . . .
>
> . . . the theatre would benefit greatly if musicians were able to produce music, which would have a more or less exactly foreseeable effect on the spectator. It would take a load off the actor's shoulders; it would be particularly useful, for instance, to have the actors play *against* the emotion, which the music called forth.[43]

These ideas could easily be reversed, and instead of the actors playing against the emotion suggested by the music, the music could play against the emotions suggested by the actors. They point to a possibility only rarely explored in conventional film scoring. Finally, he writes about film: "The silent film gave opportunities for a few experiments with music, which created predetermined emotional states. . . . But sound films, being one of the most blooming branches of the international narcotics traffic, will hardly carry on these experiments for long."[44] The importance of these works is that they were challenging the orthodoxy of the relationship between music and image/narrative. Film music criticism for the next decades primarily focused on detailing the ways in which composers explored the parallelism/counterpoint dichotomy, without ever questioning its fundamental assumption.

Alternative Film Music Thought in the Contemporary Sound Film Era

Throughout the history of film music in the sound film era, composers have, on some occasions, found ways to subvert traditional assumptions about the relationship between film and music, though these examples are in the minority. There are cases where, often due to a fortuitous sympathetic relationship between director and composer, more adventurous ideas for film music are allowed to come into play. It is worth looking briefly at just a few examples, because they point the way to more expanded possibilities. This can include the use of unexpected and avant-garde styles of music in film: the Ligeti-inspired orchestral scores of Radiohead's Jonny Greenwood in P.T. Anderson's *There Will Be Blood* (2007), *The Master* (2012), and *Phantom Thread* (2017) are more recent examples. In addition, Greenwood's musical cues often emerge and disappear at unexpected times that don't seem to mirror the structure of the narrative, similar to those seen in some of the work of French filmmaker Jean Luc Godard.

Godard's randomly appearing and disappearing orchestral music in *Le Mepris* (Godard 1963; composer: Georges Delerue) and *Détective* (Godard 1985; licensed music) breaks one of the most foundational rules of film scoring. Both the entrances and exits of the music cues upend traditional expectations of the way the score's structure is meant to mirror that of the narrative (as do Jonny Greenwood's). In addition, the relationship to individual scenes/characters is often fairly puzzling in terms of Gorbman's/Kassabian's analysis of the music's responsibility to the narrative. Annette Davison cites *Pré-Nom: Carmen* (Godard 1983; licensed music) as offering "a deconstruction of sound and image proposed by the classical Hollywood film" in which a "diegetic string quartet produces both diegetic and nondiegetic music cues" (2004), revealing their artifice.

John Williams's score for *The Long Goodbye* (Altman, 1973) breaks so many of the conventions of film music that it could also serve as a guide to alternative possibilities for film scoring. It introduces the theme song for the film almost inaudibly, and as an instrumental, a jazz piano trio improvisation that only barely states the melody, as diegetic[45] music coming from a party next door to the apartment of 1970s anti-hero Philip Marlowe (Elliott Gould), the film's protagonist. When the audience first hears the full version of the eponymous Main Titles theme (lyric by Johnny Mandel), it cuts randomly back and forth between two arrangements featuring different vocalists (Clydie King and Jack Sheldon); in both cases, the film makes a half-hearted effort to imply that they are being listened to on car radios by the two main characters. From this point on, after being interrupted by a sequence in which the theme is played in a Muzak version in a supermarket where Marlowe is shopping for cat food, the theme is *the only music in the entire film*.[46] Every music cue in the film consists of different (and almost always diegetic) versions of the song "The Long Goodbye": several jazz and blues versions, played by a cocktail lounge pianist in the bar where Marlowe collects his messages,[47] on Spanish guitar, a two-chord jam at a beach party, a Mexican funeral brass band, and being whistled or hummed under the breath of both Marlowe and various gangsters.[48] Altman, in an interview with himself,[49] modestly says, "I'm not much interested in music that just goes along with the action," but his relationship with music in film throughout his career puts him in a league with Sergei Eisenstein as an enabler of inventive relationships between film and music.

While best known as a multi-instrumentalist and founding member of the English rock band Radiohead, Jonny Greenwood has established himself as a distinctly original composer of art music and film scores. Strongly influenced by the contemporary orchestral scores of Ligeti, Penderecki, and Messiaen, he combines virtuosic (and glissandi-rich) string writing with his knowledge of programming, software synths, and skill with the Ondes Martinot. He has established a number of close relationships with directors, but foremost with Paul Thomas Anderson: their body of work together, at this writing, including *There Will Be Blood* (2007), *The Master* (2012), *Inherent Vice* (2014), and *Phantom Thread* (2017), which was nominated for an Academy Award for Best Original Score, has already joined the ranks of Hitchcock/Herrmann, Fellini/Rota, and Leone/Morricone as game-changing director/composer collaborations. What is particularly remarkable about his body of work is that Greenwood remains resolutely experimental, despite his success, and continues to work in a uniquely personal film music language.

Film Music as Music for Film

Film music differs from other musical genres in an important way: it is ultimately defined by function, not by stylistic attributes. While it can contain elements of classical music, jazz, rock, electronic, or popular songs, as a body of work, it has amorphous borders. "Analytical methods in general are challenged by the wide variety of musical styles employed in film—indeed, nearly every kind of music written or performed in the twentieth century has appeared in movies."[50] What defines it is its relationship to the image/narrative of film. No other form so interdependently draws its structure and content from an outside source. The only comparison that could be made would be to a composer who sets words written by someone else not originally intended to be musicalized (e.g., a poem) to music. Yet, in that case, the composer has the freedom to alter the structure and rhythm of those words from their original intent. But the film composer is not free to reedit the film to match his or her music.

And the interdependence is mutual. Barthes, discussing the relationship between text and images (in photographs), uses the term "anchorage" to describe the limitation of interpretation that text places upon images.[51] Music cannot help but "anchor" the film image purely by juxtaposition. But he uses the term "relay" to describe "text and image in a complementary relationship,"[52] comparing them aptly to cartoons and comic strips. In film, this "relay-text" is generally expressed by spoken dialogue, but in silent film, music takes its place (except for a few title cards). This imposed structure leads the composer in different directions than they would have gone in otherwise. While film music historians agree that Golden Age composers were strongly influenced by the nineteenth-century European classical music practices,[53] it is hard to imagine the music that Max Steiner wrote for the "Approach to Skull Island" scene in *King Kong* (Cooper & Schoedsack 1933) in a live performance context without the film in the 1930s: it lacks a compelling melody, slowly simmers, creating an ominous atmosphere, and gradually fades in the diegetic sounds of the "native" drumming and chanting from a distance. Yet, in the context of the film, it is absolutely right and does not strike us as having anything unusual about it. And it is almost unheard of for a composer to write a piece of music that lasts eleven seconds, yet short cues are very common in film music. Many of the formal rules of music composition are made irrelevant by the primacy of the relationship of music to image/narrative. The genesis of each musical decision is motivated by its task in relationship to this image/narrative. The function of film music, as described by Gorbman and Cohen (signifying emotion, providing narrative cues, delineating structure, etc.), suggests that each musical decision is made in relationship to each cue to be scored. Chion speaks of the possible relationship between music (and sound) and music as being inherently *empathetic* ("taking on the scene's rhythm, tone and phrasing"[54]) or *anempathetic* (music which exhibits "conspicuous indifference to the situation").[55] But this relationship, which is unavoidable once one decides to juxtapose film and music, does not need to remain trapped in stasis: that there is a relationship is definitive, but the nature of that relationship is potentially fluid.

The early silent film era featured multiple scores for every film. But as film history progressed, studios continued to increase their control over the music that accompanied film: first through the creation of "cue books," then through "compiled scores," and finally through the creation of original scores (for more detail on these, see Chapter 2). The sound era fixed films with one score and one score only. Not until the era of contemporary scores for silent film did the score revert to being a variable and diverse element. As discussed, it is beyond the scope of this book to address all of the issues connected with the difference between a film score being performed "live" and one that is prerecorded. But the relevant issue here is one of plasticity. There is an infinite variety of possible scores for a single film, and each live score is never performed exactly the same way twice.[56] As seen earlier in the work of Godard/Williams/Greenwood et al., it is possible to create music in a contemporary sound film with an innovative approach, and clearly, there are some composers, particularly those who have the trust and support of their directors, who have created rich, imaginative, and innovative work in the synchronized sound context. However, throughout the history of film and film music, it has been fairly rare for a composer to pursue an approach that reexamines the foundational functional role of film music. The contemporary professional film/TV composer must measure their professionalism in respect to their ability to meet the expectations of director + producer + editor + music editor + music supervisor + audience + self. In moments of candor, film music composers have acknowledged that the opportunities for free play in what John Zorn called "the challenging and restrictive world of film music"[57] are, in fact, rare.[58] In fact, in his discussion of the creation of Breil's score for *Birth of a Nation*, one of the first important orchestral original films scores, Cooke reports that director D.W. Griffith and the composer "had many disagreements over the scoring of the film,"[59] rendering Breil "among the first to have his painstakingly musical solutions cut to conform to the demands of the director."[60] Since the middle of the silent film era, film music has been largely tethered to the narrative, and it substantially remains so today, as it must. But the contemporary score for *silent* film is a form that is tailor-made for new opportunities and interventions.

The Polysynchronous Possibilities Inherent in Contemporary Scores for Silent Film

Structurally, contemporary scores for silent film give the composer a chance to work in a long-form musical development and to give the music a much more prominent position in the combined new art form; sound films are restrained by the twin restrictions of dialogue and the necessity of being "unheard." Because of the absence of the original director and producer, the composer is free to interpret, or reinterpret, the work as they see fit. However, it is not enough to merely be "against" something; one must be "for" something else:[61] that is to say, the composer must have a clear intention and the ability to express it in order to make a reinvention of the role of film music meaningful and effective. Even if the intention is "no intention" (cf. Cage/Vandermark,[62] that is, the application of aleatory techniques), this indeterminacy must be clearly indicated to the audience. The polysynchronous film music composer can make use of all the techniques of the history of music composition but *to different ends*. This requires the recognition of, and facility with, the semiotic associations of various styles, attributes, and conventions of music, in order to potentially use them as tools in order to accomplish these alternative goals. In choosing from a body of work in which it is a given that none of the original principals are still attached to the film, the composer is potentially freed from a rigid responsibility to these multiple collaborators. In order to discuss the nature of these possibilities, I have suggested the term "polysynchronous."[63] The use of this term is not only to distinguish itself from the pervasive dichotomy of the terms "synchronous" versus "asynchronous" (that is still an important element of critical/academic discussions of film music) but *also* to create a category that includes a wide variety of unorthodox film music practices. Polysynchronicity, while embracing both synchronicity and asynchronicity as part of the fabric of an overall film score, opens to include a different currency, which is not measured based on its relationship (for or against) with the film's "original" intent, but on its own terms.[64]

In this book, I will illustrate what I mean by the term "polysynchronicity" in this context, show its precedents and current practice, show its application (or lack thereof) in contemporary music for silent films, and finally, show how I have applied it in my own creative practice. In the process, I give an overall portrait of a vital art form (contemporary scores for silent film) about which there has been relatively little academic or critical writing.[65] The polysynchronous film score is one that is not limited to synchronicity or asynchronicity, but chooses freely between the first two and includes a third category. This includes, first of all, music that (i) does not clearly express an easily defined point of view (happy versus sad, safe versus threatening), but is rather more complex and open, and (ii) is free to make more playful juxtapositions between music and image/narrative, including, but not limited to, irony, historical references, puns, asides, parallel narrative, and other forms of subtext. In addition, in the context of contemporary scores for silent film, it includes scoring practices which upend the expectations and traditional practices of "silent film music." It can also make direct use of the learned associations of various types of music (Kassabian's "competence"[66]) for purposes other than their usual film music conventions. This could involve instrumentation, genre, or musical memes. The goal is to take learned associations and repurpose them with other ends in mind. A simple version of this idea could be the use of slow, languorous music for a scene that features fast-paced action, such as a scene of silent film comedy players, the Keystone Cops. A more complex version might be to use Bernard Herrmann-esque suspense music to create tension systematically throughout a film in unexpected places, with a different goal in mind than a conventional suspense film: perhaps with political, comedic, or anarchic goals in mind. It could involve using unexpected instrumentation, for example, instruments that could not have existed in the silent film era (electric guitar, electronics); the use of styles that had not developed in the silent film era; (rock, electronica, modern jazz, minimalism); or the use of attitudes that are not traditionally associated with the silent film era (irony, doubt, referentialism). None of these, in and of themselves, create polysynchronicity, but they are tools that could be put to apt use in its realization.

It is important here to clarify the difference between asynchronicity and polysynchronicity. By definition, the polysynchronous film score as a whole *may contain* both synchronicity and asynchronicity. However, the fact that certain relationships clearly elude classification into the parallelism/counterpoint dichotomy makes the third category of polysynchronicity necessary. Polysynchronicity is, by one definition, that which cannot be clearly categorized as synchronous or asynchronous. It has no paradigmatic structure; it is borderless.

One of the foundational attributes of polysynchronicity is intent. First, the composer does not accept primary allegiance to the (perceived) intentions of a director or feel that the score's primary role is to express the original narrative of the film. A contemporary silent film score may, at times or throughout, choose to express a different narrative. Second, in all cases, regardless of what final decision is made, the composer takes nothing for granted and considers afresh the relationship between music and film. This can include the content, structure, or even existence of the music (it is an expectation of silent film accompaniment that the music will occur continuously throughout the film: to stop and leave sudden silence of any length is unexpected and potentially disruptive to the audience). Likewise, it is expected that the structure of the music will mirror the structure of the film, begin at the beginning of the scene, end or change at the end of a scene, or at lease crossfade into it in order to support continuity and mask the editing. The polysynchronous score may draw awkward attention to the editing or ignore the scene structure altogether.

A fundamental tenet of polysynchronicity is the rejection of film music as background music per se: that the primary role of the music is to support the narrative from its position of "invisibility." A widely held belief among both composers and audiences is that music in a film must not draw attention to itself (see composer interviews in Chapter 9). Instead, the polysynchronous film score potentially functions as an equal, a cocreator of a complete (new) artwork of combined film and music, one that is, in its most pure form, performed live in front of an audience. It clearly draws attention to itself, at least in the hands of some practitioners. Music *does* have meaning, both absolute and referential[67] and that meaning is a tool that may be deployed in different ways, and toward different goals. It does not necessarily need to be used in preordained ways, dictated by previously established assumptions about its purpose, in order to have a meaningful role. However, polysynchronicity also opens up more complex relationships between music and film—sometimes more difficult to define—than a comparison of the music's narrative and the film's narrative. In discussions of Eisenstein in *Image/Music/Text*, Roland Barthes posits a "third meaning,"[68] which is "not in the language system."[69] It describes this third meaning as a result of the friction between various levels of meaning, including the "obvious meaning,"[70] the "obtuse meaning"[71] (the creator's intention), and other possible levels of interpretation. This same idea can be applied to the relationships between music and image/narrative, opening to resonances far more complex than music that merely has a single message to impart regarding the film (especially when the music does not fall into easily demarcated stylistic boundaries). In fact, this "third meaning" of the intersection of text and image, which he describes as "evident, erratic, obstinate,"[72] is where the obvious/informational and obtuse/symbolic rub up against each other, and the three align in interesting ways with the concept of synchronicity/asynchronicity/polysynchronicity. He later describes the obtuse meaning as "the epitome of a counter-narrative."[73]

Criteria for Polysynchronicity

It has been established that the term "polysynchronicity" is inclusive; that is to say, a polysynchronous film score can contain *elements* that can be described as synchronous, asynchronous, or polysynchronous. The following criteria, I feel, are among those that invite a discussion of polysynchronicity. However, it is not necessary that an entire film score embody *all* of these characteristics in order to qualify for discussion.

1. The work cannot be easily categorized within the synchronous/asynchronous model.
2. The work powerfully challenges the generally accepted (by both composers and critics/academics) relationship between music score and narrative film.
3. The music interacts as an equal partner with the film, rather than merely "supporting" it, through its "visibility." A new, multimedia art form is created, with equal emphasis on film and music.
4. The orchestration, dynamics, musical idioms/references, and other compositional elements at times create a feeling of surprise that draws attention to the score through its audacity.
5. The music breaks the "fourth wall" supporting the perceiver's immersion in the film.
6. The music suggests a different interpretation of the events on screen than the expected perception, including those that may be in apparent contradiction to that ostensibly intended by the original filmmaker. This interpretation could be one specifically guided by the composer, or the intention could be to open the film more widely to the viewer's own experience and interpretation.

In addition, when looking at contemporary scores for *silent* films, a discussion of polysynchronicity will ask the additional questions: What is the music's relationship to conventions of film scoring? And what is the music's relationship to conventions of *silent* film scoring? These questions must be applied to both the score as a whole and individual cues. Marco Bellano's "The Tradition of Novelty—Comparative Studies of Silent Film Scores: Perspectives, Challenges, Proposals" articulates the value of comparative studies of different contemporary scores for the same silent film:

> What then would be the aim of this kind of approach? A deep comprehension of film language, I would argue. In fact, audiovisual functions can bring into focus both the visual and the narrative content. An audiovisual function works like a gloss on the director's work: it is the result of a musical interpretation of the images. It conveys a composer's point of view on a certain fragment of a film. It is, of course, the point of view of an individual; a different musician could see the same fragment in a completely different way—and completely different would be the audiovisual message that reaches the audience, too. To compare two different musical readings of the same sequence is like starting to draw a map of the hidden potential of a film, better of rationalizing its dramaturgical value.[74]

There are practitioners, some of whom who are involved at the intersection of research and restoration of historical scores (both original and compiled) and the creation of new scores, who cite the importance of being *faithful* to the films (and to their directors). This school of practitioners has a clear passion for the art form, a deep knowledge of the history and does wonderful and essential work. They also feel strongly about their approach to silent film scoring.[75] However, I would suggest that there is another way to look at the situation which stands not in opposition to but alongside the work of these composers, performers, and researchers. Call it modernist, post-modernist, or experimental, but I feel that there are other potential tasks for music other than "serving" the film. There are other potential times for silent film to live in besides the historical past. And there are other potential relationships between music and film. As Marco Bellano writes,

> as it is impossible to reconstruct the complete "tradition" of different musical interpretations pertaining to each silent film, it must be stressed once again that the term "tradition" needs to be understood without historical implications: what is "traditional," in this case, is not a certain repertoire of silent film scorers but practice that is continued until the present days. The idea of the "tradition of

novelty" does not identify a historical series of musical documents, but a way of looking at a silent film as *a potentially perennial source of musical inspiration*.[76] (My italics)

Tieber and Windisch identify "three modes of musical accompaniment for silent films today: (1) the reconstruction of historical scores; (2) modernizing the film with the help of contemporary music, no matter what the genre; and (3) "improvisation," which generally means to illustrate the images with the recycling and reuse of proven musical material."[77] I would argue that many modern scores combine modes 2 and 3, and that the definition here of improvisation is a limited one; but I do agree with them that "every accompaniment is an interpretation of the film."[78] So let it be said from the outset that these polysynchronous contemporary scores for silent film are not meant to replace traditional silent film scores that seek to express the "director's intentions" or to create a modern simulacrum of what we think we know of historical practices (though ultimately we can neither know either of these nor can the audience experience them in the same way as the audience of 100 years ago).[79] They are a different animal that functions in "parallel." The goal is to create a new hybrid work of art, which is aimed not at reviving a much-beloved historical artifact (though that often happens inadvertently in the process) but rather to explore through free play some of the unexplored relationships between music and film. In the following chapter, I will discuss some of the history of silent and sound film scoring, as well as critical/analytical writing on the topic, in order to provide some context for the further development of these ideas.

Notes

1. "[W]hen it comes to early film music scholars are typically reduced to, at best, educated guesses." Anderson, "Reforming 'Jackass Music,'" 51.
2. Rick Altman, *Silent Film Sound* (New York: Columbia University Press, 2004), 8.
3. Sergei Eisenstein, *The Film Sense* (London: Faber and Faber Ltd., 1943).
4. See Kassbian's notion of "competence" discussed later in this chapter in more detail (Anahid Kassabian, *Hearing Film: Tracking Identifications in Contemporary Hollywood Film Music* [New York and London: Routledge, 2001], 23).
5. The term "licensed music" here refers to preexisting music for which the filmmaker has acquired a "sync license" for the right to reproduce it in synchronization with the film.

6 Gregg Redner, *Deleuze and Film Music: Building a Methodological Bridge between Film Theory and Music* (Chicago: Intellect Ltd. University of Chicago Press), 7.

7 "This is not to say that the parallelism of sounds and images which embody these qualities represents the only possible manner in which different media may be combined; if the picture gestures up, so to speak, the music can always gesture down. The point, however, is that this does not represent an alternative *principle*; seen this way, oppositional scoring, as its designation implies, represents merely the opposite of parallelism. It is the inversion of a principle, a parasitic concept, and its practice represents no more than the exception which proves the rule." Nicholas Cook, *Analysing Musical Multimedia* (New York: Oxford University Press, 1998), 65.

8 In response to George Burt, *The Art of Film Music* (Boston: Northeastern University Press 1994) viii.

9 Kathryn Kalinak, *Settling the Score: Music and the Classic Hollywood Film* (Madison: University of Wisconsin Press, 1992), 29.

10 For example, as early as 1915, D.W. Griffith's *Birth of a Nation*, sanctioned by the director himself, had a different score for its West Coast and East Coast premieres. Its Los Angeles premiere in February of 1915 featured a compiled score by Carli Elinor, whereas the New York premiere in March of that same year featured an "original" score by Josef Breil, which contained a combination of compiled classical and popular music cue, and original music by Breil, largely drawing upon his themes and motifs. See Martin Marks, *Music and the Silent Film: Contexts and Case Studies 1895-1924* (New York: Oxford University Press, 1997), 109–66 for a detailed analysis of Breil's score.

11 The term "non-diegetic" is used in film music discourse to describe music that is not part of the narrative world of the film. The term "underscore" is sometimes used as a synonym in this context.

12 Claudia Gorbman, *Unheard Melodies: Narrative Film Music* (Bloomington, IN: Indiana University Press, 1987), 73–91.

13 Ibid., 153.

14 Scott Lipscomb and Roger A. Kendall, "Perceptual Judgment of the Relationship between Musical and Visual Elements in Film," *Psychomusicology* 13 (1994): 60-98.
Scott Lipscomb and D.E. Tolchinsky, "The Role of Music Communication in Cinema," in *Music Communication*, ed. D. Miell, R.A.R. Macdonald and D. J. Hargreaves (London: Oxford University Press, 2005), 383–404.
Annabel J. Cohen, "Music as a Source of Emotion in Film," in *Music and Emotion: Theory and Research* (2001), 249–72.
Annabel J. Cohen, "How Music Influences the Interpretation of Film And Video: Approaches from Experimental Psychology," in *Perspectives in Systematic*

Musicology, ed. Roger Allen Kendall and Roger W.H. Savage, 15–36. Selected Reports In Ethnomusicology; V. 12, Los Angeles, CA: Dept. of Ethnomusicology, University of California, 2005.
15 Cohen, "Music as a Source of Emotion in Film," 258.
16 Kassabian, *Hearing Film*, 38.
17 David Neumeyer and James Buhler, "Analytical and Interpretive Approaches to Film Music (II): Analysing Interactions of Music and Film," *Film Music: Critical Approaches*, ed. K.J. Donnelly (New York: Continuum, 2001), 19.
18 Redner's work is based on that of Gilles Deleuze (*Cinema 1: The Movement-Image*, 1986 and *Cinema 2: The Time-Image*, 1989), which in turn draws on that of Henri Bergson (*Matter and Memory*, 1911, and *Creative Evolution*, 1911). Bergson's comparison of the functioning of the intellect to the artificiality of the cinema and the creation of images by the film camera/projector (cf. projector image metaphor in score for *Faust*, Chapter 5) provides the foundation for Deleuze's concepts ("sensation, nomadology, the refrain, the eternal refrain, becoming utopia, smooth space, and duration"), which Redner uses to create a new "flexible analytical methodology" to reconcile film theory and music theory (Redner, *Deleuze and Film Music*).
19 Ibid., 7–16.
20 Annette Davison, *Hollywood Theory, Non-Hollywood Practice: Cinema Soundtracks in the 1980s and 1990s* (Leeds: University of Leeds, 2004), 16.
21 A.L. Rees, *A History of Experimental Film and Video* (New York: Bloomsbury Academic, 1999), 65–75.
22 Jason Weiss, *Always in Trouble: An Oral History of ESP-Disk* (Middletown, CT: Wesleyan University Press, 2012), 142–3.
23 Jeff Smith, "Unheard Melodies? A Critique of Psychoanalytic Theories of Film Music," in *Post-Theory: Reconstructing Film Studies*, ed. David Bordwell and Noel Carroll (Wisconsin: Wisconsin University Press, 1996), 236.
24 Emilio Audissino, *Film/Music Analysis: A Film Studies Approach* (Southampton, UK: Palgrave Macmillan, 2017), 26–7.
25 Kalinak, *Settling the Score*, 24.
26 Audissino, *Film/Music Analysis*, 54–60.
27 Ben Winters, "Musical Wallpaper? Towards an Appreciation of Non-narrating Music in Film," *Music Sound and the Moving Image* 6, no. 1 (2012): 52.
28 K. J. Donnelly, *Occult Aesthetics: Synchronization in Sound Film* (Oxford, UK: Oxford University Press, 2014), 1.
29 Marc Ribot, in an email to the author, October 5, 2020.
30 Mervyn Cooke, *A History of Film Music* (London: Cambridge University Press, 2008), 34–5.
31 Eisenstein, *The Film Sense*, 159–60.

32 For example, "Songs of Maidens" from Rubinstein's *Demon*: sadness; Schumann's *Fantasiestuecke*, no. 2: inspiration Barcarolle from Offenbach's *Tales of Hoffman*: love etc. (Eisenstein, *The Film Sense*, 159–61).
33 Eisenstein, *The Film Sense*, 86, as quoted in Petter Frost Fadnes, "Improvising the Deluge: Live film scoring and improvisational practices," *Jazz-Hitz*, 01 (2018): 112.
34 V. I. Pudovkin, *Film Technique and Film Acting* (USA: Lear, 1949), 311.
35 "Marxists know that in every defeat of the workers lies hidden a further step toward victory." Ibid.
36 Ibid.
37 Gorbman, *Unheard Melodies*, 99.
38 Hanns Eisler and Theodor Adorno, *Composing for the Films* (New York: New York University Press, 1947), xxxiv.
39 Cook, *Analysing Musical Multimedia*, 63.
40 Hanns Eisler and Theodor Adorno, *Composing for the Films* (New York: New York University Press, 1947), 90.
41 Gorbman, *Unheard Melodies*, 109.
42 Bertolt Brecht, *Brecht on Theater* (London: Bloomsbury Methuen Press, 2014), 151.
43 Ibid., 130.
44 Ibid.
45 The term "diegetic" is used to refer to music that is part of the narrative world of the film (see footnote 10), also known as "source music" because the audience can see the real or implied source of the music.
46 Composer John Williams credits Altman for the idea: "The music was a terrific idea—entirely Bob's. He said, 'Wouldn't it be great if there was one song, this omnipresent piece, played in all these different ways?'" quoted in Gayle Sherwood Magee, *Robert Altman's Soundtracks* (Oxford, UK: Oxford University Press, 2014), 76. But Williams's execution of the idea must also be cited for its wit, execution, and detail.
47 Marlowe (Elliott Gould) to cocktail pianist, "You practicing for the Hit Parade? Pianist: "I gotta learn this goddamn thing. Herbie [the owner] thinks it will beef up the lunch trade. . . . Cheap as I work he cannot lose." (*The Long Goodbye*, 1973).
48 The one exception is a tinny recording of "Hooray for Hollywood," which bookends the film.
49 *Altman on Altman*, ed. David Thompson (London: Faber and Faber, 2005), 73, as quoted in Kate McQuiston's excellent study of this score, "The Soundtrack Doth Repeat Too Much: Or, the Musical Spectacle of Keeping Up Appearances in Robert Altman's *The Long Goodbye*," *Film Literature Quarterly* 44, no. 2 (2016): 132.
50 David Neumeyer and James Buhler, "Analytical and Interpretive Approaches to Film Music (I): Analyzing the Music," in *Film Music: Critical Approaches,* ed. K.J. Donnelly (New York: Continuum, 2001), 19.

51 Roland Barthes, *Image/Text/Music* (New York: Hill & Wang, 1977), 40.
52 Barthes, *Image/Text/Music*, 41.
53 Roy Prendergast, *Film Music: A Neglected* Art, 2nd ed. (New York: Norton, 1992), ix.
54 He adds that "obviously such music participates in cultural codes for things like sadness, happiness, and movement." Michel Chion, *Audio-Vision: Sound on Screen* (New York: Columbia University Press, 1994), 8.
55 Ibid.
56 "Music for the silent film was an independent, ever-changing accompaniment." Martin M. Marks, *Music and the Silent Film*, 6. "[F]rom theater to theater, many different musicians worked on the same single silent picture. As a result, each film could have many different 'scores.'" Marco Bellano, "The Tradition of Novelty," 208.
57 John Zorn, "Ennio Morricone Was More than Just a Great Film Composer," *New York Times*, (C1), July 9, 2020.
58 See, for example, Elmer Bernstein, *Elmer Bernstein's Film Music Notebook: A Complete Collection of the Quarterly Journal, 1974-1978* (Sherman Oaks, CA: Film Music Society, 2004), for anecdotal discussions of these limitations by numerous film composers, including David Raksin, "Whatever Became of Movie Music?" 1, no. 1 (Fall 1974): 24–9. Also, Elmer Bernstein, "Whatever Happened To Great Movie Music?" *High Fidelity*, July 1972, 55–8 reprinted in *The Routledge Film Music Sourcebook*, ed. James Wierzbicki, Nathan Platte, and Colin Roust (New York and London: Routledge, 2012), 178–82.
59 James Wierzbicki, *Film Music: A History* (New York: Routledge, 2009), 61.
60 William Darby and Jack DuBois, *American Film Music: Major Composers, Techniques, Trends, 1915-90* (Jefferson, NC: McFarland & Company, 1990), 3. (In Wierzbicki, *Film Music: A History*, 61.)
61 Barthes, on this related topic (see Chapter 2), continues, "the *contemporary* problem is not to destroy the narrative, but to subvert it; today's task is to dissociate subversion from destruction." Barthes, *Image/Text/Music*, 65.
62 See Chapter 3.
63 I have found no other use of the terms "polysynchronous" and "polysynchronicity" in relationship to film music's framing of the dichotomy of synchronous and asynchronous scoring. I have found the term used an various analytical contexts, in articles such as "Emergence of Hierarchical Networks and Polysynchronous Behaviour in Simple Adaptive Systems" (Botella-Soler & Glendinning, 2012), "Negotiating Teacher Identity and Power in Online Poly-Synchronous Environments: A Heuristic Inquiry" (Miles & Mikulec, 2008), "Mechanistic studies of *Microcystic aeruginosa* inactivation and degradation by UV-C irradiation and chlorination with poly-synchronous analyses" (Ou, Gao et al., 2011). But none

64. of these use it in the same context or even the same theoretical domain as my discussion. There is also a computer game called Polysynchronicity.
65. And, as improvised silent film music practitioner Petter Frost Fadnes says, "From Brecht to Eisenstein and Kubrick, there is a case for how music as an independent entity may shift our experience of audiovisual expressions (film or stage) from unobtrusive blandness to individual reading and experience." Fadnes, *Improvising the Deluge*, 111.
66. By way of illustration, I informally asked all of the composers in my interviews (Chapter 9) if there had been any critical or academic writing about any of their work, other than the occasional review. They all replied in the negative.
67. "Competence is based on decipherable codes learned through experience. As with language and visual image, we learn through exposure what a given tempo, series of notes, key, time signature, rhythm, volume, and orchestration are meant to signify" (Kassabian, *Hearing Film*, 23).
68. cf. Meyer 1956 et al.
69. Barthes, *Image/Text/Music*, 52–3. He also describes it as "indifferent to moral or aesthetic categories . . . it is on the side of the carnival."
70. Ibid., 60.
71. Ibid., 54.
72. Ibid., 56.
73. Ibid., 53.
74. Ibid., 63.
75. Bellano, "The Tradition of Novelty," 212.
76. Not all historically based scholars feel this way. Rick Altman performs a show called "The Living Nickelodeon," arguably the most historically deep "resurrection" (his words) approach to recreating music for silent films. Altman plays the piano and sings, encourages the audience to sing along, and to be noisy and boisterous for that matter. Yet he says, "I love what you characterize as the 're-mix' approach, I am in favour of ANY approach that increases spectatorship for early films." Paul Flaig, "The Living Nickelodeon and Silent Film Today," in *New Silent Cinema*, ed. Katherine Groo and Paul Flaig (New York: Routledge, 2015), 133–4.
77. Bellano, "The Tradition of Novelty," 213.
78. Manuel Deniz Silva, "'The Sounds of Silent Films': An Interview with Claus Tieber and Anna K. Windisch," *Aniki: Portuguese Journal of the Moving Image* 5, no. 1 (2018): 173.
79. Ibid.
80. And, as illustrated in the next chapter, not completely divorced from historical practices. Donnelly writes that "Silent cinema had a certain amount of autonomy for images and music respectively. . . . there is certainly a case for the survival of the aesthetics of silent cinema in the margins of mainstream cinema." (Donnelly, *Occult Aesthetics: Synchronization in Sound Film*, 212).

2

Scores for Silent Film

Then and Now

Historical Music for Silent Films

Music has accompanied film since its earliest inception.[1] Emile Maraval played piano at the first Lumière Brothers screening in Paris in 1895,[2] and Dr. Leo Sommer's Blue Hungarian Band accompanied the first American public film projections on Thomas Edison's Vitascope in New York in 1896.[3] Georges Méliès himself accompanied the first performance of his *Voyage dans la lune* in Paris.[4] What is generally not known, despite years of research by film music historians, is exactly what music they played.[5] The collective improvisations of the world's early film accompanists constitute a vast lost body of work that continues to tantalize the imagination. However, the evolution of music for film during the life of the pre-sync-sound era (approximately 1896–1927) went through a number of phases, beginning with improvised scores and culminating in through-composed original scores.

The term "improvised scores" is not used here in the sense of a jazz improvisation but, rather, to indicate that each film did not necessarily have an exactly detailed musical accompaniment prescribed for it; instead, the choice of music was left to the organizers of each individual performance. The most common practice was to use precomposed music, drawing on both classical repertoire and popular songs, and assembled in a cut-and-paste fashion, often on the fly, in order to provide the musical background for the film.[6] Classical music was generally used for its emotional or connotative content. A description by early film director Cecil Hepworth of some of the earliest musical accompaniment during the mid-1890s goes as follows: "The sequence opened with a calm and peaceful picture of the sea and sky. Soft and gentle music (Schumann, I think)."[7] Marks goes on to describe the complete recollection as "a type of accompaniment used throughout the silent period: the compilation of pre-existent music, matched in mood and in the style of performance to the images it accompanies."[8]

Each accompanist therefore drew upon their own repertoire (or collections of sheet music and cue books).[9] But as Bellano points out, "The use of fragments from a repertory is absolutely not in contrast with the idea of improvisation."[10] In fact, it is much in tune with the contemporary postmodern approach of appropriation (sampling/looping): my choice of existing materials, and the way I assemble them, is my composition.[11]

It is impossible to say exactly what constituted the exact content of these earliest accompaniments (and sometimes they were just juxtapositions, with no direct connection to either the narrative or the visuals). They varied tremendously from venue to venue, and very soon critics, audiences, and directors began to feel unhappy with them. In addition to wildly inappropriate music and questionable performance practices, orchestras were known to collectively rise from their seats and go on a break in the middle of a film.[12] The evolution of the silent film score during the thirty years of its history comprised four basic stages: the Wild West of its origins, the development of "cue books" and then "compiled scores," and finally, the gradual acceptance of a (mostly) unique original score for each film as a necessary ingredient that added prestige and depth to the cinema experience. Tracing the path of this development shows the ways in which contemporary scores for silent film draw upon the diverse stages of this history, both as technique and as historical reference.

Discontent with Early Film Accompaniment

In his 2003 essay "Reforming 'Jackass Music,'" Tim Anderson describes nickelodeons (local movie houses) as "potentially disruptive and heterogeneous spaces of spectacle and distraction"[13] and documents a desire by critics, audiences, and film producers to "reform both the sound and musical accompaniment of film from a potentially excessive, 'music hall' aesthetic of collective performance into a more formalized theatrical regime of film exhibition whose elements are dedicated to the needs of the master narrative."[14]

The early environment of film music production was marked by both carelessness and deliberate disruption, not necessarily respectful to the authority of narrative.

Anderson cites four areas of film music accompaniment as problematic for critics, producers, and audiences that were in need of reform: "(i) the aesthetic reformation of music vis-à-vis film narrative; (ii) the propriety and limits of musical performance; (iii) the professionalization of the musician; and (iv) the undefined site of exhibition/participation."[15]

One of the most objectionable habits to producers was "funning" the film: the practice of playing humorous or incongruous music or sound effects to evoke laughter from the audience, whether in a comedy or melodrama, often in direct contradiction of the clear narrative intent. "They play comic songs in classical pictures (the spectators often join in singing these), the drummer injects some fool noise in a serious scene and your 'jackass audience' is delighted."[16]

As much an issue as the deliberate subversion of the narrative was a systematic lack of professionalism and care paid to film music creation and performance.

> Louis Levi . . . recollects how the little cinema orchestras round the period of 1912 were quite satisfied to play selections of light café music quite unrelated to film on the screen—and, after a given period of *The William Tell Overture*, Rubinstein and Tchaikovsky, get up and leave the film and its audience to the deathly hush of silence.[17]

The ultimate aim of these criticisms was to provide a "proper" (i.e., high class/legitimate, as opposed to low class/jackass) musical accompaniment, which inherently implied one that "served" the narrative. Part of the conflict reflected the fact that film was evolving from being, at least in part, a spectacle-based entertainment into one in which narrative was considered to be the central interest (cf. Gunning's quote in the Introduction to this book regarding "attractions that escaped the demands of formal narrative structures"[18]).

As narrative became preeminent, the role of film music in supporting that narrative became more formalized, and film producers wanted more control over it. Dissatisfaction with the heterogeneous (in both quality and content) film music performance practices led to two parallel and related solutions: cue books and compiled scores. But some of the earliest possibilities for alternative approaches to film music were laid where the carnivalesque mood and setting of early film presentation enabled rupture, borderless sound worlds, and non-paradigmatic music making.

Cue Books

Cue books were collections of suggested music for film musicians and music directors, often collected and/or composed by well-known silent film musicians/composers. Some of the most well known of these authors (Ernö Rapée and Hugo Reisenfeld, for example[19]) became some of the first composers of original scores for films. These cue books were organized by topic and usage. This catalog of film music libraries by George W. Beynon claims that it "covers the field and has stood the test of severe trial without failure."[20] It groups the suggested music excerpts under the following headings:

> Agitation, Anguish, Barcaroles, Battles, Brightness, Chasing, Children, Complacency, Characteristic, Daintiness, Dancing, Death, Despair, Dramatic, Dramatic (semi), Dramatic tension, Excitement, Fear, Fights, Fires, Foreboding, Forgiveness, Galloping, Gladness, Grief, Grotesque, Hunting, Hymns, Jealousy, Joy, Lamentation, Love, Lullabyes, Military, Mystery, Neutral, Pastoral, Pathos, Pathetic (semi), Pleading, Prayer, Religion, Remembrance, Sorrow, Triumph, Tumult, Vivacity, Witchery, Weddings.[21]

A similar list from star actress Geraldine Farrar offers specific suggestions drawn from classical repertoire:

1. Contentment — L'apres-midi d'un faun — Debussy
2. Joy — Coronation scene, Boris Gudunov — Mussorgsky
3. Melancholy — Meditation, *Thaïs* — Massenet
4. Humility — Ave Maria — Bach-Gounod
5. Love — Libestod [sic], *Tristan and Isolde* — Wagner
6. Courage — Ho yo To ho!—2nd act *Walküre* — Wagner
7. Desire — Sicilliana, *Cavalleria rusticana* — Mascagni
8. Hope — Duet, finale 1st act, *Madame Butterfly* — Puccini etc.[22]

However, in addition to forming an important step in the progression from freely improvised scores to composed scores, these books helped formalize the organization of music into "style topics" (what Gorbman calls "cultural musical codes").[23]

> The decisive intervention is the way these books organize musical thought: they were highly influential not only because musical directors, pianists and organists of the early cinema turned to them to locate specific pieces but also because those pieces helped delimit or conform boundaries of topics, fitting newly

composed music into them as well as a substantial percentage of the standard repertory after roughly 1850.[24]

Compiled Scores

Compiled scores (sometimes called *cue sheets*[25]) are lists of precomposed music that give a musician or theater music director a guide to specific pieces of music to play along with each scene of a specific film. It is still up to each musician to arrange, orchestrate, and perform the excerpts, so this still provided room for a variety of musical backgrounds for each film. But it began to give the film companies a greater control over the musical accompaniment and reduce the possibilities for musical mishaps of the types described earlier.

The earliest compiled scores were very basic, being only organized by suggested type of music and could be used as shorthand in connection with either a cue book or an improvised score. For example, consider music cues for *How the Landlord Collected His Rents* (1909), a 230-foot reel that lasted three and a half minutes.

Scene 1—March, brisk.
Scene 2—Irish jig.
Scene 3—Begin with andante, finish with allegro.
Scene 4—Popular air.
Scene 5—Popular air.
Scene 6—Andante with lively at finish.
Scene 7—March (same as No. 1)
Scene 8—Plaintive.
Scene 9—Andante (use March of No. 1)[26]

But they soon developed into much more detailed documents, often directing the music director exclusively to popular music works whose copyrights were owned by the film production company. A cue sheet issued by Warner Bros. for *The Desired Woman* contains a list of cues that change every one to three minutes, each followed by descriptions ("Maestoso, Sentimental, Romantic, Fight"), and both "tax-free" and "taxable" suggestions of existing compositions, including works by classical composers (Saint Saens, Sibelius) and by contemporary cue book composers (Axt, Rapée).[27] This allowed film companies to have greater control over the musical accompaniment to films, for both artistic and financial reasons, although it must be added that certain theater musical directors would still substitute their own choices for certain pieces or even ignore the compiled score altogether. However, especially in the larger venues, which required that compiled scores be assembled from massive musical libraries of parts for full orchestra, the sheer volume of new films coming through would make using the compiled scores the most practical solution.[28]

Original Scores

There would always be occasions where an appropriate passage of precomposed music could not be easily found at hand for a certain section of film, and the musician or music director would be forced to improvise or compose an original piece of music. But original music in films was initially viewed unfavorably in the United States and only used as a last resort.[29] At a time when American music was viewed as inherently inferior to European classical music, why use new music written by an inferior American composer when works of the great European composers were available to be assembled into new film scores? In a scathing review of Mortimer Wilson's groundbreaking score for *The Thief of Baghdad* (Walsh 1924), one Los Angeles reviewer wrote, "when the music of the world is at the disposal of an arranger and the libraries are rich in beautiful numbers, written by renowned composers, suitable for accompanying such a delightfully fantastic picture, why worry any one man to write a 'new note for every gesture?'"[30]

The first significant original silent film score is often cited as Camille Saint Saëns's score for *L'Assassinat du duc de Guise* (1908). And a true film score it is: Martin Marks writes that, "Analogous to the film's use of [inter]titles, each musical tableau is set apart from the others by a pause; and each begins with a clearly defined meter, tempo, theme, and key that contrast with those that precede and/or follow."[31] And Royal S. Brown notes that "the climactic moments that back up the assassination remarkably foreshadow film-music tropes still in use."[32]

Joseph Carl Breil's score for *The Birth of a Nation* (Griffith 1914) is considered by many to be the first important original American orchestral film score.[33] However, influential as it was in this respect, it contained large amounts of precomposed music, including both classical and popular songs and folk music. This sequential list of music cues for the opening ten minutes of the film, drawn from Martin Marks's deep reading of the film's score, gives a sense of the interpenetration of original and precomposed music:

1. Fanfare for opening credits (Breil)
2. "The bringing of the African . . ." theme 1 (Breil)—The Theme of Barbarism
3. Abolitionist meeting—Hymn (Breil)
4. Title and scene introducing Austin Stoneman and Elsie—theme 2 (Breil)—"Stoneman and Lydia Brown—The Mulatto"
5. Scene between father and daughter—theme 3 (Breil) Elsie Stoneman Motif (in three parts)
6. Introduction of Camerons of Piedmont—The Old Folks At Home (popular song)
7. Arrival of Stoneman sons—repeat of music from iv
8. Horseplay—Where Did You Get That Hat? (popular song + Breil music from iv)
9. A walk through the cornfields (Breil) + In The Gloaming (Harrison)
10. A visit to slave quarters—Zip Coon/Turkey In The Straw (popular song)[34]

A list of symphonic excerpts used in Breil's score for *Birth of a Nation* includes works by Bellini, Grieg, Mozart, Suppé, Tchaikovsky, Weber, and, infamously, Wagner's Ride of the Valkyries (to accompany the rescue by the Ku Klux Klan). Folk/popular tunes included "America (My Country 'Tis of Thee)," "Auld Lange Syne," "The Bonnie Blue Flag," "Comin' Thru the Rye," "I Wish I Was in Dixie," and many other Civil War-era tunes. Breil's score was succeeded by such landmark scores as Wilson's for *The Thief of Baghdad* (1924), William Axt's for *Don Juan* (1926), and Leo Pouget and Victor Alix's for *La Passion of Joan of Arc* (1928).[35]

Today, there are some original scores that are known and have been reconstructed with some degree of dependability. Gottfried Huppertz's score for Fritz Lang's *Metropolis* (1927), Hans Erdmann's score for Murnau's *Nosferatu* (1922), and Chaplin's scores for his own films still exist in some form and are occasionally performed with the films. Gillian Anderson notably has worked with the US Library of Congress in restoring and performing silent film scores, including some of the aforementioned scores, as well as those for Griffiths's *Intolerance* (Breil, 1916), *Broken Blossoms* (Gottschalk, 1919), *Way Down East* (Peters/Silvers, 1920), and others. While these scores exert an irresistible pull of historical interest, many of them are combinations of original and compiled music and have had a long and complex journey to their present forms,[36] and few can claim irrefutable evidence of historical veracity.

In the thirty years of history of the silent film in its original incarnation, the film score had gone from a complete no-man's-land of unpredictability, through a series of forms in which greater control was gradually exercised over the nature and content of the music associated with each film, to its final stage: the original film score. While the vagaries of performance still left some room for uncertainty,[37] the original score resulted in the one-film/one-score convention that would be technically codified by the development of synchronized sound. "The coming of sound further standardized the already industrialized mode of film production."[38] Whereas at the birth of film any individual work could be seen with any number of different musical accompaniments, now it could be seen with only one: until the rebirth of the art form of multiple scores for silent film in the 1980s.

Silent Film Music Conventions

The preceding discussion of historical silent film music composition can be summarized in the following list of conventions:

1. **Live performance**. By necessity, silent film music was performed live, on site, coincident with the projection of the film. Whether improvised on the spot, drawn from an assemblage of cue books and compiled scores, or composed specifically to be played in synchronization with the film, the music was delivered in person.
2. **Duration**. The music lasted throughout the duration of the film, and with a few short gaps for emphasis or scene changes, was continuous from beginning to end (early unsatisfactory practices cited earlier notwithstanding). The ostensible goal of this practice is to keep the perceiver "immersed" in the diegetic world of the film.
3. **Mimetic music** (musical sound effects). "Mimetic music, usually in some rhythmic way, mimes or imitates action."[39] This technique is described in the earliest writing about film music in its first era, for example, drum rim shots for gunshots or crashes, or violin glissandi for an object falling.
4. **Symbolic music** (referential). "Symbolic music, because of listeners' familiarity with its cultural usage or lyric content, makes quick reference to non-musical situations."[40] Symbolic music either (i) quotes titles or

lyrics, or (ii) quotes styles (classical music can be used to represent high-culture, punk rock can be used to represent rebellion).
5. **Structure of music/film**. The structure of the music mirrors the structure of the montage, with music cues beginning and ending (or transitioning) in sync with the editing of the film.
6. **Leitmotifs/themes**. Leitmotifs and themes are specifically connected to characters, locations, and narrative elements (chases, relationships, betrayal, etc.). In the context of film music, a leitmotif is a short melodic or rhythmic phrase that is memorable enough to be recalled when heard again and often used (notably by Richard Wagner in his operas, with whom the technique is often associated) to make connections in a film/score.
7. **Tempo/rhythm matching the rhythm of the editing/action**. Fast tempos for the chase scenes and comedy, slow, lugubrious tempos for tragedy and melodrama, a loping rhythm for a cowboy picture, and a tango/bolero for going "south of the border."
8. **Orchestration**. Music for silent films is expected to be performed by an organ or by a solo piano (preferably upright and out-of-tune). Despite the fact that large cities often featured orchestras of up to seventy musicians, this trope remains in the popular imagination.
9. **Melodic/harmonic conventions**. Diminished chords for villains, major sevenths for love themes, parallel fifths for Native Americans, and harmonic minor scales for "Arabian" settings (or virtually any other non-Western culture).
10. **Silent film era music** (1895–1927). By definition, music written or sourced for films during the silent film era was contemporaneous to that time period. It may be historical, but it is not from post-1927. Hence, music of that era is associated, from that time onward, with film of that era, and vice versa.

Of course, not every score featured all of these techniques, but then as now, speed was a primary feature of the creation of film music, and this musical shorthand made reliable connections between composers and audiences.[41]

It is beyond the scope of this book to carry on an in-depth discussion of the implications of the change in the role of music during the historical evolution from live sound to sync sound.[42] Its importance for the purpose of this discussion is that *certain* conventions from the silent film era were carried into the sound film era, by audiences, by film directors, by studio executives, and by composers, and it is these conventions that are carried into their work by *contemporary* composers of scores for silent films. It is the water they have been swimming in for their entire careers until they create their first score for silent film, and even if they don't come to contemporary scores for silent film from a substantial background in contemporary film scoring (as some do and some don't, as will be seen in later chapters), they have been exposed to these conventions as audiences of contemporary film culture, as consumers of media, including film.

While most film histories cite *The Jazz Singer* (1927) as the beginning of the sound film era, the transition from silent film to sound film was a gradual and uneven one. Indeed, attempts to synchronize sound with image began before the successful pioneering of film in the late nineteenth century, and many interim versions of various effectiveness paved the transition to sound film in which dialogue, sound effects, and music were able to be effectively recorded, mixed, and edited. In the 1920s and early 1930s, Lee De Forest's Phonophone, Warners's Vitaphone, Fox's Movietone, and many others were offering some combination of music and sound, some with only music, some with only speech, and some documentary recordings of live performances of "recitation, songs, non-narrative performances and interviews."[43]

During this period, both creators and audiences were going through a radical readjustment of their experience of film, film sound, and film music.[44] Most importantly, for the craft of film scoring and film music's role in the "realism" of film, the maintenance of the audience's immersion in the narrative world of the film had to change at a fundamental level. No longer was the music performed live in the theater, with the characters and setting of the film remaining up on the screen. Now it was all up on the screen. And, most significantly, now music had to share the aural space with dialogue, and with production sound, sound effects, and, eventually, sound design.[45]

Silent Film Music Conventions Applied to Sound Film Scoring

Just as the musical techniques associated with both spectacle and narrative films were carried into silent film scoring from previous performance traditions such as theater, magic, circus, and magic lantern shows, composers for the sound film did not invent the film scoring language from scratch. They were too busy with the considerable task of solving technical challenges, reimagining conceptual relationships, and adapting established practices at a breakneck pace to keep up with the demand for a new commercial product.

Claudia Gorbman has written illuminatingly about some of these challenges, for example, in her analysis of Max Steiner's score for *King Kong* (1933). Early in one of the first important film scores in sound films, occupying 75 of the 103 minutes of the film, the (diegetic) sounds of native drumming and chanting are accompanied by the (non-diegetic) RKO orchestra: when the chief discovers he is being observed, he cuts off the drumming, and the orchestra stops as well. The music is anything but "invisible," yet it is clear that filmmakers and audiences were still not sure what the proper role of musical underscore should be in relation to the film narrative. Gorbman asks,

> Are we to believe that Denham is shooting a *silent* film of all this dancing, chanting and drumming? No sound recording apparatus gets caught *in flagrante delicto* along with the camera. If a microphone and a soundman were accompanying Denham, what would the mike pick up? Would it record the drumming, the chanting, and the RKO orchestra? We know the "obvious" answer to this question, but this scene seems to test its very obviousness in eliminating, on the diegetic level, a soundman along with Denham and his camera. It is as if sound in a film has no technological base, involves no work, is natural, and will simply "show up."[46]

Davison asserts that "a number of the scoring functions which gradually became standardized after the coming of sound can be traced back to practices which developed during the silent era."[47] She includes music's role as a continuity device, "sneaking in and sneaking out," and music as a narrating device.

The following list is an examination of the ways in which the distinguishing conventions of the silent film score, as enumerated earlier in the chapter, were, and were not, carried into the sync-sound film era of scoring.

1. **Live performance**. By definition, sound film music is not performed live; it is prerecorded and edited and mixed with the other sound elements. The relationship between the musicians and the audience is no longer part of the performance/spectacle tradition, and much that goes with it is lost. The "excessive, 'music hall' aesthetic of collective performance" and "potentially disruptive and heterogeneous spaces of spectacle and distraction" become a "more formalized theatrical regime of film exhibition."[48] In addition, both the challenges and satisfactions of live performance practice are eliminated as well.

2. **Length**. Composers had to learn a new technique: how to get the music in and get it out without the audience noticing. Film sound had become "realistic" and the score needed to become "invisible" and achieve all the other outcomes documented in Gorbman's "Classical Film Music Principles" without being noticed. The goal of this practice is still to keep the perceiver immersed in the diegetic world of the film. But now it must be done in a series of shorter cues, sometimes interspersed with quite long periods without music, with just dialogue and production sound.
3. **Mimetic music** (musical sound effects). Mimetic music, now dismissed as "Mickey-Mousing" is mostly reserved for cartoons (notably in Carl Stalling's great scores for the Warner Brothers cartoons of the 1940s onward, and in their modern progeny *Animaniacs* (Spielberg, 1993–1998), *Tiny Toon Adventures* (Spielberg, 1990–1992), *The Ren and Stimpy Show* (Kricfalucy, 1991–1996) et al.), although the practice of closely following the dramatic beats persisted, especially in the practice of the "Golden Age" composers (Steiner, Rózsa, and Korngold et al.), and is still often used by composers today in some contexts.
4. **Symbolic music** (referential). Both versions of symbolic music (song quotes and styles) have survived and thrived. Some directors have repeatedly based on their entire scores on the inventive use of licensed music in this fashion; Stanley Kubrick, Martin Scorsese, and Quentin Tarantino have often done away with the composer altogether. But even in composed scores, symbolic music was, and continues to be, a prominently used technique.
5. **Structure of music/film**. The structure of the music mirrors the structure of the montage, with music cues beginning and ending (or transitioning) in sync with the editing of the film. This has continued mostly unchanged, with a very few exceptions, some examples of which are referred to in this book.
6. **Leitmotif/themes for characters, locations, and narrative elements**. This technique is as ubiquitous as ever, notably in the work of John Williams, but also by many other composers, including "A list" Hollywood composers, as well as internationally. It is a rare film score that doesn't use this technique to some degree.
7. **Tempo/rhythm matching the rhythm of the editing/action:** This technique is almost as ubiquitous as technique 6, although occasional use of the asynchronous music cue, as in the examples cited in Chapter 1, has

become a familiar trope: operatic arias are now the de rigueur soundtrack for scenes of explicit violence.
8. **Orchestration**. The orchestral film score is still the dominant Hollywood model, although a number of factors (lower budgets, digital technology, the pervasiveness of pop music) have made this less universal.
9. **Melodic/harmonic conventions.** While melodic and harmonic conventions became much broader and more widely varied in the years following the silent film era, basic tropes have mostly continued unchanged (dissonance for threat or evil, minor scales for sadness or ethnicity, major tonalities for happiness or innocence).
10. **Music of the era**. Much of the music of the 1920s, particularly ragtime piano, became associated with the silent film era, and thus became a semiotic cue for historicity. Films like *The Sting* (Hill 1973) and *Bugsy Malone* (Parker 1976) use 1920s music, especially jazz and ragtime of that era, to place their setting historically and geographically.

Practitioners of Sound Film Scoring

Throughout the sound film era, the tropes identified by Claudia Gorbman in her "Classical Principles" have remained dominant. This is not only reflected in after-the-fact analyses of film music, but it is enshrined in every technical instructional text, and often in composer interviews therein. Two widely used technical manuals for film scoring are still Earl Hagen's *Scoring for Films* (1971)[49] and Karlin and Wright's *On the Track: A Guide to Contemporary Film Scoring* (1990).[50] In *Scoring for Films,* Hagen conducts "A Symposium on the Composer's Views Towards Psychology" in which he asks questions of a number of "A List" Hollywood film composers of his time about their approaches to composing for films (this roundtable includes Alfred Newman, Hugo Friedhofer, Jerry Goldsmith, Quincy Jones, Leonard Rosenman, and Lalo Schifrin). Questions include, "What contribution do you feel that the composer must make for his film?" and "To what extent does the picture dictate the necessities and style of the musical score?"

Newman says, "I would say, without equivocation that the picture dictates the necessity and style of the musical score, totally . . . the film must always dictate the spirit, style and psychology of any score." To the second question, Hugo Friedhofer replies, in a word, "Completely." It's worth noting that while

Newman and Friedhofer are Golden Age composers, the interview also includes Silver Age composers Jerry Goldsmith, Quincy Jones, and Lalo Schifrin, who are also in agreement on this topic. Lalo Schifrin comments that "[film music] creates the perfect psychological climate for the audience to be absorbed by what is going on in the scene," while Jerry Goldsmith says, "We should write music that underlines the basic emotions of the film, the story, the drama—we should tie together sequences." These composers, particularly Goldsmith (*Planet of the Apes*, 1968, and *Chinatown*, 1974) and Jones (*The Pawnbroker*, 1964, and *In Cold Blood*, 1967), are among the most creative and innovative in film music history. However, these quotes make clear that certain assumptions are taken for granted and remain in place from generation to generation.[51] In 1995, John Williams in an article in *Time* magazine said, "Movie scores have changed very little over the years. The fundamental grammar comes from operatic incidental music of the 19th century. That is still the accepted language of the popular film era."[52] Karlin and Wright go on to write that "music must fulfil the expectations generated by the film."[53] They go on to report that a study in the December 2002 issue of *Science* reported that "the abstract knowledge about the harmonic relationships in music inscribes itself on the human cortex, guiding expectations of how musical notes should relate to one another as they are played."[54] They quote David Huron, head of the cognitive and systematic musicology laboratory at Ohio State University, concluding that "our brains have adapted to the way music is."[55] And finally, "This addresses the issue of audience expectations and is very relevant to the art and science of film scoring."[56] And, as recently as 2009, *The Reel World: Scoring For Pictures* instructs the aspiring film music composer: "First and most important, is to speak with your director and see what types of music she or he thinks are the most appropriate for the film."[57] In 2017, Andy Hill posits the attributes of the dramatic music of the ancient Greeks and assures the aspiring film composer, "If your music hasn't met all of them, you can be sure that any director who knows what he or she is doing will object."[58] And remember the professional advice of blockbuster composer Hans Zimmer quoted in the Introduction to this book: "Stick with the story like glue."[59]

These are the basic beliefs that contemporary composers bring to the table when beginning a silent film score: established music scoring practice, based both on established conventions and on expectations about silent film music and about film music in general.

Writers about film music also bring assumptions and reference points to both their experience and their critical writing. It is pertinent here to look at what *these* assumptions and conventions are, and how they compare with those of practitioners.

Film Music Analysis: Further Discussion

In "The Hidden Heritage of Film Music: History and Scholarship," K.J. Donnelly suggests semiotics and musicology as the two basic approaches that have historically been used to critique film music.

> Semiotics is concerned with cultural coding, with the way that film music can communicate with an audience through its recognisable elements within certain contexts . . . and is concerned with music as a functional item that exists within the film purely for its communicational value. . . . Musicology, on the other hand, suggests that there are other contexts in which to situate the music, particularly that of its production and relations to the traditions of orchestral music in the classical concert hall.[60]

These reflect Redner's historical analysis (see Chapter 1), and other film music writers who focus on how *meaning* is created in film music, either from a technical (how do they do it?) or semiotic (what does it mean?) point of view.[61] Donnelly goes on to point out that "music is never a simple transitive communication between 'text' and audience, but a more complex process where the music's 'meaning' is imprecise, always excessive to its context, and can never be seen as finite."[62] The mechanical process of film music-making has traditionally been to try to sharpen the meaning (of the film) so that the audience "gets it," and the meaning is clear.

The duality of musicology and semiotics runs parallel to the distinction made by Leonard B. Meyer in *Emotion and Meaning in Music* (1956) between absolutists (those who feel that musical meaning lies within the "context of the work itself"[63]) and referentialists (those who believe music has additional aspects that refer to "concepts, actions, emotional states and character").[64] Particularly relevant is his contention that the two are not mutually exclusive and that "arguments are a result of a tendency toward philosophical monism rather than a product of any logical opposition between types of meaning."[65] What is useful for film music analysis is for both of these viewpoints to be freed from presumptions about their potential application.

Many writers on meaning in music agree that the notion of *expectation* is pivotal in the listener's experience,[66] regardless of whether that expectation is created through absolute or referential means. Nowhere is this more true than in film music, where not only both learned and inherent musical meaning comes into play but also reference to a life of experiencing film music (as well as television shows, commercials, and music videos), what Kassabian calls *competence*; this is reflected in both the self-perpetuating repetition caused by the use of other film music in contemporary film score temp music and, for example, the use by the band Darth Vegas of classic film music cues as referential music in their score for *Nosferatu* (Murnau 1922) (see Chapter 4 for details).

In his book *Film Music* (2005), Peter Larsen points out that music analysis "is an interest-controlled activity . . . we always analyse with a specific purpose."[67] Both the musicological and semiotic approaches still take as given the assumption that the major purpose of film music is to underscore the presumptive narrative of the film. The issue of whether this is the best, or only, objective is not explicitly questioned. To a certain extent this is natural in a contemporary sound film, because, for reasons given in Chapter 1, inevitably the mutual goals of the director and the composer result in a close collaboration. It is only in contemporary scores for historical silent films that these two goals have the potential to diverge. This is where Kassabian's distinction between *assimilating* and *affiliating* identifications comes into play. "Assimilating identifications track perceivers toward a rigid, tightly controlled position that tends to line up comfortably with aspects of dominant ideologies. Affiliating identifications track perceivers toward a more loosely defined position that groups or affiliates several different narrative positions with a fantasy scenario together."[68] Kassabian's notion of affiliating identifications points the way to an alternative approach to film scoring.[69] It is some of the first critical writing to suggest that it is a desirable quality to score a film with music that has a wider potential for affect and interpretation by the audience. Up to this point, most critical writing shows how music leads the perceiver to a particular understanding or emotional state, with the highest praise reserved for the music that leads most compellingly.

The assumption that the desires of the film director and the audience coincide, based on previous experience and practice, is expressed by Tim Anderson's comment, "[Gorbman's thesis that 'music binds an audience together'] posits a focused analysis of the performance of film music that embraces a dialogical relationship between the desires of the 'film' and the moment-to-moment pleasures of the audience."[70] However, it is possible that an audience could be delighted by unexpected music that would give them pleasure precisely because of the element of surprise, and by its more idiosyncratic offerings. "Rather than sound creating a binding response by the audience (somewhat like a voice-over moderator explaining to the audience what they are supposed to be seeing/experiencing), couldn't . . . film music offer the audience members an individual experience in their own response to the sound/image relationship?"[71]

Emilio Audissino rejects the "form/content split" which he sees as inherent in most contemporary academic film music theory. Building upon the film theory concept of Neoformalism associated with Kristin Thompson and David Bordwell,[72] he builds his *Film/Music Analysis* approach on the foundation that music cannot be considered as either in cooperation with or in opposition to the film (synchronous/asynchronous), but must be seen as an integral part of a single entity which *is* the film (see Kalinak, Chapter 1).[73] However, while he builds a compelling case, it lives in the world of synchronized sound films. Central to the conceptual liberation of contemporary scores for silent film is abandoning the idea of music and image/narrative as parts of a single entity (the sound film), but rather to see them as (at least potentially) two independent elements, each capable of moving freely, in terms of meaning and in terms of their relationship to each other. Sound films are static in this way; silent films are fluid.

Writing About Contemporary Scores for Silent Film

Until very recently, relatively little has been written about contemporary scores for silent film as a distinct art form, apart from sporadic reviews of performances. The writing there mostly addresses the effect of contemporary music on audiences viewing silent films, and the advantages of "familiar" music.

In a study done at McGill University in 2008, Blair Davis used contemporary electronic scores as a way of provoking deeper engagement with silent films from students in her film history class. Using four films (*The Cabinet of Dr. Caligari* [Wiene, 1920], *Man with a Movie Camera* [Vertov, 1929], *Ballet Mechanique* [Léger/Murphy, 1924], and *Haxan: Witchcraft Through the Ages* [Christensen, 1922]), she shows, by way of a written "spectatorship survey" and subsequent discussion groups, that students both prefer and are more engaged by silent films, when experienced with contemporary scores, rather than "old" music (both orchestral and organ scores). While the survey is a fairly informal one, without proper control groups, this article does advance the notion that the very anachronism that some would fear to cause disengagement had the opposite effect on many students—imbuing the films with a sense of "modernity" and helping them find a way into films they might have otherwise rejected out of hand.[74] In the survey, Davis used both music that was juxtaposed at random, such as DJ Spooky's "Songs of a Dead Dreamer" with *The Cabinet of Dr. Caligari* (1920), and composed scores, such as the Cinematic Orchestra's score for *Man with a Movie Camera* (1929). The article does not address the issue of the composer's intent (only present in the second selection), but it does indicate that there is a cumulative new experiential result derived from the juxtaposition of the semiotic associations with both silent black-and-white film and contemporary electronic music. It is this kind of relationship that is brought on by scores such as Black Francis's (The Pixies) score for *The Golem* (Wegener/Boese, 1920), performed by a rock band, and Gary Lucas's score for the same film, performed on solo guitar with extensive electronic processing, Giorgio Moroder's disco score for *Metropolis* (Lang, 1928) or Philip Glass's minimalist score for *Dracula* (Browning, 1931).

"Alternate Soundtracks: Silent Film Music for Contemporary Audiences"[75] explores the practices of the Motion Picture Company, a contemporary ensemble that performs an interpretation of compiled scores for silent films. Under the heading "Recognisable Music," Thorp and McPhee explain,

> In choosing music for the shows that we produce, we are particularly aware of the historical context of the films' production and narrative setting, and the fact we are using music that was actually played as an accompaniment to the films shown in Sydney theatres during the silent era. If they were devised as strictly musically accurate, the shows would risk offering little emotional engagement for a modern audience.[76]

One practice was to

> use music that a modern audience recognises as belonging to the era of the film. Thus, in Harold Lloyd comedies of the 1910s and 1920s we use music such as "What'll I Do" by Irving Berlin that was used in *The Great Gatsby* (Jack Clayton, 1974—US release) and is recognisable as belonging to the 1920s. For earlier comedies we use rags such as "Twelfth Street Rag" by Euday Bowman,[77] composed in 1914. This was one of the best-selling rags of the World War One era and the style and, to a large extent, the tune is familiar to contemporary audiences.[78]

They assert that "popular music of the period does not fit in well" (presumably because this music is unknown to contemporary audiences), but classical music excerpts, such as von Suppé's "Light Cavalry Overture" or Rossini's "William Tell Overture," are still recognizable, and, as such, effective. Overall, their technique is to use contemporary tools to accomplish the goals of early silent film music: leitmotif, improvisations based on cue sheet riffs, and traditional dramatic scoring "to be as historically accurate as possible, while offering an entertaining presentation." But just as music in film was once a neglected topic in writing on film theory, there is the very beginning of a body of work of serious analysis of contemporary scores for silent film by academics and practitioners alike. Parts II & III of *Today's Sounds for Yesterday's Films* (2016), edited by K.J. Donnelly and Ann-Kristin Wallengren ("Novel Music and New Issues"/ academics, and "Current Practices and New Traditions"/practitioners),[79] and Part IV of *Music and Sound in Silent Film* (2019), edited by Ruth Barton and Simon Trezise,[80] which also contains work by both academics and practitioners, as well as journal articles by Bellano, Donnelly, and others,[81] all over the last five years or so, are hopefully the beginning of a larger examination of this art form and the theoretical/practical issues at hand. Hopefully, this book will contribute to this list.

But despite the lack of extensive critical and academic attention, there is an incredibly rich body of work, developed around the world, of contemporary musical accompaniment for silent film, performed at film festivals, silent film festivals,[82] arts centers, and even local film theatres. Some of these works investigate possibilities for alternative relationships between music and film image/narrative. In the following chapter, I will begin to discuss some of the existing body of work in the art form of contemporary scores for silent film.

Notes

1 Wierzbicki, *Film Music: A History*, 19.
2 Ibid., 19., and Cooke, *A History of Film Music*, 7–9.
3 Wierzbicki, *Film Music: A History*, 19.
4 Cooke, *A History of Film Music*, 7–9.
5 Some excellent research has been done, despite the lack of audio recordings, notably in John Whiteoak's *Playing Ad Lib: Improvisatory Music in Australia 1836–1970*. In his second chapter, which looks in detail at silent film accompaniment practices, he quotes 100-year-old pianist Carmen Naylor, "You would just put your hands on the keys and play, or start in a certain key—and the key itself [pause] . . . I can't explain it to you" (Whiteoak, *Playing Ad Lib*, 66–8). Despite some much more detailed descriptions of practices, these can't possibly do justice to the (potential but inevitable) diversity and idiosyncrasy of improvised silent film accompaniment

practiced by hundreds, if not thousands, of musicians around the world over the thirty-year history of silent film.

6 Cooke, *A History of Film Music*, 13. There were exceptions. Martin Marks has made a careful study of music that has survived (in part) for films by Emil and Max Skladanowski that were shown in 1895 at the Wintergarden Theatre in Berlin. The accompaniment for these films included both precomposed music (Glinka, Gillet) and new music composed specifically for the films (Kruger, Hoffman) (Martin Marks, *Music and the Silent Film*, 29–48). What is not known is how this music directly related to the film.

7 Roger Manvell, and John Huntley, *The Technique of Film Music* (New York: Communications Arts Books, 1967), 20, cited in Marks, *Music and the Silent Film*, 28.

8 Marks, *Music and the Silent Film*, 29.

9 Sergio Micelli, *Musica per film. Storia, estetica—analisi, tipologie* (Milano: Ticodi, 2009), 40: "Everyone relied upon their own repertoire, reading the music or playing by heart, with little and more or less questionable adjustments to the film. So it should not be excluded that the definition [of improvisation], especially when used by a musician, was used as a reference more to the etymological root than to the musical practice, identifying thus a performance staged with an improvisational mindset, that is to say without preliminary preparation." As quoted in Bellano, "Silent Strategies," 52.

10 Bellano, "Silent Strategies," 52.

11 See, for example, Negativland, Plunderphonics and the Avalanches, among many others.

12 Gillian B. Anderson, *Music for Silent Films 1894-1929: A Guide* (Washington, DC: Library of Congress, 1988), xix.

13 Anderson, "Reforming 'Jackass Music,'" 49.

14 Ibid.

15 Ibid., 53.

16 C.E. Sinn, "Music for the Picture," *Moving Picture World*, July 1, 1911, 1509, cited in Anderson, "Reforming 'Jackass Music,'" 50.

17 Levi, cited in Manvell and Huntley, *The Technique of Film Music*, 19.

18 Anderson, "Reforming 'Jackass Music,'" 50.

19 Ernö Rapée, *Encyclopedia of Music for Pictures* (New York: Belmont, 1925) and Hugo Riesenfeld, "Music and Motion Pictures," in *The ANNALS of the American Academy of Political and Social Science* 128, no. 1 (November 1926): 58–62.

20 George Beyon, *Musical Presentation of Motion Pictures* (New York: Schirmer, 1921) in Altman, *Silent Film Sound*, 368.

21 Ibid.

22 Ibid.
23 These codes evolved into the contemporary practice of using music libraries, and then sample libraries in contemporary music production.
24 Neumeyer and Buhler, "Analyzing the Music," 24.
25 See Wierzbicki's more detailed study of this practice in Wierzbicki, *Film Music: A History*, 36–41.
26 "Incidental Music for Edison Pictures," *Edison Kintogram* (September 15, 1909): 12–13. Reproduced in Charles Merrell Berg, *An Investigation of the Motives and Realization of Music to Accompany the American Silent Film, 1896-1927* (New York: Arno Press, 1976), 103, quoted in Altman, *Silent Film Sound*, 265.
27 Anderson, *Music for Silent Films*, 32.
28 Van Vechten, 1916, in Marks, *Music and the Silent Film*, 11.
29 In Australia, the habit of commissioning original scores for films never developed; my research has not been able to turn up a single historical original score composed for an Australian silent film.
30 Medcalfe, "Hollywood Theater," *The American Organist* 7, no. 11 (1924): 642–4, quoted in Anderson, *Music for Silent Films*, xxxix.
31 Marks, *Music and the Silent Film*, 53.
32 Royal S. Brown, *Overtones and Undertones: Reading Film Music* (Berkeley and Los Angeles: University of California Press, 1994), 53.
33 For example, Marks, *Music and the Silent Film*; Cooke, *A History of Film Music*; Wierzbicki, *Film Music: A History*, etc.
34 Marks's book *Music and the Silent Film: Contexts and Case Studies 1895-1924* contains a detailed analysis of all the original cues in the film, as well as popular/folk songs and classical excerpts.
35 Anderson, *Music for Silent Film*, xl–xlii.
36 See Emilio Audissino's "Gottfried Huppertz's *Metropolis*: The Acme of 'Cinema Music,'" in *Today's Sounds for Yesterday's Films* (2016), ed. K.J. Donnelly and Ann-Kristin Wallengren (UK: Palgrave Macmillan, 2016), 45–63, or Paul Cuff's "Presenting the Past: Abel Gance's *Napoléon* (1927), from Live Projection to Digital Reproduction," *Kinétraces Editions* 2 (2017): 120–42.
37 Ibid. *Birth of a Nation* was circulated with a different score to Breil's on the West Coast, and Wilson's score for *The Thief of Baghdad* was considered too technically challenging for any but the musicians in the largest city and was thus subsequently circulated with an alternative compiled score.
38 Davison, *Hollywood Theory, Non-Hollywood Practice*, 19.
39 Wierzbicki, *Film Music: A History*, 22.
40 Ibid.
41 Prendergast, *Film Music: A Neglected Art*, 10.

42 For a more in-depth discussion of this topic see Nancy Wood, "Text and Spectator in the Period of the Transition to Sound" (PhD diss., University of Kent, 1983).
43 Gorbman, *Unheard Melodies*, 46.
44 Interestingly, this transition is has been the subject of films great and small, from *Singing in the Rain* (Donen and Kelly, 1952), and *The Artist* (Hazanavicius, 2011) to Mel Brooks's *Silent Film* (1976).
45 As Gorbman puts it, "music in the sound film does not occupy the soundtrack in isolation. Rather, background music shares the soundtrack with other acoustic phenomena (dialogue, effects, music) whose ostensible source is located in the diegetic space" (Gorbman, *Unheard Melodies*, 41).
46 Gorbman, *Unheard Melodies*, 75. Itaics in original.
47 Davison, *Hollywood Theory, Non-Hollywood Practice*, 20.
48 See footnote 13.
49 Earl Hagen, *Scoring for Films* (Van Nuys, CA: Alfred Publishing Co. Inc., 1971.)
50 Fred Karlin and Ray Wright, *On the Track: A Guide to Contemporary Film Scoring* (New York: Schirmer/MacMillan, 1990.)
51 Like Goldsmith, Leonard Roseman is acknowledged as one of the true innovators and boundary-breakers in the Silver Age of film music. Here he says, "The music can contribute a great deal; in support of an overall shape, *but this shape originates with the film itself, not the music*" (my italics). (Burt, *The Art of Film Music*, 5).
52 Michael Walsh, "Music: Running Up the Scores," *Time Magazine*, September 5, 1995.
53 Karlin and Wright, *On the Track,* 129.
54 Ibid.
55 Ibid.
56 Ibid.
57 Jeff Rona, *The Reel World: Scoring for Pictures* (Milwaukee, WI: Hal Leonard Books, 2009), 6.
58 Hypothesizing what music was written for *Oedipus Rex* (429 BCE), he writes, "The music was homophonic, modal and rhythmically simple, but we can make a reasonable guess that it met the following three requirements: it entered and exited the scene at dramatically appropriate times; it was tonally appropriate (in the sense of both mode and color); it supported rather than intruded upon or conflicted with the story. These remain, more than two millennia later, the basic criteria for dramatic music." Andy Hill, *Scoring the Screen: The Secret Language of Film Music* (New York and London: Rowman & Littlefield, 2017), xx.
59 Zimmer, "Zimmer Teaches Film Scoring."
60 K. J. Donnelly, "The Hidden Heritage of Film Music," in *Film Music: Critical Approaches,* ed. K.J. Donnelly (New York: Continuum, 2001), 2.

61 Redner, *Deleuze and Film Music*, 7.
62 Donnelly, "The Hidden Heritage of Film Music," 2.
63 Leonard B. Meyer, *Emotion and Meaning in Music* (Chicago: University of Chicago Press, 1956), 172.
64 Ibid.
65 Ibid.
66 Ibid. plus, Annabel Cohen, "Music as a Source of Emotion in Film," 263 and Annabel Cohen, "How Music Influences the Interpretation of Film and Video."
67 Peter Larsen, *Film Music* (London: Reaktion Books, 2005), 39.
68 Kassabian, *Hearing Film*, 141.
69 Interestingly, she tracks these identifications across both purpose-composed and licensed music; in earlier writing licensed music is mostly viewed only as a threat to the assumed more valued music by a film composer. Yet by the twenty-first century licensed music has become so firmly entrenched in film music (indeed has been so for decades) that it must be dealt with as a subgroup of the form.
70 Anderson, "Reforming 'Jackass Music,'" 51.
71 Filmmaker Tim Kennedy, in personal communication with author, December 25, 2014.
72 Audissino builds this theoretical development across numerous works of contemporary writers on film music theory, including works by Bordwell and Thompson, in Chapter 4 of his *Film Music Analysis*, 67–94.
73 "Hence, the method focusses on how music functions in these three areas. I call this Neoformalist method Film/Music Analysis to mark the strong audio-visual interrelation subtended to it it is not a musical analysis of 'film music' but a filmic analysis of how film and music interact to produce an interconnected audiovisual system." Audissino, *Film/Music Analysis*, 88.
74 Blair Davis, "Old Films, New Sounds: Screening Silent Cinema with Electronic Music," *Canadian Journal of Film Studies* 17, no. 2 (2008): 77–98.
75 Jan Thorp and Eleanor McPhee, "Alternate Soundtracks: Silent Film Music for Contemporary Audiences," *Screen Sound: The Australasian Journal of Soundtrack Studies* 2 (2010): 64–74.
76 Ibid., 69.
77 Here is yet another association of ragtime music with the silent film era.
78 Thorp and McPhee, "Alternate Soundtracks," 69.
79 *Today's Sounds for Yesterday's Films*, ed. K.J. Donnelly and Ann-Kristin Wallengren (UK: Palgrave Macmillan, 2016).
80 *Music and Sound in Silent Film: From the Nickelodeon to the Artist*, ed. Ruth Barton and Simon Trezise (New York and London: Routledge, 2019).

81 See citations throughout this book.
82 The Pordenone Silent Film Festival (Le Giornate del cinema muto), the Avignon/New York Film Festival, and the San Francisco Silent Film Festival are but three that regularly present silent films with contemporary scores.

3

Opportunities in Contemporary Scores for Silent Film

The contemporary score for silent film, as a hybrid art form,[1] derives from a number of points of origin. On the one hand, it is often a composer-generated art project, born of a love of film, a dissatisfaction with the strictures of the contemporary film scoring industry, or a search for new outlets and audiences. But in a parallel stream, DVD releases of silent films need music, and whether the producers turn to contemporary composers, license preexisting music, or turn to composer-generated projects (which are often focused on live performance), they necessarily reflect *someone's* concept of what silent film music is, and should or could be.

A fortuitous recent trend, though still more the exception than the rule, is the release of DVDs of early films with multiple scores, often contrasting in style, orchestration, and approach. The 2006 Eureka!/Transit Film release of F.W. Murnau's *Faust* (1926) features a contemporary orchestral score by Timothy Brock, and also a solo harp score by Stan Ambrose; the 2009 Kino International release features a compiled score by the Mont Alto Orchestra, a "piano score by Pérez de Azpeitia, adapted from the original 1926 orchestral arrangement" and Timothy Brock's new orchestral score. The 2011 Criterion Collection release of Victor Sjöström's *The Phantom Carriage* features two scores: one by Swedish composer Matti Bye and the other by experimental duo KTL, and the 2012 BFI release, *Fairy Tales: Early Colour Stencil Films from Pathé* (1901–8), features multiple commissioned scores from experimental composers from the Touch label. There are a number of reasons why the contemporary score for silent film is a particularly hospitable environment for these diverse and innovative film scoring practices.

In his influential paper "Now You See It, Now You Don't: The Temporality of the Cinema of Attractions,"[2] Tom Gunning makes a powerful case for treating the silent film era as a distinct art form from the subsequent history of sound film. He cites three major assumptions that held sway over critical writing on film through the 1970s: (i) that "early cinema [was] a preparatory period for later film styles and practices, the infancy of an art form"; (ii) that the development of film was an evolution of its true essence, an evolution from reproduction and theatricality to "a uniquely cinematic essence" (focusing on editing and a moveable camera, for example); and (iii) that this evolution led to the primacy of narrative or storytelling.³ While a case can be made for the first assumption on one level, in that it traces film music conventions through the silent film era into the sound film era, the positing of the silent film as an art form with unique characteristics is profound, especially regarding the role of music. The silent film has no other sound permanently connected with it, other than a live music (and potentially sound effects) score. There is no dialogue, no "atmospheric" sound, no sound effects, no sound design, and, of course, no music. This inherently gives the added music a greater role as the total sound aspect of the film experience.

Gorbman suggests the following reasons for music's original accompaniment of silent film:

> (i) It had accompanied other forms of spectacle before and was a convention that successfully persisted, (ii) It covered the distracting noise of the movie projector, (iii) It had important semiotic functions in the narrative: encoded according to late nineteenth-century conventions, it provided historical, geographical, and atmospheric setting, it helped depict and identify characters and qualify actions. Along with intertitles, its semiotic functions compensated for the characters' lack of speech. (iv) It provided a rhythmic "beat" to compliment, or impel, the rhythms of editing and movement on the screen, (v) As sound in the auditorium, its spatial dimension compensated for the flatness of the screen, (vi) Like magic, it was an antidote to the technologically derived "ghostliness" of the images. (vii) As music, it bonded spectators together.⁴

Music in silent film took on roles that were later, in the sync sound era, replaced by dialogue, sound effects, as well as, particularly in the digital era, sophisticated sound design, panning, EQ, and other digital audio postproduction techniques. In addition, possibly because of this large role taken on by music, the convention in silent film is that music runs through the entire length of the film.⁵ During the "Golden Age" of film music (the early 1930s through the early 1950s), music continued to play during a large majority of the length of the film. Scores like Steiner's for *King Kong* (Cooper/Schoedsack, 1933), Franz Waxman's for *The Bride of Frankenstein* (Whale, 1935), and Korngold's for *Captain Blood* (Curtiz, 1935) contained vast swathes of wall-to-wall music. However, as films moved toward greater naturalism through the second half of the twentieth century, music receded in most films to a smaller role in the film—in minutes, if not in importance. The composer's challenge became to create shorter music cues and discreetly sneak them in and out of the soundscape without the audience noticing.[6] However, the silent film score provides a chance for a composer to create a large-scale work, potentially with a long-form structure, albeit wrapped around the structure of the film. Finally, the unique quality of the silent film itself—the heightened style of acting, the silent film shooting techniques (such as lengthy close-ups), the fantastic improvisations of technical imagination in films like Lang's *Metropolis* (1927) and Murnau's *Faust* (1926) (later replaced by digital animation), and the sheer level of invention in the creation of a new art form/technology—made the silent film a rich terrain for innovation. In parallel to this journey of discovery, early practitioners were also inventing the role and technique of music in films, for example, the constantly shifting relationship between source music and underscore (diegetic vs. non-diegetic) in Gorbman's discussion of *King Kong* cited in Chapter 2.

Contemporary scores for silent film build upon this unique foundation by introducing elements newly brought into film in the advent of the last 100 years of film and music history. They have another century of the historical development of music to draw upon, from blues and jazz to rock and roll, aleatory and serial composition, minimalism, electronica, and black metal. They can assume the audience's familiarity with the movie-going experience and our collective familiarity with the cultural tropes of the film scoring language. They have the resources of new instruments, new styles, and new technologies. The contemporary score for silent film is most often an "art" project, and as such, not bound by commercial considerations. As the original creatives in making the film (director, producer) are no longer involved, this composer-driven project, for better or worse, is not bound to other collaborators. Their embodiment of multimedia potentially reorders the roles of film and music (especially when they are performed live), creating a cumulative spectacle in which the balance can be shifted between foreground and background. Silent film performances with live contemporary music are *happenings*: performative events.

In 1980–1, a peculiar thing happened. Two different composers, in two different countries, participated in large-scale projects in which a live orchestral score was performed in sync with the same silent film, Abel Gance's 1927 historical drama *Napoléon*. They were Carl Davis, a British composer of music for film, theater, dance, and concert works,[7] and Carmine Coppola, an American composer known primarily for his music for the films of his son, Francis Ford

Coppola (including *The Godfather* trilogy [1972, 1974, 1990] and *Apocalypse Now* [1979]). They were both commissioned to draw attention to a new restoration of the three-part epic by film historian Kevin Brownlow (Davis's in the United Kingdom and Coppola's in the United States).[8] Both scores used large swathes of precomposed classical music, in the style of the original "compiled scores," as well as folk music, French revolutionary songs, and a song from Napoleon's favorite opera (*Nina* by Giovanni Paisiello). They also both featured the French national anthem *La Marseillaise*, which features centrally in the narrative of the film. And both scores also contained their own newly composed original music.[9] The ongoing collaboration of Brownlow and Davis led to a rebirth of interest in silent film with live orchestral accompaniment (twenty-nine silent feature films between 1980 and 2007 for Thames Television),[10] and a reevaluation of both the silent film art form itself and silent film music performance practice, that is, the performance of live orchestral scores. Paul Cuff quotes music critic Michael Walsh saying at the time that "the live element of the performance commands a certain respect and attention" and that "the 'absence of spoken words' makes audiences all the more attentive to the art before them."[11]

It is true that historical silent films were projected in movie theatres from time to time between 1927 and 1980. In small repertory houses or on Saturday afternoons on programs with cartoons and newsreels, silent films would be shown for the entertainment of children and the occasional silent film enthusiast, often accompanied by solo pianists or organists, who would improvise musical accompaniment, often in (what was perceived as) the classic silent film style. It is possible that some of these accompaniments were not in a "silent film style"—though it's difficult to say absolutely, as these form a continuum with the "lost history" of the early improvised scores of the original silent film era. These accompaniments would inevitably have been influenced by the history of sync-sound film music as well. But I have so far not found any documentation of newly composed original silent film scores after the silent film era and before 1980.[12]

The real beginning of reinvention and playfulness in contemporary silent film scores began in earnest, to the best of my knowledge, with the American ensembles Club Foot Orchestra in San Francisco and Alloy Orchestra in Boston. In the case of the former, some of the scores performed by the group are written by the leader Richard Marriott and others are composed collectively. Marriott writes:

> I became interested in doing something visually that further expressed the ideas behind the music; something that would help put the music in context. I

considered projecting slides of experimental art on a screen behind us. Then a friend suggested, after catching our show: "The music is so cinematic, why don't you take outtakes of 1950s sitcoms and score them." I put it under my hat. Later that night I saw a Lily Tomlin skit on Saturday Night Live. She was reading the Dow Jones averages of various art trends. She reported, "Pop Art up 10 . . . Op Art up 20 . . . Expressionism down 30." I turned the channel. And there was *The Cabinet of Dr. Caligari*. The distorted sets and dreamlike atmosphere in the film were the qualities that I always envisioned accompanying our music. The subversive plot was drenched in the unconscious. I was obsessed to write for that film.[13]

That score was premiered at the 1987 Mill Valley Film Festival.[14] In 1991, the Alloy Orchestra was invited by a local film programmer to create a score for a screening of *Metropolis* at the Coolidge Corner Theater in Boston. Leader Ken Winokur writes, "We had done a wide variety of music for theater, installations, performance pieces etc., so this seemed like a fun and logical thing for us to do. We didn't have any expectations about doing this more than just a weekend but got really interested in the medium immediately."[15] Both groups have gone on to score many different silent films of all styles, nationalities, and genres and are regarded widely in the field as among the finest and most serious practitioners.[16]

However, since that time, the art form of contemporary scores for silent film has grown exponentially into a form that has attracted composers of all genres and has become a regular feature at film festivals, arts institutions, and concert halls. Composers identified with classical, jazz, folk, electronica, rock, hardcore, avant-garde, and many other genres have created scores for silent films, and there are a number of ensembles who have joined the Club Foot and Alloy orchestras in devoting themselves largely or virtually exclusively to performing new scores for silent film. In addition, the historical recreation of silent film scores in their original form, either by assembling compiled scores from original sources or by performing historical orchestral scores has also grown. The Mont Alto Motion Picture Orchestra is one such ensemble that uses instrumentation and source material that aspires to be a faithful reflection in spirit or fact of the historical silent film music experience.[17] They are both practitioners and historians of silent film music. The Moving Pictures Show is an Australian nine-piece chamber ensemble that screens films from 1912 until 1929 and performs accompaniment from compiled scores discovered in Australia, the United Kingdom, and the United States.[18] Gillian Anderson is a conductor, musicologist, and scholar who restores and performs historical original orchestral silent film scores.[19] Acknowledging the range and variety of every aspect of contemporary silent film scores (including style, instrumentation, historicity, technique, and intent), it is useful to compare a series of scores by different composers for the same film.

In the next section, I contrast and compare six scores for a segment[20] from Georges Méliès's most famous film *Voyage dans la lune* (1902) and discuss them both in terms of historical practice (of both silent and sound film scoring) and modernism (referencing the criteria for polysynchronicity). This will provide a snapshot of contemporary practice upon which subsequent analysis can be based. Fortunately, there exist multiple DVD recordings[21] that derive from both origins (live performances and the requirements of DVD releases), and the styles, approaches and conceptions of the music vary widely. Each score is discussed in terms of the tools used by the composers and in terms of what they say about the producer/creator's conception of what contemporary silent film music is or could be. The criteria discussed are as follows:

Mood: What is the feeling that the composer/producer is trying to create regarding what we are watching?
Genre: What style of music does the composer use to express that mood?
Orchestration: What instrumentation does the composer use to express or invoke that mood?
Attitude: What do these choices tell us about the attitude of the practitioner toward what we are watching?
Historicity: Is the score meant to be in the style of historic silent film music, or is it unrepentantly contemporary? Does it use any of the techniques of historic silent film scoring as a way of acknowledging that it is silent film music?
Synchronicity: Does the music follow the dramatic beats of the editing? Does it use trapping and/or musical sound effects?[22] Does it express (or attempt to express) the director's presumed intent?

Voyage dans la lune (Méliès, 1902): A Case Study[23]

Georges Méliès was one of the earliest and is still one of the most experimental of all filmmakers. Beginning his career as a cartoonist and then a magician, by 1888 he had taken over the theâtre of the master magician Jean-Eugène Robert-Houdin. Méliès's magic performances combined a flair for dramatic narrative with skilled sleight of hand and ingenious mechanical devices. It was in the pursuit of new spectacles for his stage show that he attended the first showing of the Lumière brothers' Cinématographe on December 28, 1895. He tried to buy the device but was turned down—he soon built his own version. From simple short films that showed magic illusions, he soon evolved into one of the first and greatest innovators of film special effects and trick photography. His films covered every known genre, including documentary, comedy, newsreel, melodrama, erotica, fairy tales, and science fiction, and included among his over 500 films such titles as *The Four Troublesome Heads* (1898), *The Merry Frolics of Satan* (1906), *The Wizard, the Prince and the Fairy* (1900), *Eight Girls in a Barrel* (1900), *Divers at Work on the Wreck of the "Maine"* (1898), and a series of nine films about the Dreyfus affair.[24] His 1902 film *Voyage dans la lune* (*Trip to the Moon*) is probably his best-known work: the iconic image of the rocket crashing into the eye of the "Man in the Moon" has been referenced in contemporary films (*From the Earth to the Moon* [Mostow, 1998] and *Hugo* [Scorsese, 2011]), used in rock videos (Queen, the Smashing Pumpkins, Katy Perry), and homaged on TV shows *The Simpsons* and *Futurama*.

While it is known that there was a piano player performing at early performances of *Voyage*, it is not known exactly what music was played.[25] Over the years, piano players at local movie houses surely performed diverse improvised scores. But the film has been released on and off over the years on DVD by various companies, varying from respected archivist preservationists Flicker Alley to smaller lesser-known companies (A-1 Video, Unknown Video, Arte Video). All of them include recorded music as part of the DVD package. A comparison of these scores gives an interesting perspective on the modern silent film score. The various releases of the film on DVD reflect a wide variety of ideas of what silent film music should be, which in turn reflect a broad range of conventions drawn from the silent and sound film eras, and contemporary music scoring practices. These presumptions influence the instrumentation, style, structure, tempo, and historical context of the music. For purposes of space and focus, I have chosen one particular sequence from the film to analyze.[26]

The first third of the film has followed the planning, construction, and preparation for building the rocket and taking off for the moon. As the scene in question begins (about one-third of the way into the film), a formal gathering awaits the prospective travelers to the moon. They arrive in top hats and waistcoats and salute the gathering. The rocket itself is wheeled into view, and the travelers rowdily pile into it. The rocket is loaded into a giant cannon by a chorus of young women dressed in sailor suits, who turn and wave to the camera (and, presumably, the audience). A general in military regalia arrives and commands the rocket be fired, and the well-dressed crowd of onlookers applauds and waves them farewell. As they take off, there is a crossfade to the moon, as personified by the Man in the Moon. In one of the most iconic images in early film history, the rocket lands on the moon, crashing into his eye.[27]

The sources of the six scores examined later are as follows:

1. *Marvelous Méliès* (A-1 Video)
2. *Ballerinas from Hell: A Georges Méliès Album* (Unknown Video)
3. *Méliès the Magician* (Arte Video)
4. *Georges Méliès: First Wizard of Cinema (1896-1913)* (Flicker Alley)
5. *The Alloy Orchestra Plays Wild and Weird: 14 Fascinating and Innovative Films (1902-1965)* (Flicker Alley)
6. *Le Voyage Dans La Lune* (Astralweks)

1. *Marvelous Méliès* (A-1 Video)

This score uses various minimalist synthesizer tracks throughout the film, which make no effort to sync with the visuals in any way. Vaguely "oriental" sounding, they start and stop randomly throughout the film.

In certain ways, this is probably similar to the earliest stream of the historical performances of silent film music in that it just tries to set a mood for the show as whole and doesn't attempt to follow the film closely at all.[28] The music for the scenes in question simply continues from the previous scene, plays throughout the scenes described earlier, and then stops randomly later; after a brief pause, another track begins. There are no credits for either performer or composer (Table 3.1).

Table 3.1 *Marvelous Méliès* Analysis

Composer/Performer	Uncredited
Mood	Mysterious, exotic
Genre	Synth-pop
Orchestration	Electronic/synth
Attitude	Old movies are spooky and "other"
Historicity	Completely modern (for its time), no attempt at historicity
Synchronicity	None whatsoever, not even the beginning of scenes, or films for that matter

Comments: While this is not an attempt to mimic conventions of historical silent film music, there is a comparison to be made with some of the issues brought up by critics of early film music practices, as referenced in Chapter 2.

2. *Ballerinas from Hell: A Georges Méliès Album* (Unknown Video)

A stylishly made but inexpensive release; all of the films are accompanied by an organ score (by Bob Vaughn) that sounds as though it were recorded live at a roller-skating rink.

The music is continuous throughout the DVD, running even through the transition between one film and another. The music for the scene in question begins in the previous scene with a sort of generic fanfare, and then once we are into the scene, moves onto a bouncy tune that one might associate with a happy outing in the park (or roller-skating rink). The music throughout is often somewhat tentative, as if the organist is seeing the film for the first time. In keeping with that suggestion, changes in the direction of the music often lag behind the scene changes. As the scene changes to the rocket launch, the music jumps to an explicit fanfare, and once it takes off again is in a transitional mode, nondescript, as though waiting to see what will happen next. It remains in this holding pattern until the rocket lands, at which point it returns to a jaunty bounce (Table 3.2).

3. *Méliès the Magician* (Arte Video)

Some early films were at times performed with narration—*Voyage* is one of them. The next few versions have narration, which is treated in different ways. A well-made DVD for its time, this one also contains a substantial documentary about Georges Méliès.

Table 3.2 *Ballerinas from Hell* Analysis

Composer/Performer	Bob Vaughn
Mood	Fanfare, bouncy, hesitant
Genre	Roller-skating rink organ
Orchestration	Theater organ
Attitude	The scene is charming, possibly because of its "antique" quality
Historicity	Implied historical accuracy (use of organ)
Synchronicity	None, not even beginning of scenes, or film

Comments: In some ways, this is quite a faithful reenactment of some early film music practices. The theater organ, which was widely used in silent film accompaniment, is what many people today expect for music for a silent film. But even more historically resonant is the sense that the accompanist is seeing the film for the first time and thinking on their feet. This is probably the context in which many silent film musical accompaniments outside of the major cities took place [a].

[a] See James Wierzbicki, *Film Music: A History* and Anderson, *Music for Silent Films*. This is why the lengthy composing/rehearsal process, and rigorously detailed synchronicity, and trapping of contemporary silent film artists the Alloy Orchestra and the Blue Grassy Knoll already merit recognition as at least an element of polysynchronicity.

Table 3.3 *Méliès the Magician* Analysis

Composer/Performer	Eric Le Guen
Mood	Mysterious, exciting
Genre	Light classical, ragtime
Orchestration	Solo piano
Attitude	Old movies are spooky
Historicity	Implied historical verisimilitude
Synchronicity	Multiple trapping, follows scene changes and dramatic beats

Comments: It reflects a common traditional approach by silent film accompanists today.

The musical accompaniment is solo piano, clearly composed for the film. It is in a "silent film music" style, being a combination of turn-of-the-century light classical and ragtime music. The scene in question begins with some vaguely Debussy-esque fanfares and then moves to a fast 2/4 tune when the scene switches to the launch. It then increases in tempo until it programmatically culminates in a big glissando to the bass register as the rocket takes off and stays in a low register tremolo throughout the space scene, including the moon impact. Music credits are "With original music by Eric Le Guen" (Table 3.3).

4. *Georges Méliès: First Wizard of Cinema (1896-1913)* (Flicker Alley)

This is the definitive set of Méliès films, a five-DVD edition (later followed by a sixth).[29] The version of *Voyage dans la lune* here has an orchestral accompaniment that can only be described as "light classical." It sounds like something from *Snow White and the Seven Dwarfs* (1937) or another Disney animated cartoon of that era. It begins with a light, cheerful strolling song as the crowd assembles and the travelers approach; there are several variations and a key change, but the theme is basically repeated until we cut to the cannon and the general. At this point, the music changes to a military march, ending with a timpani hit as the cannon is fired (not mixed convincingly with the rest of the music—this is treated as a sound effect). As the rocket flies up to the moon, we are treated to piano tremolos, suggesting mystery and wonder (stopping for a cymbal crash when the rocket goes into the Man in the Moon's eye).

In addition, there is a voice-over narration, complete with a French accent and numerous mispronunciations of words. The music is faded down during the narration and faded up during pauses (Table 3.4).

Table 3.4 *First Wizard of Cinema* Analysis

Composer/Performer	Robert Israel
Mood	Playful, charming, military
Genre	Light classical/theater music
Orchestration	Orchestral
Attitude	Innocent and exciting
Historicity	Implied historical accuracy
Synchronicity	Trapping on cannon and moon hit

Comments: Includes voice-over narration, under which music is raised and lowered (known as "dialogue-dodging" in contemporary film scoring parlance).

Table 3.5 *Wild and Weird* Analysis

Composer/Performer	The Alloy Orchestra
Mood	Exciting and fun, playful
Genre	Military march, sci-fi synth
Orchestration	Drums, keyboard synth
Attitude	It's a glorious undertaking, outer space is mysterious
Historicity	Modern in instrumentation and style, but historically referenced
Synchronicity	It traps the launch, but not the moon impact. It follows the dramatic beats and the scene changes.

Comments: This score, at least, is not really very wild or weird. It also has narration (no accent), which is consistent with historical practice. It is clearly meant to be in the silent film style, yet with some modern styles and references. The implication is that the accompanists use silent film-era practices but reflected through the lens of their own (contemporary) musical style.

5. *The Alloy Orchestra Plays Wild and Weird: 14 Fascinating and Innovative Films (1902-1965)* (Flicker Alley)

Despite their reputation for "garbage-can percussion," their *Trip to the Moon* is a fairly conventional synth score with drum set accompaniment.

The structure is completely locked into scene changes. The scene in question begins with a stately synth march with a martial beat on the drums; it repeats its binary structure through the first part of the scene, moving from major to the relative minor. At the change to the rocket launch, it changes to a press roll on the snare drum (associated with military events and suggesting suspense and anticipation), leading up to a (synth) fanfare, "Mickey-Mousing" the visuals (four women playing trumpets to announce the take-off). A drum set hit (w/

cymbal) marks the cannon shot that launches the rocket and then silence until they begin traveling toward space. The space travel is marked by a synthesizer portamento redolent of 1950s science fiction films,[30] leading to another drum hit as they land (the eye/moon collision is not trapped) (Table 3.5).

6. *Le Voyage Dans La Lune* (Astralwerks)

This electronic score by French synth-pop group Air is the most recent described here. It uses a very contemporary sounding combination of synths/samples, electronically processed audio (including voices), and drums.

Oddly enough, this section breaks down to percussion only: tuned timpani, snare drum, and claves. It has a strong pulse and very melodic timpani, repeating a pattern. As they prepare to take off, a piano arpeggio pattern begins in 12/8, having the effect of being exciting (quasi-fanfare) and carrying us across the transition to the take-off scene, where it continues until the launch. The space scene has synthy space music of a somewhat "emo"/sentimental kind (Table 3.6).

Many, though not all, of these scores adhere to established conventions of film music for this kind of narrative/visual and for silent film music. The organ score attempts to reproduce early organ scores for silent film, which were quite common. Many of the others use various combinations of fanfares and marches for the first half (boarding the rocket) and various ideas of "space music" for the takeoff. Trapping is sometimes used for the takeoff. Several use "old"-sounding music that is generally associated with quaint old movies.

Table 3.6 *Air* Analysis

Composer/Performer	Air
Mood	Portentous, then wonder/mystery
Genre	Synth-pop
Orchestration	Percussion, piano, digital electronic samples and software synths
Attitude	Importance, excitement, mystery
Historicity	Unabashedly modern
Synchronicity	Minimal, except it changes with scenes
Comments: The film itself has also been altered. (It's been colorized.) The creation of a new score by the French pop group is, in itself, an event, and focuses attention on the music.	

Summary

The preceding case study is meant to illustrate several points. First of all, it shows diversity in approaches to contemporary scores for silent film, both in their production and in their realization. Second, it shows how contemporary scores reflect the assumptions that composers and producers carry into their creation (or juxtaposition) of music, and how they do, or do not, align with the historical tropes of silent film music. Third, they give an introduction to the contemporary silent film score as interpreted by various creators. In addition, it can be said to express one of the significant aspects of the contemporary score for silent film as a form: the existence of many scores gives a film a chance to have multiple meanings. If we accept that music influences the perceiver's understanding and experience of the film, then each of these scores presents the audience with a different film. Each brings the film to life in a new way, with a different overall content and context. And music does not always have the same meaning for each perceiver. The less specifically "referential" the music, the greater the possibilities for Kassabian's *affiliating identifications*.[31] Needless to say, being as they are prerecorded, not all of these scores represent the apotheosis of the contemporary film composer's art. In fact, it's likely that some of them were not even composed specifically for the film: the creative choice may have been that of the producer of the DVD who chose the music to be juxtaposed with these films. The case can be made that the truest expression of this art form is when a contemporary composer chooses a film, applies all of their knowledge, skill, experience, and creativity to creating a new score, and most often these scores are often, at least initially, performed live. Contemporary composers for silent film have investigated a number of new and creative ways to juxtapose music and film, and the composers and films I have chosen to discuss in the next chapter represent several different varieties of experimentation.

The Alloy Orchestra uses an instrumental palette that would have been both technologically impossible (synthesizers) and stylistically baffling (contemporary music styles) in the silent film era. The Club Foot Orchestra uses musical jokes and the reinterpretation of the narrative content of the film. Richard Einhorn as well has formed a passionate relationship with the film he chose and created a score that expresses his own feelings about it. And the Blue Grassy Knoll use the various folk and popular music styles at their disposal, as well as a free-wheeling humor, to fête the films of Buster Keaton. In addition, all of these practitioners have spent a tremendous amount of time crafting their scores (The Blue Grassy Knoll and the Alloy Orchestra often spend months working full-time on a single feature-film score), and this gives them the ability to apply levels of technique and detail that were probably only rarely seen in the silent film era, due in part to the haste with which the music was usually created.

Looking back to the list of silent film stylistic conventions from Chapter 2, several seem to remain less often investigated. In the interviews I conducted with the four practitioners who are discussed later in Chapter 9,[32] every composer began by breaking the film down into scenes and began with the presumption that their music would be structured around these scenes. The assumption that the structure of the music would mirror the structure of the film is not really questioned. Every composer then begins to create themes and motifs. The idea that the basic Lego blocks of a film score are themes and motifs is taken as a given. The Alloy Orchestra and the Blue Grassy Knoll are basically oriented toward expressing the narrative as originally conceived, though they are occasionally willing to depart from that on a special occasion, when they feel it is justified. But the Club Foot Orchestra and Richard Einhorn seem less concerned about the original artist's intent. Einhorn is not concerned about it in the least; he's more involved with his own relationship with Joan of Arc, the historical/mythic figure. This is where these two pairs separate into slightly different camps, although there is plenty of overlap. Alloy and BGK see themselves as contemporary versions of classic silent film score composers, with their primary allegiance to the directors and actors in the films they score. Club Foot and Einhorn see themselves as contemporary creators of music as multimedia, and while respectful and extremely passionate about the work they celebrate, they are not originalists; they are more concerned with realizing their own artistic visions.

In the next chapter, I analyze and compare a few specific music cues whose approaches differ in some profound ways. They showcase the way certain assumptions underpin the most basic building blocks of the contemporary silent film score, and that reflect notions of how to score film, how to score silent film, and what the task of film music is or might be. They also show some possibilities for stepping outside those boundaries.

Notes

1 A hybrid of film music, silent film music, and contemporary music.
2 Tom Gunning, "'Now You See It, Now You Don't': The Temporality of the Cinema of Attractions," in *The Silent Cinema Reader*, ed. Lee Grieveson and Peter Krämer (London: Routledge, 2004), 41–50.

3 Ibid., 41–2.
4 Gorbman, *Unheard Melodies*, 53.
5 One of the most important responsibilities of film music's "invisibility" is its role in assuring continuity and the audience's immersion in the film-going experience. One of the most powerful tools at the film composer's disposal, in both silent and sound film, is the sudden introduction of silence. But in the silent film lexicon, it is only used rarely, briefly, and with a very specific intent in mind, much like a drum break in a jazz arrangement, usually to highlight a moment for humorous or dramatic effect, or between scenes. See the discussion of *Page of Madness* (Kinugasa, 1926) in Chapter 5 for one exception.
6 "Writing a movie score is like a boy sitting in the balcony seat with a girl. He must be forceful enough to impress the girl—but not loud enough to attract the usher!" Victor Young, *Chicago Sun-Times*, 1955, http://brandeisspecialcollections.blogspot.com/2008/04/victor-young-collection-39-linear-feet.html.
7 Simon Trezise, "Carl Davis Interview," in *Music and Sound in Silent Film: From the Nickelodeon to the Artist*, ed. Ruth Barton and Simon Trezise (New York and London: Routledge, 2019), 149.
8 Coincidentally, the film had two scores in its earliest incarnation: one by Arthur Honegger and one by Werner Heyman, both 1927.
9 For a wonderful article detailing the far more complex history of the film and its music than it is possible to recount here, see Cuff, "Presenting the Past," 120–42.
10 Ibid., 134.
11 Ibid..
12 Post-silent film era, in its widest interpretation, for example, late Chaplin. James Wierzbicki discusses "mute" (as opposed to "silent") film—films with diegetic noise, sound effects, and even the sound of the human voice, but no dialogue, such as Chaplin's *Modern Times* (1936). These, and the films of Jacques Tati, such as *Mr. Hulot's Holiday* (1953), are referenced in Chapter 7. James Wierzbicki, "The 'Silent' Film in Modern Times," in *Music and Sound in Silent Film*, ed. Ruth Barton and Simon Trezise (New York and London: Routledge, 2019), 198–208.
13 Club Foot Orchestra, "Club Foot Orchestra: Pioneers of Modern Music for Silent Film," accessed April 3, 2014, http://www.clubfootorchestra.com/.
14 Ibid.
15 Ken Winokur, interview with author, April 10, 2012.
16 As for how this regard is determined, since there are no awards for contemporary scores for silent film, no annual best-of lists, and little academic or critical writing about them, with the exception of a few concert reviews, I would point to a very wide record of performing at international festivals, a long perseverance in the field, and the fact that, when asked to name their favorite other performers in the field, they often named each other.

17 Mont Alto Motion Picture Orchestra, "The Mont Alto Motion Picture Orchestra," accessed May 10, 2014, http://www.mont-alto.com/.
18 Thorp and McPhee, "Alternate Soundtracks: Silent Film Music for Contemporary Audiences," 64–74.
19 Gillian Anderson, "Gillian Anderson: Conductor," http://www.gilliananderson.it.
20 The segment comprises two scenes: the launch of the rocket and the beginning of the voyage through space, including the iconic scene of the rocket crashing into the eye of the Man in the Moon. I chose these two scenes in order to illustrate both the approaches to two contrasting dramatic/narrative moments and to illustrate contrasting approaches to structure (moving from scene to scene, cf. Gorbman's "formal demarcations," classical principal #4, under narrative cueing).
21 I began collecting these recordings years ago because I scored the film myself in 1997 as part of my second set of silent film scores, *The Georges Méliès Project*.
22 The term "trapping" is here used to mean music that explicitly follows visual events in the film. Goldmark calls it the "literal . . . synchronization of sound and image" (2005), and it is also referred to, often pejoratively, as "Mickey-Mousing," invoking the practice as commonly used in animated cartoon scoring.
23 Some of this material, in a somewhat altered form, was given as a paper at the Musicological Society of Australia Annual Conference, Canberra, Australia, 2012, and later at the 2013 Another World of Popular Entertainments conference in Newcastle, Australia.
24 Paul Hammond, *Marvelous Méliès* (London and Bedford: Gordon Fraser Gallery Ltd, 1974).
    John Frazer, *Artificially Arranged Scenes: The Films of Georges Méliès* (Boston: G.K. Hall &Co., 1979); Elizabeth Ezra, *Georges Méliès: The Birth of the Auteur* (Manchester, UK: Manchester University Press, 2000).
25 Wierzbicki, *Film Music: A History*, 18.
26 The length of the film in its entirety varies widely on different DVD releases depending on projection speed and differing prints. The shortest in my collection is under eight minutes (*Ballerinas from Hell*); the longest is close to sixteen minutes (the Air score).
27 The film draws on a wide variety of contemporary sources, including Jules Verne's *From the Earth to the Moon* (1865) and H.G. Wells's *First Men in the Moon* (1900). John Frazer writes, "the Méliès film is finally as much of a satire of nineteenth century scientific achievement as it is an adventure tale to be swallowed whole." Frazer, *Artificially Arranged Scenes*, 98–9.
28 Anderson, *Music for Silent Films*, xv.
29 In 2008, Flicker Alley released a five-CD set entitled *Georges Méliès: First Wizard of Cinema 1896-1913* containing beautifully digitized version of 173 films, curated by

David Shepard and Eric Lang. This was followed in 2010 by *Méliès Encore*, which contained an additional twenty-six films.
30 Invoking the early association between the Theremin and aliens/outer space created in *Rocketship X-M* (Neumann, 1950), *The Thing from Another World* (Nyby, 1951) and *The Day the Earth Stood Still* (Wise, 1951)
31 Kassabian, *Hearing Film*, 141.
32 See Chapter 9.

4

Contemporary Scores for Silent Film

Four Case Studies

Comparing varieties of approaches can be a useful lens through which to examine contemporary scores for silent film in order to investigate how they do or do not take advantage of creative possibilities for innovation in film scoring. Alternative styles, instrumentation, compositional techniques, and structures are but a few of the areas ripe for reexamination. It is useful to examine in depth a few scenes or films from some important contemporary practitioners in order to see some of these issues in practice. The following four case studies all show different possibilities for innovation (and embody some aspects of polysynchronicity), yet many of them also adhere in other ways to previous film-scoring practices.

Sherlock Jr. (1924): Buster's Meta-Geographical Jump

> When its hero jumps before our incredulous eyes through a two-dimensional nickelodeon screen into the inner sanctum of cinematic space, we are spectacularly taken aback by Keaton's epistemological modernity and critical wit. In a single leap of reflexive faith, his film enters upon, and its hero with it, an inquest into its own constitution and—because it is all a dream—into the vexed connection between cinematic art and the unconscious.[1]

The setup: Buster, a shy and lovelorn amateur detective, is seen at his job as a projectionist at a movie theater. We see the audience watching the film (entitled *Hearts and Pearls*, a creaky melodrama involving a stolen pearl necklace set in the world of the wealthy), and a pianist and small theater orchestra accompanying the film. He has just been falsely accused of stealing the watch of his beloved's father and dozes as we watch the film on the screen, an arch melodrama with a crime subplot that mirrors the plot of *Sherlock Jr.*, substituting stolen diamonds for the watch, and a similar cast of characters, albeit of much higher social status. The director uses a multiple exposure technique to show Buster separating from his sleeping self. At 17.42, the melodrama characters in the film-within-the film turn into the characters from *Sherlock Jr.*, now wearing tuxedos. The ghostly Buster witnesses this from the projection booth and reacts with alarm (seeing his amour apparently being fooled by his rival) and tries to awaken his sleeping self. As the rival engages in further subterfuge, Buster leaves the projection booth, first sitting in the audience, seemingly unobserved, so as to get a closer look. Finally, he climbs up over the piano and jumps into the diegetic world of the film in order to confront his rival, who immediately throws him back out of the film into the theater and goes back to menacing the girl. In the theater, the band plays on unperturbed, even though Buster falls across the piano and into the middle of the orchestra pit. Undeterred, he climbs onto the stage again and jumps back into the film, but now the scene has changed, and he is standing outside the front door of the mansion (Figures 4.1–4.2).

Thus begins one of the most postmodern and experimental sequences in film history.[2] It is useful to compare two different contemporary scores for this sequence in order to see how the composers (or groups of composers) approach a sequence which is nonsequential: the scene consists of a series of purposefully jarring cuts from one seemingly random geographical location to another, expressing the manic possibilities of film editing. The groups are San Francisco's Club Foot Orchestra and Melbourne's Blue Grassy Knoll.

Figures 4.1–4.2 *Sherlock Jr.* (Keaton/Bruckman, 1924).

The Club Foot Orchestra and the Blue Grassy Knoll

The Club Foot Orchestra was founded in 1983 in San Francisco by composer/trombonist Richard Marriott. They were originally an instrumental ensemble, who took their name from a performance art nightclub in the Dogpatch neighborhood of San Francisco where they were the house band. The original members included Snakefinger, Beth Custer, Eric Drew Feldman, Dave Barrett, Dick Deluxe Egner, Josh Ende, Arny Young, Julian Smedley, Dave Kopplin, Raoul Brody, and Opter Flame. In 1987, the group premiered Marriott's score for *The Cabinet of Dr. Caligari* (1920)—see Chapter 3—and from that period on, they specialized in creating and performing original scores for silent films.[3] Portions of Marriott's next score, *Nosferatu* (1922), were composed by CFO band member Gino Robair, and this led to a system of collaborative composition, in which individual members of the group composed the music for different sections of the film. They continued this format successfully through subsequent scores for *Sherlock Jr.* (1924), *Pandora's Box* (1929), and *The Hands of Orlac* (1924). The band member composers who worked on these scores included Steve Kirk, Sheldon Brown, Nik Phelps, Myles Boisen, Matt Brubeck, Elliot Kavee, and Beth Custer, some of whom have gone on to score silent films and animation on their own.

The Blue Grassy Knoll is a five-piece gypsy/bluegrass band from Melbourne that specializes in scores for Buster Keaton films, although they have also scored the 1922 Chinese silent film *Labourer's Love*. Their first Keaton score, for *Our Hospitality* (1923), was performed in 1996, and since then, they have created scores for *The General* (1927), *Sherlock Jr.* (1924), *Go West* (1925), and a number of shorts. They have toured internationally and in 2014 premiered a reorchestration of their score for *The General* for the Australian Silent Film Orchestra (consisting of BGK + sixteen additional players) at the Melbourne Recital Centre. The core members of the group are Gus Macmillan (who was my interview subject), Mark Elton, Phil McLeod, Simon Barfoot, and Steph O'Hara.[4]

The "scene change sequence" (my designation) is a montage of jump cuts in which comical effect is made of the fact that Buster, now ensconced within the diegetic world of the film, is tossed from scene to scene as the backgrounds behind him change in an ever more bewildering series of seemingly random geographical scene changes. After a sight gag in which he takes a pratfall off the front steps of the mansion where the film is set, he is then transported in rapid sequence to the middle of a busy street, the edge of a cliff, a jungle (surrounded by lions), the desert (almost run over by a speeding train), a reef in the ocean, a snow-covered field, and finally back outside the mansion. There is no explanation for any of these cuts; they are a series of sight gags that reflect the pleasure in the possibilities of the medium of film. At the end of this sequence, the audience is returned to the diegetic story of the film-within-a-film, without any explanation.

Scene Change Sequence, with Music by the Club Foot Orchestra

Before the sequence to be analyzed formally begins, there is the sequence where Buster enters the screen. This begins at 17:22 when Buster's ghostly body first separates from his sleeping body leading to the transition in which the characters in the film-within-a-film turn into the characters in the film that is part of Buster's diegetic (i.e., "real") world. While the CFO music that runs through the entire following sequence up until the "scene-change-sequence" could be described

Table 4.1 Club Foot Orchestra, Scene Change Sequence (*Sherlock Jr.*)

Timing	Narrative	Music
19:15	Buster in front of house	A meandering, chromatic solo clarinet
19:37	Buster in back garden	Electric guitar arpeggios over a noirish horn section (Steve Kirk)
19:47	Buster on the street of a country town	A juxtaposition of the Tristan theme and "Camptown Races," Marriott's arrangement
19:58	Buster on a mountain top	Mountain Harmonica and Fiddle, Sheldon's idea
20:11	Buster in jungle with lions	Lions, by Nik Phelps, remembered from an old insurance commercial (horn fanfare with bells)
20:25	Buster in desert	"Indian" tom-toms, accompanied by "Old West" guitar, until horns do "danger/chaos" musical sound effects as the train almost runs over him. Tom-toms persist afterward with "world music" clarinet
20:56	Buster on reef in ocean	"Little Grass Shack," Hawaiian guitar rag: two guitars (Myles's idea)
21:12	Buster dives off reef and lands in snow	"Jingle flutes" very abstract idea with jingle bells (Beth's idea), multiple flutes are nonrhythmic and chromatic
21:27	Buster back to original scene, end of sequence	Trumpet for Stravinsky's *Histoire du Soldat* (Chris's idea)

Source: Analysis by author, supplemented by notes from Richard Marriott.

Contemporary Scores for Silent Film 73

Figures 4.3–4.11 *Sherlock Jr.* (Keaton/Bruckman, 1924) scene change sequence.

as "strange" or "otherworldly," stylistically, it is not like any identifiable style or form of music that is familiar. It combines elements of minimalism, atonality, jazz, and rock, in a slowly developing progression involving accumulating layers of sustained guitar chords, an eighth-note ostinato on the glockenspiel, and chromatic flute and string parts, a complete wash of polytonality. It eventually moves into thematic material from the score, a "Western/Spanish" motif, but a flute fluttering atonally above it accompanies even this more identifiable style. Finally, the solo chromatic clarinet brings us through Buster's entry into the film-within-a-film, and into the first section of the sequence analyzed later in the chapter (Table 4.1; Figures 4.3–4.11).

Scene Change Sequence, with Music by the Blue Grassy Knoll

The Blue Grassy Knoll version begins in the prelude with more conventional "spooky" music: minor chords in the accordion, free percussion punctuation,

Table 4.2 Blue Grassy Knoll, Scene Change Sequence (*Sherlock Jr.*)

Timing	Narrative	Music
19:15	Buster in front of house	Faux baroque music guitar and violin, a folk waltz
19:37	Buster in back garden	Banjo plays "In An English Country Garden," after trapping Buster's fall
19:47	Buster on the street of a country town	Musical sound effects of car horns as cars drive by, and of noisy city sounds
19:58	Buster on a mountain top	Musical sound effects of light wind, suggesting a great height
20:11	Buster in jungle with lions	"Jungle" tom-toms, and world music flute, along with some animal sound effects
20:25	Buster in desert	Harmonica suggests the "Old West," until train is trapped by shrieking horn on harmonica, fast bluegrass on banjo traps train passing, returning to empty "Old West" harmonica
20:56	Buster on reef in ocean	Sea chantey on accordion, ¾ time
21:12	Buster dives off reef and lands in snow	Jingle bells as the tune "Jingle Bells" is played freely on the upright bass, and a voice says "Ho, ho, ho" and "Merry Christmas!"
21:27	Buster back to original scene, end of sequence	Banjo plays "In An English Country Garden," after trapping Buster's fall

and a ghost-like Theremin, with some freer elements, especially with arco violin and bass, as Buster tries to enter the screen, with lots of trapping. There is an immediate cut as the sequence begins (Table 4.2).

Summary

Both of these accompaniments reflect originality and playfulness in their approach. The Blue Grassy Knoll's use of bluegrass as a basic musical language, their use of extended techniques in their lightening-quick and extremely numerous and inventive musical sound effects, their quick changes from section to section, and an overall good-humored irreverence, clearly show an example of a musical accompaniment that is not likely to be mistaken for being contemporaneous with the film. But with its use of familiar tunes to convey information (including in their titles), the literalness of the musical associations, the close following of dramatic beats, and the use of musical sound effects, this score draws quite heavily on traditional silent film scoring techniques. The Club Foot Orchestra accompaniment is much looser and more freewheeling, changing quite approximately with the scene cuts. It does use clear stylistic cueing at some points, but at others, it creates quite baffling juxtapositions (country house garden: Film Noir/electric guitar; snowy mountaintop: chromatic flutes). There are a number of cues that would be very difficult to put into any simple stylistic category and reflect quite complex compositional ideas, while the BGK cues are clear and direct in communicating their musical associations. And the CFO references (Tristan, Histoire du Soldat, a 1960s insurance commercial) are much more obscure. The BGK cue is modernist, but the CFO cue is postmodern and surreal.

The Golem: Two Contemporary Rock Silent Film Scores

Figure 4.12 *The Golem: How He Came into the World* (Wegener/Boese, 1920).

Der Golem, wie er in die Welt kam (*The Golem, How He Came into the World*) (1920) was the obsession of German actor/director Paul Wegener. Not only did he cowrite, codirect, and star (as the Golem) in the film, but he had made two previous versions of the story—*The Golem* (1915) and *The Golem and the Dancing Girl* (1917), both of which have been lost—ultimately leading to his final and most successful telling of the story in 1920. Based on a Jewish folk tale, the film is set in the sixteenth-century Jewish ghetto of Prague. Designer Hans Poelzig (a protégé of Max Reinhardt) and cinematographer Karl Freund (F.W. Murnau's *The Last Laugh*, Fritz Lang's *Metropolis*, and E.A. DuPont's *Variety*) collaborated with Wegener to create one of the greatest silent films of German Expressionism. It has been cited as an inspiration for James Whale's *Frankenstein* (1931), with which it shares several plots and character elements.

Laurence Kardish summarizes the plot as follows (Figure 4.12):

> From his study of the position of the stars, Rabbi Loew suspects that the Jews are about to suffer a catastrophe. As it happens, the Kaiser commands that they leave his dominion. To protect his congregation from the forced expulsion,

Loew, with his assistant, Famulus, creates the Golem out of a piece of clay, following an ancient ritual. The Kaiser summons Loew to a celebration at court in order to entertain the public with magic. Loew presents the Golem and reminds the Kaiser and his noble entourage of the wandering of the Jews in the wilderness. Because one of the participants in the celebration ignores his admonition to be silent during talk of the Exodus, the imperial palace nearly collapses. Loew has the Golem support the roof. In gratitude, the Kaiser rescinds his edict against the Jews. The Golem has thus fulfilled his function; Loew changes him back to a shapeless clump of clay. But Famulus secretly brings the creature to life again in order to kill the hated nobleman Florian, who enjoys the affections of Loew's lovely daughter Miriam and who has already spent the night with her. Florian flees from the powerful monster into a tower, falls to the ground, and dies. Suddenly the Golem takes on a life of its own and sets fire to the ghetto. In the end a little girl is able to subdue the monster and save the Jews.[5]

The original score, by Hans Landsberger, has been lost; the 2002 Kino DVD has a more recent orchestral score by Alijoscha Zimmermann. However, the scores looked at here are both rock-based and feature the electric guitar as their string section.

Black Francis and Gary Lucas

Black Francis is best known as the leader of the rock group the Pixies and has also performed under name Frank Black. His score was originally commissioned by and premiered at the San Francisco Silent Film Festival in 2008. It was later recorded and released both on DVD with the film and as an audio CD.[6] The score features a rock band consisting of Black Francis (vocals and rhythm guitar), Duane Jarvis (lead guitar), Joseph Pope (bass), Ralph Carney (horns), Eric Drew Feldman (keyboards and "synthetics"), and Jason Carter (drums and percussion) and was produced by Feldman. The score consists almost entirely of rock songs, with a few interstitial instrumental passages based on the songs. Black Francis is most prominently known as a rock performer and recording artist, and his score for *The Golem* is his only work in creating music for silent films, though his songs have been widely used as licensed music in film and television.

Gary Lucas is a guitarist known both for his collaborations with Captain Beefheart and Jeff Buckley and for his work as a composer and guitarist in his own right. He has created scores for other films, both sound and silent, the latter including *The Unholy Three* (Browning, 1925), *Vampyr* (Dreyer, 1932), and *The Goddess* (Yonggang, 1934). His score for *The Golem* was commissioned by the Brooklyn Academy of Music Next Wave Festival and premiered in 1989. It was originally co-composed with keyboardist Walter Horn and has subsequently been performed as a solo by Lucas on electric guitar. The score is entirely instrumental and consists of elaborate multilayered soundscapes created with an array of pedals for looping, delay, distortion, and chorusing effects. Gary Lucas is well known internationally for his live performances with film and has also had considerable experience creating recorded music for film and television. He is known as an improviser and a virtuoso instrumentalist, as well as a songwriter. The score was subsequently recorded at a live performance and released on DVD.

The Golem (Black Francis)

Black Francis's score for *The Golem* consists almost entirely of songs, interspersed with occasional short transitional instrumental passages, usually based on the themes from the songs. From my research, the use of songs with lyrics as a silent film score is, if not unique, extremely rare.[7] He does not use precomposed songs from his existing repertoire but instead has written songs whose lyrics refer very explicitly to the content of the film, often quite literally. For example, when we see the title card "This is my new servant, Golem," a song begins, entitled "Obedient Servant":

> You be my master
> I'll be your servant
> Live in my shadow
> I'll be observant
> Hurt he who hurts you
> Yay I will be fervent
> Don't cry
> It's they who die

When we first see Miriam and Florian together, we hear the song "Miriam and Florian," which begins:

> Miriam and Florian
> When no one's around

Long black curls
And small white pearls
Together found
Lovers drowned

The lyric to "Miriam and Florian" is not completely literal; it reflects a songwriter's penchant for poetic expression. While "long black curls, small white pearls" is a literal description of Miriam's appearance, they are never found drowned together. That is a poetic description of their existential position as forbidden lovers. There is extensive use of reprises of songs, similar in function to the way reprises are used in musical theater to advance the narrative. The song "Miriam and Florian" is used five times, as is the theme titled "The Golem." Other songs are used more than once as well.

The uses of the "Miriam and Florian Theme" in Black Francis's score for *The Golem* (Table 4.3).

The parallel narrative expressed by the songs, while in no way contradictory to the ostensible original narrative of the film, is nevertheless framed by the lyrical content. The song "You're Gonna Pay" introduces the film (and score) during the opening credits; it invokes the theme of retribution and punishment explicitly expressed throughout the film in Prince Florian's

Table 4.3 Uses of "The Miriam and Florian Theme" (*The Golem*)

Title	Timing	Narrative	Music
"Miriam and Florian"	16:10	They first see each other from afar.	Song with lyric (see above).
"Miriam and Florian Theme (Version 1)"	23:27	First illicit meeting.	Instrumental, slow, and sensual.
"Miriam and Florian Theme (Version 2)"	44:00	Florian's secret note is delivered to Miriam while Rabbi Loew takes the Golem to show the emperor.	Song with new lyric, steady folk rock. "The road is choked with dust.... My throat's choked up with lust."
"Miriam and Florian Theme (Version 3)"	47:00	Miriam receives the note and reacts with joy.	Instrumental, slow distorted guitar and organ.
"Miriam and Florian Theme (Version 4)"	51:49	Florian comes to Miriam and they go off together.	Instrumental, slow distorted guitar and organ.

death (for dishonoring Miriam), in the rebellion of the Golem (the Rabbi's punishment for calling upon the dark forces of sorcery) and the emperor's threatened doom (for condemning the Jews). The song is reprised, close to the end of the film (01.05.23), when Famulus (the Rabbi's assistant, who loves Miriam) realizes that Miriam is in a tryst with Prince Florian, her illicit lover, and reactivates the Golem, inducing him to kill Florian. The lyric in the reprise follows the action very closely.

The song "Custom All the Way" sums up the narrative arc of the entire film:

And I conjured in the dark / And I spoke with evil's son / (It's like custom all the way) / But I'll mash your perfect parts / When your task is done / (It's like custom all the way) / We frightened all the people / And we freaked 'em all at court / (It's like custom all the way) / But your master is so evil / So we gotta cut this short / (It's like custom all the way).

The chorus repeats, "Blow on the shofar tell everyone / God He has saved us tell everyone / God He has saved so celebrate / Go to the temple / And give him thanks."

The lyric "We freaked 'em all at court" is clearly representative of the composer's lack of concern about, and even embrace of, anachronism. It is part of the frisson of the score that it superimposes a rock aesthetic on a film made almost 100 years earlier. This potential to make the film accessible to a younger audience, who might reject the film as archaic and irrelevant with a different kind of score, is a perfect example of what Blair Davis discovered in her research discussed in Chapter 2.[8] A shot in the film shows an ancient text: "If you have brought the dead to life through magic, beware of that life. When Uranus enters the house of the planets, Astaroth will demand his creature back. Then the lifeless clay will scorn its master and turn to destroy him and all it meets." Black Francis sings: "And I conjured in the dark."

Unlike some of the lyrics in my score with librettist Hilary Bell for *Faust* (see Chapter 5), which impart quite a different meaning to some

Figure 4.13 *The Golem DVD* (Black Francis). Used by permission of Black Francis.

of the scenes from the visual narrative, these lyrics shadow the narrative as expressed in the title cards, albeit adding a layer of subtext and detail, as well as a modern vernacular (cf. Davis). So, on the one hand, they function—as textual content—in a relatively traditional film-scoring context: supporting the narrative and providing some audience members with an additional level of emotional engagement. Yet, on the other hand, the score's unexpected instrumentation and musical style and its position at the forefront of the audience's attention defy traditional expectations for a silent film score (Figure 4.13).[9]

The Golem (Gary Lucas)

Unlike that by Black Francis, Gary Lucas's score is entirely instrumental. Whereas a band performs Black Francis's score, Lucas's score is performed by a single musician. Although both performers bring a unique presence and history to their performance, it is clear that Lucas's performance could *only* be performed by him due to both its virtuosity and its complex instrumental techniques, utilizing a large array of pedals that modify his guitar sound, and crossing a broad swathe of musical styles, ranging from fingerpicking country blues and folk, slide guitar, and Hendrix-esque hard rock soloing, to pure improvised music noise. (A traditional orchestral film score can be performed equally well by any properly trained group of musicians.)

A compositional technique for contemporary silent film scores often used by improvisers, jazz or otherwise, is to prepare a series of musical motifs and/or themes that express the major narrative and/or dramatic themes of the film. The score then does not exist as a static through-composed document but remains in a fluid state, which changes with each performance.[10] When accomplished improvisers are performing, these scores have an excitement and spontaneity equal to a great jazz performance in a nightclub, with the added bonus of watching a wonderful film. Many great contemporary silent film and music performances have utilized this approach, such as Don Byron's score for *Scar of Shame* (1927), Matt Dariau's Paradox Trio score for *Battleship Potemkin* (1925), and Tom Cora's score for *Man with a Movie Camera* (1929).[11] Lucas utilizes this approach to great effect in his score for *The Golem*. Unlike Byron or Dariau, whose scores use arranged/composed thematic material for an ensemble and then use improvisations on these themes to connect different scenes, as a soloist Lucas is much freer to blend precomposed and improvised content. That is not to say this score is any less *composed*—rather, that it is the form, techniques, and motifs that are composed, not every individual note as in a conventional orchestral score. While Lucas's score generally follows the overarching narrative contour of the film as BF's does, he sometimes follows it more loosely. Both scores begin with a short distinct musical statement (taking the place of a studio fanfare, like the 20th Century Fox theme by Alfred Newman)—BF's is an introduction to the first song, whereas Lucas's is *musique* concrete, electronic sound that almost sounds like a film slowing down when it breaks, a musical joke. But the next five minutes of the film are treated quite differently.

As we see a panorama of stars that are being studied by Rabbi Loew, Black Francis begins with an instrumental called "Little Stars Theme"; then, as the Rabbi announces his findings with a title card saying, "I must speak with Rabbi Jehuda, danger threatens our people," he begins a song with the lyric, "Bad news, that's all I bring to you . . . something in the stars says that we are through." Lucas begins the same scene with a thick, dissonant multilayered drone, upon which he unhurriedly and intermittently introduces several short motifs that he will use throughout the film. This piece develops slowly through the first five or six minutes, making no attempt to closely follow the dramatic beats, or even scene changes, of the film, as a number of characters are introduced, events take place, and scenes are shown. The overall atmosphere is one of strangeness and otherworldliness. Rather than trying to reinforce or support the narrative, he establishes the music as part of an overview that places the film in the context of German horror film, Jewish mysticism, and German Expressionist silent film.[12] It also announces clearly that this will be a nontraditional silent film score, with few, if any, silent film music tropes, and that the music will be placed front and center in the audience's attention.

In both of these scores, the music and film are placed in an equal relationship: the music is not merely serving or supporting the narrative and the film as a whole; it is part of a complete spectacle comprised of the two. However, Lucas does adhere to several of the traditional tropes of film scoring. He generally follows the larger scene structure of the film, though he changes musical direction much less often than a traditional composer would, or than Black Francis does. On a few rare occasions, he does indulge in "trapping," for example, creating sound-effect-like synchronicity with the appearance of the spirits conjured by Rabbi Loew or the violence of Golem breaking down the door to pursue Prince Florian. And he has created themes that are connected to the larger themes of the film: the dense drone and slow-moving motifs for the plight/fate of the Jewish people, the country blues and ragtime for the physical/the body (both for the illicit affair of Miriam and Florian and for the strength/demise of the Golem), a chromatic eighth-note line for scenes of subterfuge and plotting, and a deeply abstract/dissonant sound for scenes connected with the mystical demonic world from which the Golem has emerged.

The one episode of musical quotation is the invocation of Wagner's "Ride of the Valkyries," the opening passage from act 3 of *Die Walküre* (which is also the leitmotif of the Valkyries), in an anthemic rock interpretation that invokes the abandon of Jimi Hendrix's performance of "The Star-Spangled Banner," which occurs directly after the introductory drone section. Whether Lucas is invoking creatures who travel between the netherworld and the human world, setting up the plight of the Jews as an epic battle, or referencing the use of the piece as source music in the Vietnam War film *Apocalypse Now* (Coppola, 1979) as inspirational music for the beginning of a helicopter invasion, it is clearly functioning (polysynchronously) for a modern audience on a multiplicity of levels, depending on each audience member's cultural references (Figure 4.14).

Figure 4.14 *The Golem* DVD (Gary Lucas). Used by permission of Gary Lucas.

Summary

The two scores, while quite different from each other, are linked by several similarities. The most immediately apparent is their instrumentation: they both use contemporary instrumentation, featuring the electric guitar and a rock style, although both bring in other stylistic elements as well. They both reject the idea of suggesting either the historical period (sixteenth century) or the cultural milieu (Jewish) for the most part; neither do they musically suggest the style or instrumentation typically associated with the silent film era. These attributes already move them far from the expectation of ragtime piano or even a quasi-historical score. In addition, neither of them makes extensive use of mimetic music (trapping), though Lucas makes some very occasional use of moments that follow dramatic beats so closely as to be the equivalent. Neither do they make much use of symbolic music, with the single exception of Lucas's quote of Wagner's "Ride of The Valkyries" from *Die Walküre*, which is used only twice. Instead, they both follow the larger structure of acts and scenes, albeit in different ways, as we will see below. They both also rely very heavily on the repetition of thematic material for their structure and development, though, again, in different ways. Black Francis uses song themes and lyrical refrains (often repeating chorus lyrics verbatim) and occasionally uses instrumental versions of songs as connectors. Lucas employs both motifs and themes, using them to make connections between different larger themes of the film, but also as starting points for lengthy improvisational developments that often take the form of flights of improvisational invention. Like Bernard Herrmann's score for *Vertigo* (1958), he creates an entire score from a relative handful of themes and motifs, through both repetition and development, and uses them to draw the score together into a cohesive whole.[13]

Where they differ significantly is in Black Francis's use of traditional song form and lyrics, and Lucas's level of abstraction and dissonance. BF's songs fall squarely into the indie-rock genre with which he is associated, and while they show a stylistically appropriate level of musical roughness, they follow the idiomatic treatment of musical form and content (verses and choruses, recurring sections, mostly consonant diatonic harmony). Lucas's use of themes and motifs is generally quite loose, sometimes consisting more of a texture or a technique than a literal melodic theme. His score is most often a dense fabric of multiple layers of pure sound: dissonant, abstract, and built on layers of feedback, loops, and distortion. In live performance, much of it is performed at an extremely high volume.

These two contemporary scores for silent film both challenge preconceptions of what silent film music should be: by their style, by Black Francis's use of songs, and by Lucas's use of dissonance and abstraction. They both act as a substantial partner to the film, functioning as equals, because of their volume, their independence, Francis's lyrical content, and the backgrounds of their creators. Their instrumentation defies the expectations of a silent film audience. Where they are less polysynchronous is in their relationship to the narrative. While they support the narrative to different degrees, neither offers a substantial counter-narrative, although both by their nature bring in references beyond the diegetic and non-diegetic worlds of the film. They don't explicitly break the "fourth wall" and draw attention to the perceiver's position as such. Only for one brief moment when Black Francis sings, "Miriam loved Florian / And his white horse / She thinks of them / Especially when the line of force / Takes its course," does he come close to a meta-commentary. They adhere to the general scene structure of the narrative, though sometimes quite loosely, but are fairly traditional in their use of thematic material: it is inevitably tied directly to the narrative. In this way, the scores remain firmly tethered to the narrative and visual structure of the film.

The Alloy Orchestra

The ensemble that filmmaker Guy Maddin called "the maestros of sproing-and-chunk grandeur" are America's preeminent silent film music makers. They have the largest original repertoire, they tour the most, and they have arguably been consistently devoted to contemporary scores for silent film for longer than any other group. They began their career with a score for *Metropolis* (Lang, 1927), premiered on December 31, 1991, at the Coolidge Corner Theatre in Brookline, MA. Since that time, they have become the best-known performers of original scores for silent film, devoting themselves full time to the pursuit for most of the last thirty years.[14] They have, at the time of this writing, completed original scores for thirty feature films and over forty shorts, including many of the most well-known classics of the silent film era.[15] They have performed live all over the world, enjoying ongoing relationships with the Telluride Film Festival, the San Francisco Silent Film Festival, and the New York Film Festival. The original group consisted of leader Ken Winokur (percussion, clarinet), Terry Donahue ("junk percussion," musical saw, accordion), Caleb Sampson (keyboard); Roger Miller (Mission of Burma) joined on keyboard after Sampson's death in 1998 and the personnel has remained consistent to this day.[16]

    The Alloy Orchestra's website describes their instrumentation as including "electronic synthesizers" and "state-of-the-art electronics," but the use of the keyboard in their scores is most often used in playing orchestral samples of acoustic instruments, often using a split keyboard to play different samples in the bass and treble clef. In a sense, their scores are similar to orchestral scores in that they often deploy string and brass sections in idiomatic roles, as well as various keyboard sounds. They more rarely use the keyboard to create any of the abstract sounds available to both analog and digital electronic music players. But they use the synthesizer, combined with each musician's instrumental versatility, to create a varied sound palette with only three musicians. The most remarked-upon aspect of their orchestration is their use of what they call "junk percussion": brake drums, hubcaps, truck springs, and other found metal objects.[17]

Like Melbourne's Blue Grassy Knoll, the Alloy Orchestra's approach to scoring silent films is fairly traditional in many ways. While their music is original and contemporary, it is not at all stylistically jarring when combined with the circa-century-old films they score. In form, they follow the act and scene structure, and they follow the dramatic beats of the narrative extremely closely, making regular use of trapping. In fact, one could make a case that watching a silent film with a Blue Grassy Knoll or Alloy Orchestra score has much in common with watching one in its original time.[18] However, one thing that makes these scores different from any that could have occurred in the 1920s is the very high level of detail with which they follow the film. Scores prepared by local music directors with small ensemble accompanists would have had only a very little amount of time to prepare, whether using cue books, compiled or original scores.[19] Both the BGK and the Alloys prepare for months to perform a new film score, using a meticulous process involving improvising to the film, documenting it, and then little by little formalizing the score and practicing it. Neither group relies on written scores: they perform all of their film scores from memory.[20]

Ken Winokur recounts:

> Alloy scores do incorporate some improvisation, but they are largely composed and are repeated almost note for note, night after night. In order to get to the point of being able to accurately perform a score, we rehearse relentlessly. We usually take about three months to compose and rehearse a score before we premiere it. The composition develops throughout that entire period—we continue fine-tuning the music up to the premiere (and then it continues to be modified and improved over time as we perform it).[21]

This level of detail is part of the appeal of their scores, and the clever use of trapping, both literal and dramatic, particularly enhances Alloy and BGK scores for comedies (in which the BGK specialize). In Alloy's score for *The General* (1926), the events which are trapped by drum hits, cymbal effects, or keyboard flourishes include trains crashing, wheels spinning, windows shutting, chairs falling over, soldiers getting knocked unconscious, ax blows, train brakes, animal traps shutting, water pouring, soldiers falling down, rifle, pistol and cannon shots, trumpet fanfares, and an entire bridge collapsing into a river. Often when trapping is not done as a literal sound effect (like the rim shots for gunshots and cymbal scraping for machinery grinding), a sequence of dramatic beats will be followed so closely by the music that the same effect is achieved. However, in the case of *The General*, their ability to work at this level of detail and specificity yields a unique rhythmic correlation, to the point that obsessive synchronicity becomes polysynchronicity through their use of a traditional technique taken to an extreme.

The Alloy Orchestra's Score for Buster Keaton's *The General*: Tempo as Melody

The narrative of *The General* takes place during the American Civil War and is based on a real event. In the fictional story of *The General*, Buster Keaton plays Johnny Gray, a hapless locomotive engineer who wants to join the Confederate Army in order to please his beautiful but somewhat shallow love interest, Annabelle Lee. When he is rejected from the army, he is disgraced, but he ends up pursuing Union spies who have stolen his train (named "The General") into Union territory. Annabelle has been inadvertently kidnapped in the train hijacking: he rescues Annabelle and retrieves the train but, in escaping, is pursued by the Union soldiers on a second train. In the end, Johnny saves the train, the Confederates best the Union Army, and Johnny becomes a hero and gets the girl.[22] The majority of the film comprises two lengthy (train) sequences: first, the two trains racing north with Johnny in pursuit of the Union soldiers, and then the two trains racing south, with the Union soldiers in pursuit of Johnny. Early on, the sound of the train is identified with the drums, playing a locomotive rhythm, accompanied by an eighth-note figure in the bass clef of the piano.

This would be expected, in keeping with the silent film trope of trapping and appreciated as a musical joke. However, what distinguishes the score for *The General* is that, from that point on, the drums, piano, and any other instruments follow the rhythm of the train—and any related machinery or form

Figure 4.15 *The General* drum motif (Alloy Orchestra).

of transport—relentlessly, speeding up and slowing down when the train does, stopping when the train stops and starting up again when the train starts up, in minute detail. With pinpoint accuracy, the entire ensemble (of three musicians) syncs the tempo of their performance to the tempo of the train throughout the entire length of the film, which contains endless set pieces about one side or the other's effort to delay the train with various obstacles and incursions, all the while dishing out multiple rim shots, tom-tom rolls, and cymbal scrapes with unequivocal accuracy. Rather than shamble along after the film, following it closely enough, as many silent film scores do, it brings the trope of following the tempo of the film to a highly refined level.[23] The result is a score whose primary focus is rhythm: the most important tool used here is the tempo, while still making ample use of themes and motifs.

Alloy's score for *The General* does make liberal use of these themes and motifs connected to characters, locations, and narrative elements: in fact, with a few exceptions, it consists mostly of music that incorporates them. There is a sentimental waltz associated with Annabelle, which we hear when we are first introduced to her character (1:29),[24] and for a final time in the last scene in the film, as he kisses her while saluting an endless parade of soldiers. There are various fanfares, accompanied by martial snare drums, associated with different military outfits, both Union and Confederate. There is a lament associated with loss in battle (64:50, 65:38), which we hear again as Johnny thinks he is going to be humiliated once more at the end for "impersonating a soldier" (72:42). But the most oft-used theme is the Pursuit Theme,[25] which accompanies the racing trains, each pursuing the other back and forth between sides in the battle. The Pursuit Theme is an assemblage of motifs, initially rhythmic, including a few short melodic motifs superimposed on them, with various forms of development. But even the melodic elements are kept fairly short to yield maximum flexibility in order to serve the rhythmic ends of the score. It begins with the eighth-note rhythm shown earlier, which is soon joined by an eighth-note ostinato in the left hand of the piano. To this are sometimes added various melodic elements that can be varied, transposed, reordered, or extended in order to give the rhythmic motifs some feeling of both development and continuity. They all recur consistently throughout the two lengthy chase scenes. But the interest is really mainly in the rhythmic parallels between the train and the music.

Table 4.4 is a schematic of one five-minute sequence of a chase scene in which Johnny is pursuing the Union spies (Figure 4.16).

Table 4.4 Use of Motivic Material and Application of Tempo Changes (*The General*)

Time code	Narrative	Music score
23:10	Johnny's train slows down to push the extra boxcar off the tracks.	Pursuit Theme (snare, strings) slows down with them.
23:15	Johnny's train is not moving.	Silence
23:21	The train starts up, at first just with snare, then piano left hand.	The tempo starts up, accelerando, following the speed of the train. It returns to a medium tempo. Pursuit Theme and superimposes a new motif: Suspense/Pursuit.
24:25	Box car runs off track.	Drum cymbal crash
24:57	Johnny's train slows down to move timbre off track.	Pursuit Theme slows down. It thins out to only mysterious, minor key synth chords.
25:30	Johnny's train speeds up.	Pursuit Theme and drums speed up.
25:56	Johnny is diverted to a side-track.	Pursuit Theme and drums slow down.
26:09	Throwing of track switch	Scraped cymbal mimics metal grinding sound effect.
26:19	Wheels spin helplessly	Mysterious (minor key) synth chords.
26:34	The train takes off without Johnny.	A snare tremolo for suspense, then music accelerando.
26.39	Both trains continue pursuit.	Pursuit Theme continues at a tempo.
26:57	The train slows down in the covered bridge.	Cont'd, tempo slows down.
27:00	Train it takes off again.	Cont'd, tempo speeds up.
28:02	Burning train slows down.	Cont'd, tempo slows down.

Figure 4.16 *The General* (Keaton/Bruckman, 1926).

Summary

With virtuosic control, the entire ensemble meticulously follows every change in the narrative tempo of the film. Their form of virtuosity is not a display of instrumental virtuosity; it is a virtuosity of ensemble playing, which is reflected in the amount of time they spend creating and rehearsing their scores. A similar case can be made for the Blue Grassy Knoll, who employ a similar process, a similar lack of written scores, and a similar ensemble cohesion.

An interesting comparison can be made between the Alloy score for *The General* and Joseph Carl Breil's score for D.W. Griffith's *Birth of a Nation* (1915).[26] Both scores use extensive repetition of thematic material, and both use music that closely reflects the narrative content of the film. However, Breil's themes mostly use repetition and a bit of reorchestration, rather than development and rarely change tempo, especially in the course of a piece. In Breil's score, there is little attempt at following the dramatic beats of the film; rather, he makes his comment with the content of the music: once it begins, the statement just plays out. The Alloy music is much more fluid and is much more closely aligned with the narrative. Their score for *The General* is not one that challenges the original narrative or reinvents the foundational relationship between music and film. Rather, it is one that takes an established technique (trapping, following dramatic beats, mimetic music) and refines it to a degree that far surpasses the professional practice of the historical silent film era.

Richard Einhorn's Score for Dreyer's *The Passion of Joan of Arc* (1928):

Reinterpretation/Reframing

When the French Société Générale des Films offered the great Danish filmmaker Carl Dreyer a chance to make a film in France, they offered him a choice of three subjects: Catherine de Médecis, Marie-Antoinette, and Joan of Arc. The script he finally wrote was based partly on a novel by Joseph Delteil but based more on the original transcripts of the trial of Joan of Arc during her imprisonment and execution by the English in the fourteenth century.[27] While an immediate critical success, the film was not a financial success and significantly hampered Dreyer's career. However, subsequently, it has come to be considered one of the masterpieces of the silent film era and appears on many lists of the greatest films of all time.[28] The film proceeds to tell the story of the trial and execution of Joan of Arc with relentless intensity and focus: Joan's five-month trial is here compacted into a single day. The performance of actress Renée Jeanne Falconetti is one of wrenching intensity as she enacts Joan's "tragic predicament and her courageous decision to accept death rather than spiritual and physical imprisonment."[29]

There is an original score for the film composed by Leo Pouget and Victor Alix, two of the more well known of the early composers of original scores for silent film. But the film has inspired contemporary composers of many genres to compose scores for it, including symphonic (Jon van de Booren, 1988; Tõnu Kõrvits, 2009; Bronius Kutavičius, 2009; Stefan Smulovitz, 2010), pop (Nick Cave and the Dirty 3, 1995; Cat Power, 1999; Joan of Arc, 2011[30]), electronic (Ugress, 2003; In The Nursery, 2008), ambient (Rob Byrd, 2003), and Richard Einhorn's oratorio, "Voices of Light" composed for orchestra, chorus, and solo voices, written so as to be able to be performed in synchronization with the film.[31] It is no wonder that the film has attracted multiple composers with multiple approaches. The stark nature of the film suggests a canvas on which a number have been tempted to paint. The film historian Roger Manvell has written, "The first impression one gains from seeing this film is its silent cry for sound. . . . The great ecclesiastical heads with their gesticulating mouths seem to require some corresponding cataclysmic uproar of the human voice."[32]

Richard Einhorn has written opera, orchestral, and chamber music, song cycles, film music, and dance scores. While he uses sequencers and synthesizers as part of his composition process, he is an orchestral composer; his score is performed by various orchestras, not by a working band, as are the scores of the Alloy Orchestra, the Club Foot Orchestra, or Black Francis. *Voices of Light* is an oratorio that can be performed either with or without Dreyer's film and has been issued both as a DVD, with the film (on the Criterion Collection), and as a CD of the music (performed by the Anonymous 4, with the Netherlands Radio Choir and Orchestra).[33] Although Einhorn began working on *Voices of Light* in the 1980s, it took him six years to bring the project to fruition. It was premiered in February 1994 as a live accompaniment to the Dreyer film at the Academy of Music in Northampton, Massachusetts, USA, performed by the Arcadia Players and the Da Camera Singers under the direction of Margaret Irwin-Brandon. It has subsequently had more than 100 performances around the world. Unlike other composers discussed here, *Voices of Light* is Einhorn's only silent film score.[34]

Dreyer spent over a year researching Joan of Arc and the transcripts of her trial before writing the script.[35] Richard Einhorn also did enormous research before he began writing *Voices of Light*, including research on Joan of Arc and her time, on mystical religious texts and writings about Joan in the original Latin and Medieval French (including that of Hildegard von Bingen); he also visited many of the historical sites in France. He sampled the bells in the church in Joan's hometown Domremy in order that they could be performed by an electronic instrument as part of the piece.[36] Einhorn says, "I like to create pieces that have many layers of meaning, some of which contradict each other. The idea, then, is for the perceiver to put together her/his own meaning, to construct a personal narrative from a shared experience."[37] On the one hand, Einhorn's score leans toward Kassabian's "affiliating identifications" that "permit resistances and allow multiple and mobile identifications."[38] On the other hand, he adds a specific subtext that is quite different in character from the one that might be presumed without it.

In an interview with this author,[39] Richard Einhorn said:

> The torture scene in *Passion of Joan* is, in many ways, very straightforward, a scene from a horror film—albeit one directed by Carl Dreyer and shot by Rudolph Maté. In doing my research, I learned that in the Middle Ages, the inflicting of pain was associated directly with spiritual ascendance—flagellation, for example. Even the application of torture during the Inquisition was considered a search for spiritual truth. In some of the texts that I found, there was not only a mystical but erotic component to the writing when they spoke about Christ's pain.

Unlike the scoring approaches taken by practitioners like the Alloy Orchestra or the Blue Grassy Knoll, who are essentially using modern musical materials to support silent films in a fairly traditional way, Einhorn has an explicit interpretive point of view which he wants to add to the film—not to the exclusion of other points of view but to the enhancement thereof. His music is specifically designed to express this additional subtext.

> Accordingly, rather than "score" the scene for the horror, I wrote some of the most rhapsodic music I could think of. The idea was to deepen and enhance and contradict the horror Dreyer portrayed, not reinforce it or underscore it.[40]

Although Ken Winokur of the Alloy Orchestra doesn't find fault with those who counter the assumed narrative of the film, he writes, "We don't do that . . . we enjoy working with and adding to the original film. We attempt to amplify the experience of seeing the film and don't derail that experience to make the film serve our own purposes."[41]

Clearly, Einhorn's initial attraction to the film was based on a lot more than its appeal as a vehicle for music scoring. In addition to a love of the music of the Middle Ages and the Renaissance (esp. Perotin)[42] and a deep, though non-evangelical, spirituality,[43] he had a profound and personal reaction to the film and wished to create his score as an expression of *his* vision (not that of the director). When asked if he thought the director would approve of his score, he replied, "It doesn't matter in the slightest."[44]

"The Torture Chamber"

Like the scores using songs for *The Golem* and *Faust*, an analysis of the music/film interaction of the scene described as "The Torture Chamber" from *The Passion of Joan of Arc* must consist of four levels: the film visuals (and this may be subdivided), the text on the title cards, the music, and the lyric/libretto. The constant interaction and overlap of these elements inherently place a score with songs into the category of a multimedia event.

The visual narrative for the sequence described here shows Joan being cross-examined and threatened with torture by the panel of judges who are exhorting her to recant her claims of divine inspiration. The scene culminates in her fainting after a graphic demonstration of the medieval torture devices that await her. The title cards feature their angry questions and her responses, which reflect both fear and faith. The libretto features quotes from a series of medieval mystics including Marguerite d'Oingt (an early fourteenth-century visionary and poet), Blessed Angela of Foligno, Na Prous Boneta (another fourteenth-century mystic, who was tried by the Inquisition), and Blessed Margarita (a disciple of St. Umiltà, fourteenth century).[45] (The lyrics are sung in the original Latin and Medieval French and only translated in the program notes.) A full orchestra, a choir, and vocal soloists perform the music.

The score for "The Torture Chamber" alternates between a full choir singing variations of the phrase "Glorioses playes" ("Glorious wounds"), taken from Marguerite d'Oingt, and a female soloist singing longer excerpts from mystical writings referring to the Crucifixion and the necessity of enduring suffering, in graphic terms. The last longer excerpt is sung by a mixture of a male soloist and the full chorus, culminating in a quiet repetition of "Glorioses playes," which both begins and ends the scene. While it is difficult to make an exact schematic of the interactions of the four elements, due to complexity of their overlap, a few excerpts will give a sense of their interaction (Table 4.5).

Table 4.5 Interaction Between Visuals, Text, Music, and Song Lyrics (*The Passion of Joan of Arc*)

Time code	Visual narrative	Title card text (trans.)	Libretto text (trans.)	Music
35:33	Judges assemble in the torture chamber	In the torture chamber	(Ah)	Full chorus, ecstatic
35:50	Joan enters		Glorious wounds!	Full chorus
36:02	Judges, looking very hostile	"Look upon your judges!"	(Cont'd)	(Cont'd)
36:22	Interrogator	"Do you not believe that these knowledgeable doctors are wiser than you?"	(Cont'd)	(Cont'd)
36:28	Interrogator/Joan	(Cont'd)	And I longed to see at least that little bit of Christ's flesh that the nails had fixed to the wood	Female soloist, lyrical
36:35	Joan/Interrogator	"... but God is even wiser!"	(Cont'd/variations)	(Cont'd)
36:47	First Judge/Judges/Joan	"Listen, Joan, we know that your revelations don't come from God ... but from the devil!"	(Cont'd)	(Cont'd)
37:10	Second judge/Judges/Joan	"How do you tell a good angel from a bad angel?"	(Cont'd)	(Cont'd)
37:23	Third Judge	"It is before Satan you, you are genuflecting and not before Saint Michael."	(Cont'd)	(Cont'd)
37:31	Joan smiles		(Cont'd)	(Cont'd)
37:33	(Cont'd)		Glorious wounds!	Full chorus
37:38	Fourth Judge (in rage)	"Don't you see that it is the devil who has turned your head?"	(Cont'd)	(Cont'd)

Source: Title card text: Translated by Latin scholar Peter Marshall, used by generous permission of Nadia Margolis. Libretto text: Translation from libretto.

While the judges have complete power over Joan, both physical and rhetorical, the lyric speaks of "Glorious wounds" and the music is lyrical (soloist) and ecstatic (chorus). The visual narrative shows Joan completely powerless, but the music expresses her spiritual power. (The only time her spiritual power is hinted at in the visual is her one-second slight smile at 37:31.) From her first entrance into the interrogation chamber, Joan is identified with the chorus of "Glorious wounds!" Even when the judges rage at her, the choir sings *her* song, not theirs.

The expression of two parallel narratives, one distinctly different from the other, and the complexity of the interrelationships among the different creative elements (visual/title cards/libretto/music), places this performance in the realm of *poly*synchronicity (Table 4.6).

Table 4.6 Tracking Parallel Narratives (*The Passion of Joan of Arc*)

Time code	Visual narrative	Title card text (trans.)	Libretto text (trans.)	Music
38:01	Joan/Judges		He showed [her] his heart, perforated like the openings in a small lantern.... From his very heart issued forth rays of the sun—no—brighter than the sun's rays.	Female soloist, lyrical
38:08	Judge	"I think she is ready to sign the act of recantation!"	(Cont'd, with variations)	(Cont'd)
38:23	Judge offers Joan the pen to sign the document confessing her repentance.		(Cont'd)	(Cont'd)
38:44	The judges scream at her in rage, but she refuses to sign.		(Cont'd)	(Cont'd)
39:04	Judge	"The Church awaits you."	(Cont'd)	(Cont'd)
39:10	Joan raises her eyes		Glorious wounds!	Full chorus
39:13		"[I]f you refuse, you will abandon the Church and you will remain alone ... alone!"	(Cont'd, with variations)	(Cont'd)

Contemporary Scores for Silent Film 95

Time code	Visual narrative	Title card text (trans.)	Libretto text (trans.)	Music
39:27	Joan	"Yes, alone . . . alone with God!"	(Cont'd)	(Cont'd)
39:44	Judge looks toward chains, knives, they prepare the torture instruments		Glorious wounds! (but more quietly)	(Cont'd)
40:36	Last chance to repent		"It is not fair to wish to taste only of my honey, and not the gall. If you wish to be perfectly united with me, contemplate deeply the mockery, insults, whippings, death and torments that I endured for you."	Male soloist and choir
40:56	Joan	"Even if you take my soul from my body, I will revoke nothing . . . and if I say something, afterwards, I will say that you made me speak by force!"	(Cont'd)	(Cont'd)
41:17	Instruments of torture		(Cont'd, at highest dynamic and intensity)	(Cont'd)
41:35	Joan collapses		Low bass pedal	Orchestra
41:50	They carry her body off		Glorious wounds! (quietly)	Full Choir

Summary

At Joan's lowest moment, when she is faced with the terrifying instruments of torture, the full chorus and orchestra are at their moment of greatest dynamic and emotional intensity. Einhorn illustrates the mystical and ecstatic attributes of torture, suffering, and spiritual transcendence. He has taken his own experience of both the film and its subject and has expressed that point of view, rather than the point of view that would be perceived without it (that Joan is a victim being tortured by evil clerics): he has turned a horror scene into a scene of erotic spirituality. Clearly, the exact meaning of the "director's point of view," and the "generally-understood point of view" will always be impossible to quantify exactly: however, just as clearly Einhorn has engaged in a relationship which makes the combination of the original film and his new music into a new work of art, with input from both Dreyer and Einhorn (Figure 4.17).

Figure 4.17 *The Passion of Joan of Arc* (Dreyer, 1928).

These studies of contemporary scores for four very different silent films clearly illustrate two central points. The first is that the art form of contemporary scores for silent film is a rich territory for experimentation and can accommodate a wide variety of approaches to the relationship between music and image/narrative. Most of these scores have been, and continue to be, widely performed throughout the world to diverse and appreciative audiences.[46] The second is that while some conventions of silent film music scoring (and film scoring in general) have been challenged by contemporary practitioners, many others have not. This leaves the field still wide open for new possibilities for combinations and recombinations of music and film.

In the following chapter, I use examples from my own work over the past twenty-five-plus years in the field of contemporary scores for silent film (and one sound film) to further illustrate the application of polysynchronicity as an approach to film music. I examine the ways I have, and have not, challenged the conventions of film music (both silent and sound) and what led me to the goals I set for myself in my score for Lotte Reineger's *The Adventures of Prince Achmed* (1926).

Notes

1 Garrett Stewart, "Keaton Through the Looking-Glass," *The Georgia Review* 33, no. 2 (Summer 1979): 348–67.

2   Woody Allen's *The Purple Rose of Cairo* (Allen, 1985), in which a character performs the reverse journey, leaving a silent film to enter the contemporary "real" world, is explicitly inspired by *Sherlock Jr*.
3   "Club Foot Orchestra: Pioneers of Modern Music for Silent Film," Club Foot Orchestra, accessed April 3, 2014, http://www.clubfootorchestra.com/.
4   "The Blue Grassy Knoll: Live Film Scores to Silent Movies," Blue Grassy Knoll, accessed April 3, 2014, http://bluegrassyknoll.com.
5   Laurence Kardish, *Weimar Cinema, 1919-1933: Daydreams and Nightmares* (New York: The Museum of Modern Art, 2010), 171.
6   The soundtrack was released in 2010 as a five-disc set. Only 500 copies were made, and it was released exclusively for purchase from Blackfrancis.net. The set included two CDs containing the studio recordings, two CDs containing the original 2008 live performance at San Francisco International Film Festival, a DVD of *The Golem: How He Came into the World* with the soundtrack synced to the film, and a book containing chord charts by Nick Vincent and lyrics by Black Francis for *The Golem*. Each of the 500 copies were signed by Black Francis, and each were wrapped in brown paper and sealed with a "Black Francis" marked wax stamp. http://en.wikipedia.org/wiki/The_Golem_%28album%29.
7   One exception is my score, cowritten with librettist Hilary Bell, for F.W. Murnau's *Faust* (1926), discussed in detail later in this book.
8   Davis, "Old Films, New Sounds," 77–98.
9   It is not at all "inaudible," because of the live performance, the celebrity of its rock star composer, and the volume at which it is performed, not to mention the unusual technique of scoring a silent film with songs with lyrics.
10 Although one of the pleasures of a live performance of a contemporary silent film score is that no two performances are exactly alike, this is far more the case in scores that contain a higher degree of improvisation.
11 All of these examples were part of the *Silent Movies: Loud Music* festival described in the Prelude to this book.
12 While there is legitimate disagreement among film scholars about whether *The Golem* is truly an Expressionist film (Wegener denied his intention to make an Expressionist film), from an audience's perspective *The Golem* clearly sits comfortably among films like Wiene's *The Cabinet of Dr. Caligari* and Murnau's *Faust*.
13 David Cooper, *Bernard Herrmann's Vertigo: A Film Music Handbook* (Westport, CT and London: Greenwood Press, 2001); Graham Bruce, *Bernard Herrmann: Film Music and Narrative* (Ann Arbor, MI: UMI Research Press, 1985).
14 "Alloy Orchestra: The New Sounds of Silent Films," Alloy Orchestra, accessed April 3, 2014, http://www.alloyorchestra.com/.
15 Among the films they have scored, in addition to Fritz Lang's *Metropolis* and *The General* by Buster Keaton, are *He Who Gets Slapped* (Sjöström, 1924), *Phantom*

    of the Opera (Julian, 1925/1929), starring Lon Chaney, *Nosferatu* (Murnau, 1922), *Man with a Movie Camera* (Vertov, 1929) Keaton's *Steamboat Bill Jr.* (Reisner, 1928), and many lesser known classics.

16 "Alloy Orchestra: The New Sounds of Silent Films," Alloy Orchestra.
17 Ibid.
18 Not in the style or content of their music, but in its relationship to the narrative/picture.
19 Anderson, *Music for Silent Films*, xxvi–xviii; Bellano, "Silent Strategies," 49–51.
20 Ken Winokur, Interview with the author, April 10, 2012. Gus Macmillan, interview with the author, October 10, 2012.
21 Ken Winokur, Interview with the author, April 10, 2012.
22 In an odd and ironic coincidence (and revisionist history), two of the most important films of the silent film era, *Birth of a Nation* (Griffith, 1915) and *The General* (Bruckman/Keaton, 1926) casually portray the Northern Army as the villains of the American Civil War, and the Southern Army as valiant heroes.
23 Harking back to Pudovkin's analysis purely on tempo matching (Redner, *Deleuze and Film Music*, 7–8).
24 Title Card: "There were two loves in his life: His engine, And– (photo of girl)."
25 Author's name for cue.
26 And, oddly, both films recount the American Civil War with the Confederate Army in the role of heroes.
27 Tom Milne, *The Cinema of Carl Dreyer* (New York: A.S. Barnes, 1970), 93.
28 It appears on Top Ten lists, or 100 Best Films lists in, among others, *Sight and Sound*, *Premiere*, the *Village Voice*, the Toronto International Film Festival, and others.
29 Roger Manvell, "Psychological Intensity in the Passion of Joan of Arc," in *The Classic Cinema: Essays in Criticism*, ed. Stanley Solomon (New York: Harcourt Brace Jovanovich, 1973), 111.
30 Joan of Arc is a Chicago-based indie-rock band.
31 The current Criterion Collection release contains three alternate scores: Three scores: Richard Einhorn's Voices of Light; one by Goldfrapp's Will Gregory and Portishead's Adrian Utley; and one by composer and pianist Mie Yanashita. *The Passion of Joan of Arc*, DVD, directed by Carl Theodor Dreyer (New York: Criterion, 1999).
32 Manvell, "Psychological Intensity in the Passion of Joan of Arc," 112–14.
33 "Richard Einhorn: Composer," Richard Einhorn, accessed April 3, 2014, http://www.richardeinhorn.com/.
34 Ibid.
35 Manvell, "Psychological Intensity in the Passion of Joan of Arc," 111.

36 From a "conversation with Richard Einhorn" on his website, http://www.richardeinhorn.com/VOL/VOLRichardInterview.HTML.
37 Ibid.
38 Kassabian, *Hearing Film*, 139.
39 Interview with author.
40 Ibid.
41 Richard Einhorn, interview with author, April 11, 2012. He implies here that he equates "making the film serve [a composer's] own purposes" with "derail[ing] the film."
42 Ibid.
43 Ibid.
44 Ibid. He goes on to say, "What I say publicly, and I believe privately as well, is that I don't know whether Dreyer would have liked my music, but I do know he would have appreciated my becoming as obsessed with Joan of Arc as he did!"
45 Attributions and subsequent quotes of lyrics for Richard Einhorn's program notes and libretto are published on his website, richardeinhorn.com.
46 Most of them are also commercially available on DVD as well; only the work of the Blue Grassy Knoll is entirely unavailable on DVD, and still can only be experienced in a live performance. The analysis here is based on an unreleased DVD given to the author by Gus Macmillan of the Blue Grassy Knoll.

Figure A Phillip Johnston. *The Unknown* Boston Museum of Fine Arts 1993. Photo by Ken Winokur. Used by permission.

Figure B Richard Einhorn, *The Passion of Joan of Arc*. Used by permission of Hampshire Gazette.

Figure C The Club Foot Orchestra, (L to R) Matt Brubeck, Sheldon Brown, Myles Boisen, Steve Kirk, Chris Grady, Deirdre McClure (back to camera), Catharine Clune, Elliot Kavee, Nik Phelps, Beth Custer, Richard Marriott. Photographer: Anne Hamersky. Used by permission.

Figure D Alloy Orchestra (L to R): Roger Miller, Terry Donahue, Ken Winokur. Photographer: Ken Winokur. Used by permission.

Figure E Blue Grassy Knoll. (L to R) Gus Macmillan, Phil McLeod, Simon Barfoot, Mark Elton, Steph O'Hara. Photographer unknown. Used by permission of Blue Grassy Knoll.

Figure F Gary Lucas, performing his score for *The Golem*. Photographer: Arjen Veldt.

5

The Application of Polysynchronicity

Five Case Studies

In Chapter 4, scores by contemporary composers of music for silent films were compared and contrasted, in order to analyze their relationship to classic tropes of silent and sound film scoring techniques. In particular, they were analyzed in terms of the criteria for polysynchronicity, as discussed in earlier chapters in this book. In this way, Chapter 4 functioned both as an expression of the practical application of the ideas discussed in earlier chapters and as a survey of some of the current work in the field of contemporary scores for silent film.

In order to further clarify the possibilities of polysynchronicity, this chapter examines five ways in which I have applied these ideas in my own work over the last twenty-five years or so, particularly in contemporary scores for silent film. Because the idea of the "poly" in "polysynchronous" implies a wide variety of approaches, giving rise to "affiliating identifications,"[1] I have chosen five *different* expressions of this open-ended approach, in scenes from five different films (one sound film and four silent films). Each of them approaches film scoring language and tropes in a different way.

Film Music as Unreliable Narrator: *Money Man* (Haas, 1992), Boggs's Motorcycle

Money Man is not a silent film; it is a contemporary American sound film, a sixty-minute documentary produced by the BBC, directed by documentary/feature filmmaker Philip Haas. Its relevance here is that the music for the scene in question demonstrates one of the primary criteria for polysynchronicity: that it cannot easily be placed into the dichotomy of synchronous/asynchronous

underscoring.[2] The film concerns J.S.G. Boggs, an American conceptual artist who draws pictures of money and spends them. He draws only on one side of each note and signs it on the back. His work questions the meaning of money, the value of art, and the relationship between money and art in the contemporary art market.

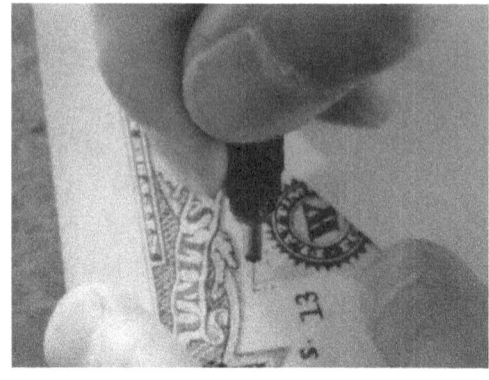

Figure 5.1 *Money Man* (Haas, 1992).

The plot of the film: the US Secret Service has raided Boggs's studio and confiscated a large amount of his artwork, saying they are deciding whether or not to prosecute him as a counterfeiter. A year has passed, and they have not prosecuted him, but neither have they returned his work to him. With a BBC camera crew in tow he travels to Washington, DC, to the home office of the Secret Service to try and get his work back.

The film begins with a series of shots of Boggs at work making his "counterfeit" money, working with artisan tools, and concentrating deeply in a seemingly deserted loft building in Philadelphia. He is then seen leaving his loft on a motorcycle, wearing leather boots and a leather jacket, driving to a motorcycle dealership, buying a fancy new motorcycle with his "counterfeit notes" and looking over his shoulder as the cashier counts the notes and gives him his change. He successfully completes the transaction and rides away from the dealership. The next scene puts the beginning of the film in context—we see Boggs with an art dealer and an art patron who is trying to buy the work (which consists of the "Boggs bills" and the receipt and change from the purchase), and learn that, ironically, because Boggs is a very successful artist, rather than having cheated the motorcycle dealership, he has benefited it, as the bank-notes-as-artwork are worth more than their face value (Figure 5.1).

However, the music leads us in another direction. Rather than being scored in a conventional documentary fashion (in which opening music traditionally sets the overall tone for the entire film to come), the music treats the opening scenes dramatically as in a feature film. The music behind the scenes in the loft is ominous minor key jazz and continues in a similar fashion throughout the scene in the motorcycle shop, which references Film Noir and implies that a crime is being committed. When Boggs leaves the store, it changes to early blues-based rock and roll (a la Chuck Berry), which in the "motorcycle film" tradition implies that he is an outlaw in the midst of an act of transgression. It ends as he returns successfully to his "hideout"—his artist's loft studio. When we see the subsequent scene, it is only then that our previous suppositions—that he is a counterfeiter and we are witnessing a crime being perpetrated—are overturned. We see that he is not a criminal but a fine artist.

The film continues with an overview of his career, documentary footage on the engraving skills involved in creating banknotes, and an erudite lecture by Boggs on the history of representations of money in art. However, as we take up the main thread of the plot—the conflict between Boggs and the Secret Service—the question is again raised of whether or not he is a criminal in some sense. Beyond the possible counterfeiting crime, there is a considerable element of showmanship to Boggs, and the question arises: Is what he does really art, or is it fakery?[3] (Figure 5.2).

Figure 5.2 *Money Man* (Haas, 1992).

Summary

For this scene, a synchronous approach would be to support the idea of Boggs as an artist practicing his craft, and there are varying ways to do that musically: in fact, it is done later in the film. An asynchronous approach would be to give information that is somehow subtextual and gives different information about the scene than we would get from just watching it without music, say, for example, that what Boggs does is humorous. But the point is that the intent of both of these approaches would be to communicate information that is *true*; that is, they would be guiding the perceiver toward a true understanding that the composer/director wants to communicate about the artist. However, the score described earlier gives information that clearly suggests an interpretation of the visuals, but that interpretation turns out to be *false* and is subsequently disproved, and the perceiver has to readjust their interpretation of what has just been understood. The perceiver has been, momentarily, deceived by the music.

This approach not only creates an unusual relationship between the film and the music but also creates "affiliating associations" of a number of types. It embodies the whole issue of truth versus falsehood that is present both in the film and in Boggs's work, but in an indirect way. It also invokes the questions of crime related to Boggs's work in a larger context—Is he a counterfeiter, not of banknotes, but of art? Does his work really qualify as art? These are questions that the film asks and, to its credit, leaves open for the viewer to answer. If there is a crime committed here, is it by the artist (who spends money which is not real money), by the Secret Service (who confiscates Boggs's artwork and will not return it, although he hasn't been charged with a crime), by the art patron (who tries to acquire the pieces of the art for as little money as possible from people who may not be aware of its true value), or by the contemporary commercial art world in enabling art and artists of questionable value? Rather than synchronous music that reinforces what we see (sad image/sad music) or asynchronous music that adds contradictory subtext to what we see (war scene, melancholy music = war is sad), this polysynchronous music cue does two things. First, it plays a practical joke on the viewer that gives very clear (but false) information about the scene. Second, it creates a network of outward-resonating references that relate in many possible ways to the content of the rest of the film, but in less-than-explicit way.

A Film Score Takes Sides: *The Unknown* (Browning, 1927), Final Scene

My original score for Tod Browning's 1927 silent film *The Unknown* (created in 1993) reflects a different inversion of expectations. It supports a narrative that directly contradicts the one ostensibly expressed by the unscored film: it reverses the roles of the hero and the villain.[4]

The plot: Lon Chaney plays an escaped killer, Alonzo, who is hiding in a circus by performing an act in which he pretends to be an armless man who does a knife-throwing act with his feet (his arms are concealed by one of the elaborate prosthetic devices for which Chaney was famous). The tangential target of this deception is the ringmaster's daughter, the beautiful Nanon (Joan Crawford), who has a terror of men's arms, and for whom Alonzo nurses an

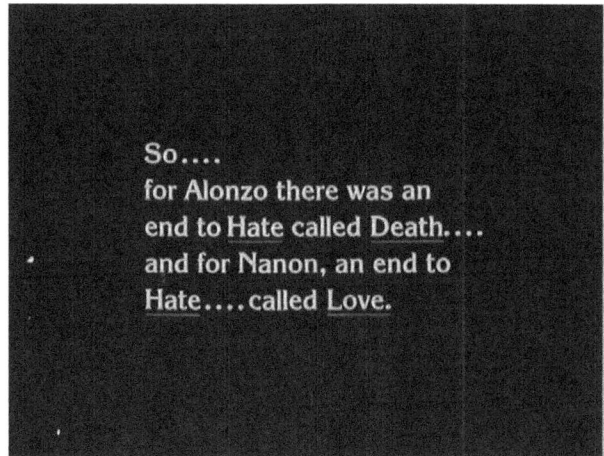

Figure 5.3 *The Unknown* (Browning, 1927).

obsessive but clandestine love. Afraid that she will discover that he has arms, Alonzo blackmails a corrupt surgeon into surgically cutting off his arms. When he returns from a lengthy convalescence, he discovers that she has gotten over her phobia and is now planning to marry the circus strongman, Malabar (Norman Kerry), because she loves his "big strong arms." Alonzo goes mad, and while pretending to be pleased for them, he plans a circus "accident" in which Malabar's arms will be torn off by wild horses. But at the last minute, Nanon runs in front of the horses to try and save her lover, and in saving *her*, Alonzo is trampled to death. In the final scene, Nanon and Malabar are happily in each other's arms, and Alonzo is dead. We are left with a moralistic title card (Figure 5.3).

However, the score supports a different interpretation, which is that Alonzo is the hero, and Nanon and Malabar are the villains. The foundation for this reinterpretation, briefly, is as follows. Alonzo is unwavering in his devotion to his love object (Nanon) throughout the film and makes first one incredible sacrifice (having his arms cut off), then another (dying to save Nanon from the wild horses). He allows his carefully wrought plan of revenge to be undone in order to save her. Nanon (and Malabar, ultimately) is narcissistic and insensitive to Alonzo's devotion, to which she is oblivious and acts only with her own desires in mind. Both she and Malabar flaunt their happiness in front of the clearly tortured Alonzo. By the end of the film, he has committed a heroic act of self-sacrifice; they have sacrificed nothing.

This interpretation is supported by the music at a number of points throughout the film. When Malabar is first introduced, the accompanying music plays his heroism ironically, implying stupidity rather than strength.[5] At the dramatic climax of the film, as Alonzo executes his plot and Malabar comes closer and closer to dismemberment,

Figure 5.4 *The Unknown* (Browning, 1927).

rather than music suggesting suspense and danger, it is accompanied by the most exciting music in the score, a fast minor key klezmer tune that celebrates Alonzo's triumph. It gains momentum and complexity with virtuoso unison passages over a fast beat as the plot races toward its completion. But once the plot is foiled and Alonzo dies, it ends. The denouement in the last scene of the moral and the lover's embrace features sinister and melancholy music, a slow tempo dirge of chromatic counterpoint, ending on an unresolved dissonance. The image/narrative/text says this is resolution and a happy ending; the music says this is the funeral music of Alonzo and does not give its blessing to this insensitive and undeserving union (Figure 5.4).[6]

Summary

The score uses the widely agreed upon associations of the traditional tools of film scoring, such as tempo, harmony, and style/genre, to achieve untraditional ends. It communicates clear semiotic cues but with a goal of superimposing a new interpretation on the narrative.

Film Score as Hall of Mirrors: *The Georges Méliès Project* (Méliès, 1899–1909)

The score for *The Georges Méliès Project* was conceived as a study in which a series of eight short films, ranging from one minute in length to about nineteen minutes, are each treated differently to some degree, regarding the relationship between music and image/narrative, some quite abstract, some very direct. My goal was to present a single program in which the relationship between film and music cannot be assumed, changes regularly, and commands attention by its very changeability.[7]

1. *Danse du feu* (*The Dance of Fire*) (1899). The music for this short film is linked to the montage structure of the film only at one moment: at the appearance of the dancer. (The opening focuses on a Satan figure.)[8] The music itself has no semiotic or musicological associations. It is unfamiliar and chromatic (nontonal), so one could make a case that it has whatever associations are connected to those two elements. But it is strongly rhythmic and contrapuntal, qualities which have a tendency to counterbalance any perceived "threat" of the first two elements. The point of this experiment is to apply music that has no particular point of view or narrative or descriptive intent, opening to both "affiliating associations" (Kassabian) and "obtuse meaning" (Barthes) (Figure 5.5).

Figure 5.5 *La danse au feu* (Méliès, 1899).

2. *The Melomaniac* (1903). The music for this two-and-a-half-minute film divides the quartet into two parts: piano and vibraphone, and soprano saxophone and bass. The piano and vibraphone are performed in strict pulse tempo (though constantly changing meter, between different divisions of 4/4, 5/4, and 11/8) and proceed relentlessly at a quick syncopated pace throughout the film. The soprano saxophone and bass play in a completely different time, freely, only following visual cues from the film. The film involves

Figure 5.6 *La mélomane* (Méliès, 1903).

a frantic choir conductor (played by Méliès himself) throwing musical notes (made of copies of his own head) up on a series of telephone wires that resemble the lines on a musical staff. The saxophone and bass slowly play the notes as they are thrown up on the staff; those notes eventually reveal themselves to be the opening melody of "God Save the King/Queen." Only in the last few seconds of the film, when the notes turn into birds and fly away, do all the instruments briefly come together in a manic repeating figure until they too fly away in a brief spasm of dissonance. The syncopated piano invokes the ragtime association with silent film, yet it is contradicted by its dissonance and chromaticism and the free chromatic improvisations of the vibraphone. The literalness of the trapping of the notes of "God Save the King/Queen" is contradicted by the fact that it is played completely out of time with the other instruments. And the relentless fast pace of the music contradicts the basic easy-going and good-humored manner of the protagonist. The music has a complex and multilayered relationship to the film (Figure 5.6).

3. *Hydrothérapie Fantastique (The Doctor's Secret)* (1909). The score for this film is based on Chopin's Valse in Ab (Opus 42), which it intersperses with more dissonant and chromatic original material. The film itself is an extended series of sight gags, based on an obese man's attempts to lose weight by visiting a rather dubious medical practice. The opening in the score is a very slow and

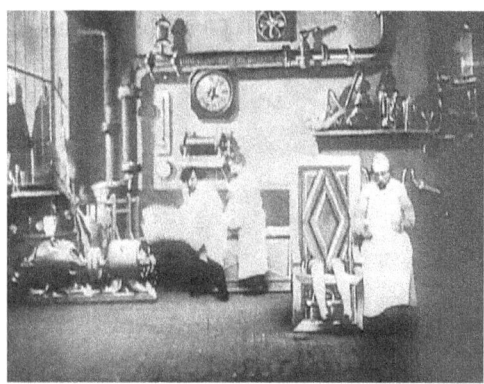

Figure 5.7 *Hydrothérapie fantastique (The Doctor's Secret)* (Méliès, 1909).

regal series of variations on the waltz theme, very beautiful and stately. This directly contrasts to the buffoonery of both the doctors and the patients. As the treatment progresses, the music transforms into a medium tempo jazz waltz with a new melody based on the harmony of Chopin's waltz. The piece goes on evolving through different sections, including baroque counterpoint (based on the Chopin harmony) and much complex chromatic counterpoint,[9] with little attention paid to the dramatic beats of the film such as they are. It finally rejoins the film as, after an infernal steam treatment explodes and the patient is blown into pieces, he is reassembled, to the tune of the Chopin waltz played as gospel tune. There is a short coda while the patient complains at the end and throws the doctors around, as the chromatic counterpoint returns, but played twice as fast. Overall, the score has manifested a very eccentric, but yet not entirely disconnected, relationship to the narrative, which reflects both humor and contrast. In addition, it flirts playfully with a number of the tropes of historical silent film scoring, including the use of classical music, the rearrangement of thematic material, and the association of dissonance with either strange or funny content. Yet, it lays out a compositional structure that maps in a contrapuntal manner with the film's montage structure (Figure 5.7).

Summary

A program of silent films with music is accompanied by a variety of musical approaches. The audience can never assume that the relationship between film and score is what they have come to expect from the previous film. Within that overall program, the music relates to the image/narrative in multiple ways that refuse to remain static and, at times, challenge conventional approaches in a variety of ways.

Silence Becomes Audible:[10] *Page of Madness* (Kinugasa, 1926) Riot Scene

One of the foundational assumptions about music for film is that its primary goal is to avoid drawing attention to itself and, in doing so, to keep the audience involved in the diegetic world of the film. The music cue chosen here not only doesn't do that, but it explicitly draws attention, not only to itself but without warning it wakes the audience up from the dream of the film, makes them explicitly aware of the artificiality of the situation they are in: sitting in a room with strangers in a darkened room[11] watching a film that is now truly "silent" and was made a century ago.[12]

The plot: A man takes a job as a janitor at a mental asylum with the hope of helping his wife, who is confined there, to escape. The film is an expressionist meditation on the inner world of the insane and contains many hallucinatory and fantasy sequences (some relating to various subplots about the past and about their family). After an abortive attempt to help her escape, he gradually accepts that he will keep his job at the asylum in order to be near her.

Sparked off by the actions of a mysterious dancer who may be an inmate at the asylum (and symbolic double of the wife), a riot develops among the inmates, and the janitor is caught up in it. The attendants are called, but they are overwhelmed by the riot. Only when the director of the asylum arrives are they able to slowly restore order.

This particular score uses a combination of carefully scored improvisation and composed material. In keeping with the film, much of the score is quite dissonant and abstract. This in itself is not remarkable. Gorbman ends her Classical Film Music Principles with "A given film score may violate any of the principals above, providing the violation is at the service of the other principals."[13] The cue builds from a quietly dissonant improvisation to a greater and greater level of volume, density, and abstraction to a wild free jazz explosion by the time the riot reaches its full fury, mirroring exactly the dramatic arc of the montage. However, at a certain cue, suddenly without warning, the music stops. There is a lengthy period of silence as the riot continues on unabated in utter silence. At another cue, the music begins again, at the same level of intensity, as if the needle had been lifted from the record and then replaced sixty seconds later in the same place (Figure 5.8).

Figure 5.8 *Page of Madness* (*Kinugasa*, 1926). Used by permission of The Museum of Modern Art.

The effect of the sudden silence is startling. The audience has been watching the film with music for about an hour at this point and is deeply involved in the diegetic world of the film. The unexpected silence breaks their bubble and draws their attention to everything artificial about the situation. The juxtaposition of frantic activity on screen and the utter silence calls into question everything about the relationship between sound and image.[14] Then just as suddenly they are jerked back into the film as the music begins again where it left off. Initially disoriented a second time and still aware of the artificiality of their position, the perceiver gradually forgets and slips back into the dream, but now haunted by the awareness that it is all a charade.

Summary

One of the most cardinal rules of film music is broken: do not disturb the audience. The musical cue described here cannot be contained by the definitions of either synchronicity or asynchronicity. Nevertheless, the score still also makes use of classic techniques such as thematic/motivic development[15] and following dramatic beats, albeit in sometimes unexpected ways.

The Music Sides with the Devil: *Faust* (Murnau, 1926), Main Titles and Ending[16]

This score for F. W. Murnau's *Faust* (1926) features a vocalist (in addition to an instrumental ensemble including cello, accordion, saxophone, piano, and ukulele). In addition to songs in a variety of styles (including classical art song, cabaret, jazz and blues, ballads, and hymns), it also includes vocal improvisation (both jazz and New Music), vocalise, and a small amount of spoken text, all written by playwright/librettist Hilary Bell. All of these are combined/interspersed with instrumental underscore.

Songs with lyrics have rarely been used in contemporary silent film scores.[17] One of the most obvious reasons is the belief that listening to words in a song, while having to read words in the intertitles,[18] would be confusing for the audience, and that the solution of fitting the songs between the intertitles is not practical: they occur too often, songs tend to be longer, and the result would be an inconvenient structural limitation. This score embraces a certain amount of sensory overload as part of its conception. The audience takes in information on four levels at the same time: the visuals, the music, the lyrics, and the intertitles. At times they have to take an active role in deciding what to "pay attention" to, as opposed to the more common passive role of the filmgoer. Usually, the filmmaker decides where the audience's attention is to be directed and is careful not to confuse them (the films of Robert Altman notwithstanding). One of the most important parts of the composer's brief is to avoid this conflict by not drawing attention to the music and to assist in directing the audience's attention.[19] More importantly, this score expresses a counter-narrative to the traditional story of Faust, as it is portrayed in the film.[20]

The plot: Mephisto (Satan) claims he can corrupt any man. The Angel of God and Mephisto make a bet: if the Angel can find a man whom Mephisto cannot corrupt, he (Mephisto) can rule the universe. The Angel chooses Faust, who is shown to be a pious and selfless man. Through trickery, temptation, and outright cheating, Mephisto succeeds in corrupting Faust. But in the end, Faust repents, and the Angel declares victory.

However, the score supports a different interpretation, in which Mephisto wins the bet. The availability of the words of the libretto, particularly in the form of additional dialogue at the end of the film, clearly gives the composer a powerful new tool in order to express an alternative viewpoint. Both music and lyrics work together to support this narrative. The reasoning behind the alternative interpretation is as follows. First, the bet between the Angel and Mephisto is about whether Mephisto can corrupt Faust or not. Mephisto *does* corrupt Faust, who behaves badly and only repents when he has lost everything, and then he is redeemed only by the forgiveness of his lover, Gretchen. There is no mention of forgiveness or redemption in the bet.

Second, the conduct of the townspeople is much worse than Faust's: Faust has been tricked by Mephisto, but the townspeople, with no prompting, behave indefensibly. Jumping to conclusions about Gretchen's guilt without investigating the evidence, they exhibit a mob mentality (which leads to a wrenching scene of the death of Gretchen's infant in the snow), and they burn her at stake. The Christian precepts of fairness, compassion, and forgiveness are absent here in a story that is ostensibly about Christian virtue and religiosity. The townspeople commit murder, which neither Gretchen nor Faust has done—Faust's supposed "murder" of Gretchen's brother is actually committed by Mephisto.

In the story told by the score (and libretto), Mephisto has won both the bet and the souls of the townspeople as a bonus. The new score supports a counter-narrative to the one expressed by the original film. This is where the opening song lifts the original story of *Faust* into a meta-narrative: Mephisto ruins people's lives and lets them die horribly: so does God. In pursuit of their agendas, they are both equally unconcerned about the fate of individuals. The Devil takes delight in suffering—God is unconcerned by it.

However, any filmmaker has a similar relationship to their characters. They cause them to live or die, to suffer horribly or escape unscathed, to be saved or damned, all in service of fulfilling the film's agenda. During the writing, shooting, and editing process, characters are killed and brought back to life, or, after all of their trials and tribulations, they may end up on the cutting room floor and might as well have never existed. So, the very first song in the film,

A Shaft of Light, establishes a meta-narrative. In a dramatic but melancholy art song, the voice of the singer is established as a one-woman Greek chorus, who comments on not only the fates of characters in the narrative but also ours as viewers, as well as the similarity of the roles of God and the filmmaker.

A Shaft of Light[21]

A shaft of light:
From the clouds;
From the projector.

The metaphor of the shaft of light—the ray of light from the Heavens—is compared to the ray of light from the film projector.

The light of creation
Piercing the dark of chaos.

The light of the movie projector shines through the darkened film theatre, illuminating the darkness, as the audience waits to be entertained by the film. The creativity of the filmmaker lightens our humdrum lives, for which solace one repairs to the cinema.

God's eye a viewfinder
Looks coldly upon his creatures.

Here is the analogy of the camera and the eye of God, introducing the idea of the filmmaker's dispassionate regard.[22]

How to heighten the stakes?
Tighten the screws?
Send a storm.
Kill the child.
Make the hero arrive too late.

The filmmaker is not concerned about the consequences for his characters: all is fair game to up the ante for a good plot.

And last,
A casual decision:
To end happily, or in tragedy?[23]

The perceiver is invited to participate in an experiment. God's eye is a viewfinder, as is the audience's: what they are invited to behold is the state of humanity—"the portals of darkness are open and the shadows of the dead hunt over the earth" (title card). By immediately establishing the role of the music as meta-narrative, the viewer is prepared for a multilevel experience. The music neither slavishly supports the on-screen narrative, nor does it merely contradict or satirize it. It exists as another element, sometimes supporting and intensifying in a traditional manner (as it does in the scene of Gretchen's sufferings), sometimes poking fun (as in the scene of the juxtaposed romances of Gretchen and Aunt Marthe), but often bringing in a different perspective, independent of both the characters and the original filmmaker, and thus eschewing the roles of both pure synchronous and asynchronous film scoring.

Thus, the composer and librettist of the contemporary film score also act as imperious gods, imposing their will upon not only the characters but the original director's vision as well. They presume to take liberties and reinterpret the film, without the director's consent or participation, and impose their own narrative on his/hers, sometimes contradicting what is presumed to be the original intent. Throughout the film, the music experiments with myriad relationships with the film, in the most ambitious embodiment of multimedia in this chapter. By the time the end of the film comes, the score has arrived at a different ending than the ostensible moral ending expressed in the visual narrative. This is where, in the parallel narrative, Mephisto has won. Over an instrumental reprise of *A Shaft of Light*, the singer, now as the voice of Mephisto, rants:

> *Okay, okay*
> *They're out of the way*
> *Now here's what it's really been about, my friend.*
> *You won two souls,*
> *Redeemed and gone to heaven,*
> *But I won thousands more!*
> *A city full of wicked souls*
> *Corrupt and sanctimonious,*
> *They drove her to insanity*
> *Then burned her at the stake.*
> *Is that not evil?*
> *They acted in my name!*
> *Take Faust with my blessings:*
> *I've won countless others.*
> *The power and the glory of the world*
> *Are mine!*

But on screen the Angel asserts victory, saying that the forgiveness of Gretchen for Faust undoes everything that Mephisto has achieved, invalidating the original

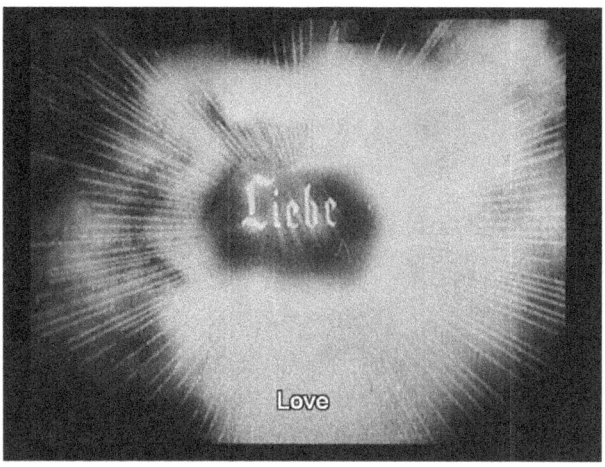

Figure 5.9 *Faust* (Murnau, 1926).

parameters of the bet. This is not argued or supported by any reasoning except the power of God to enforce it.

In the original, the Angel denies the bet (Figure 5.9):

> MEPHISTO: *My pact is binding.*
> ANGEL: *One word breaks thy pact.*
> MEPHISTO: *What word is that?*
> ANGEL: *The Word that rings joyfully throughout creation. The Word that appeases pain and sorrow; the Word that absolves all guilt, the Eternal Word, dost thou not know it?*
> MEPHISTO: *What is the word?*
> ANGEL: *Love!*[24]

The music that follows "A Shaft of Light" in the opening, which accompanies Mephisto's initial reign of evil in spreading the plague ("Chaos"), is played *forte* and is aggressive and dissonant. It is reprised here, under a dramatically spoken monologue, as Mephisto, in the parallel narrative, has the last word (Figure 5.10):

Figure 5.10 *Faust* (Murnau, 1926).

Liar!
Cheat!
Use your power, change the rules.
Invent your reasons: "Love"?!
Curse you!
Chaos! Chaos!

Summary

The music score supports a consistent narrative throughout that differs significantly from the one that would be understood from the film without the new score. On the path to doing so, it comments on itself and relates to the film in a variety of ways: combining and including synchronicity and asynchronicity, irony, and counterpoint.

The five film scores described in Chapter 5 show five more unusual approaches to the relationship between music and film and five variations of Gorbman's Classical Principles of film music.[25] *Money Man* tells us what is going on in the film, but it tells us false information. *The Unknown* identifies characters but with different roles than those intended by the filmmaker. *The Georges Méliès Project* showcases a variety of musical relationships in one program. *Page of Madness* breaks the spell of the cinema and draws our attention to its own artificiality. And *Faust* introduces a counter-narrative at the very beginning of the film, which it develops throughout.

While musical categorization is generally a fool's errand, more so today than ever, I believe that there are still qualities associated with the different traditions and techniques that are meaningful. The film scores discussed in preceding chapters derive from a variety of stylistic sources: rock, jazz, classical, folk, blues, electronic, etc. Yet, though like many of my generation I have been a genre shape-shifter throughout my career, I feel that my background as a jazz musician impacts everything I do, whether it is a classical string quartet, a loop and sample-based electronic piece or a film score. In the following chapter, I discuss why I think the techniques, history, and sensibility of jazz and improvised music are particularly useful tools for film scoring, and particularly in contemporary scores for silent film.

Notes

1. Kassabian, *Hearing Film*, 141.
2. See Criteria for Polysynchronicity, Chapter 1, criteria 1.
3. For an excellent discussion of Bogg's work, see Lawrence Weschler, *Boggs, a Comedy of Values* (Chicago, IL: University of Chicago Press, 1999).
4. See Criteria for Polysynchronicity, Chapter 1, criteria 6.
5. It is described in the score as "MOR (middle-of-the-road) Rock."
6. See Appendix 1, Figure A1 for score.
7. See criteria for Polysynchronicity, Chapter 1, criteria 1, 2, 3, 4, and 6.
8. See Appendix 1, Figure A2 for score.
9. See Appendix 1, Figure A3 for score.
10. Cf. the "inaudibility" in the second of Gorbman's Principles of Classic Film Music.
11. "The cinema? Three cheers for darkened rooms." Andre Breton (Hammond, *Marvelous Méliès*, 7).
12. See criteria for Polysynchronicity, Chapter 1, criteria 5.
13. She continues: "However unconventional or avant-garde a Hollywood musical score might be, the film always motivates it in conventional ways. Thus there is little that's progressive or subversive about jazz in the milieu of drug addiction in *The Man with the Golden Arm*, the electronic sounds that waft over the strange *Forbidden Planet*, or the electronically generated music complicit with the alcoholic dementia of Ray Milland in *The Lost Weekend*. David Bordwell, in fact, cites *Hangover Square*'s score to argue for Hollywood's capacity for 'non-disruptive differentiation,' as the film's discordant music is narratively motivated by its connection to a deranged character" (Gorbman, *Unheard Melodies*, 153).
14. "[T]he lack of synchronization between sound and images has to be characterized as potentially disturbing, perhaps even moments of textual danger." Donnelly, *Occult Aesthetics: Synchronization in Sound Film*, 8.
15. See Appendix 1, Figure A4 for score.
16. Some of this material was originally published in a journal article, Phillip Johnston, "The Polysynchronous Film Score: Songs for a Contemporary Score for F.W. Murnau's Faust (1926)," *Screen Sound Journal*, no. 3 (2012): 89–105.
17. Two exceptions are Richard Einhorn's score for Carl Dreyer's *The Passion of Joan of Arc* and Black Francis's score for *Der Golem*, discussed in Chapter 4.
18. Also known as title cards.
19. See Cohen, "Music as a Source of Emotion," and Gorbman, *Unheard Melodies*, for a more detailed discussion of this role of the composer.
20. See criteria for Polysynchronicity, Chapter 1, criteria 6.

21 Lyrics, and those which follow used by permission of Hilary Bell, from *Faust* (Murnau, 1926, original score by Phillip Johnston, with libretto by Hilary Bell (2002).
22 "I am the camera's eye. I am the machine which shows you the world as I alone see it. Starting from today I am forever free of human immobility. I am in perpetual movement." Dziga Vertov, director of *Man with a Movie Camera*, quoted in Friedrich Kittler, *Optical Media* (Cambridge: Polity Press, 2010), 189 in his "rules" for experimental cinema.
23 See Appendix 1, Figure A5 for score.
24 English intertitles are by John Stone.
25 These are discussed in detail in Chapter 1.

6

Jazzin' the Silents

Jazz and Improvised Music in Contemporary Scores for Silent Film[1]

While the art form of the contemporary silent film score runs the gamut of stylistic practice, including historical, classical, rock, jazz, electronic, folk, hardcore, world music idioms, and beyond, I'd like to suggest that both the vernacular language of jazz and the performing/composing strategy of improvisation are particularly suitable for this body of work, focusing on improvised music across a variety of styles.

A Brief History of Jazz in Film

The first twenty years of synchronized sound film music history, known as the Golden Age of Film Music, were dominated by composers rooted in the Romantic idiom of Wagner, Puccini, and Strauss, composers such as Max Steiner, Erich Korngold, Miklós Rózsa, Alfred Newman, and Franz Waxman.[2] But beginning in the 1950s, a new generation of film music composers, trained in classical composition but also friendly to jazz and popular music, arose: composers like Alex North, Elmer Bernstein, Leith Stevens, Henry Mancini, and others. These composers were not jazz musicians themselves but understood and appreciated the jazz vernacular language and were able to use it fluently in their film score writing. They sometimes also engaged collaborators from the jazz community as collaborators, such as Shorty Rogers, who contributed performances and arrangements to Leith Stevens's score for *The Wild One* (Benedek, 1953) and Elmer Bernstein's score for *The Man with the Golden Arm* (Preminger, 1955).[3] In addition, some directors also began to reach out to jazz composers themselves to score films on their own. Notable early examples include *Anatomy of a Murder* (Preminger, 1959: Duke Ellington), *Ascenseur pour l'échafaud* (Malle, 1958: Miles Davis), and *Knife in the Water* (Polanski, 1962: Krzysztof Komeda).[4]

At this time, jazz was primarily used in stories featuring jazz musicians as protagonists, such as *Young Man with a Horn* (Curtiz, 1950) and *Pete Kelly's Blues* (Webb, 1955), or stories set in seamy criminal or poverty-stricken settings, such as *The Man with the Golden Arm* and *A Streetcar Named Desire* (Kazan, 1951). At first, jazz was used primarily as source music. In North's groundbreaking score for *Streetcar*, the Dixieland jazz in the opening scenes which seems to emanate from every window and doorway sets the scene, of the location (New Orleans), the social milieu (working class, poverty) and the atmosphere of hedonism (drinking and bowling). But later in the score, powerfully in the early sexually charged scene between Stanley Kowalski (Marlon Brando) and Blanche DuBois (Vivien Leigh), the music is pure non-diegetic film music, with no justification other than supporting the narrative on screen. A bluesy piano vamp under a sultry alto sax expresses the subtext of their conversation about the weather and local geography. Leith Stevens's 1953 score for László Benedek's *The Wild One*, also starring Marlon Brando, combined vernacular jazz styles (used both diegetically and non-diegetically) and orchestral music. Stevens trades motifs and themes freely between the diegetic bop cues[5] (often played on a jukebox) and the non-diegetic full orchestral cues. This score represents a crucial step in the evolution of the use of the jazz idiom from diegetic source music to non-diegetic underscore.[6] By the 1960s, the associations of jazz had changed from sex, poverty, drug addiction, and crime to something cool, classy, and hip—the soundtrack to Hef's Playboy Mansion. Henry Mancini's scores for the Blake Edwards's films *Breakfast At Tiffany's* (1961) and *The Pink Panther* (1963) use jazz in a far more light-hearted way (albeit retaining a tongue-in-cheek association with crime) than in his dark score for the 1958 film noir *Touch of Evil* (Welles). In his very thorough *Crime and Spy Jazz on Screen, 1950–1970*, Derrick Bang documents the way in which jazz evolved into a widely used genre in a broad variety of contexts (in both film and television and on both sides of the Atlantic): by 1962 its use ranged from the Academy Award-nominated *The Manchurian Candidate* (Frankenheimer, 1962, score by David Amram[7]) to the more low-budget *Satan in High Heels* (Intrator, 1962, score by Mundell Lowe).[8] Particular mention must be made of jazz composers who also had conservatory training and created brilliant genre-crossing scores (coming to the classical/jazz synthesis from the opposite direction of composers like North, Bernstein, and Stephens), such as Quincy Jones, who studied with Nadia Boulanger (*In Cold Blood*, 1967, *The Pawnbroker*, 1964) and John Lewis of the Modern Jazz Quartet (*Odds Against Tomorrow*, 1959).

Jazz became absorbed into the musical language of film scoring and, at least occasionally, lost its lurid associations. And over time film music came to embrace all genres of jazz from Dixieland (*The Gig*, 1985, music by Warren Vaché) to bebop (*The Wild One*, 1953, Leith Stevens), to West Coast "cool-school" (*The Sweet Smell of Success*, 1957, Elmer Bernstein), to Mainstream (*Mo Better Blues*, 1990, Bill Lee), to avant-garde (*Naked Lunch*, 1981, Howard Shore/Ornette Coleman). In contemporary films, jazz is still most often used in cases in which it is diegetically tied to the film: either in biopics, such as *Bird* (Eastwood, 1988), featuring music by jazz musician/film composer Lennie Niehaus or *Round Midnight* (Tavernier, 1986), with music by jazz musician/composer Herbie Hancock. More recently, films by the team of director Damien Chazelle and composer Justin Hurwitz, *Whiplash* (2014) and *La La Land* (2016), have combined diegetic jazz and underscore. The fact that both films incited considerable negative backlash from jazz musicians, critics, and fans[9] did not prevent them from achieving widespread popular success, with *La La Land* winning Academy Awards for both best score and best original song ("City of Stars"). A more unusual example is the score for *Birdman* (Iñárritu, 2014), in which jazz drummer Antonio Sánchez performs solo on drums and percussion, the principle original scoring in the film (though the director uses a substantial amount of licensed classical music as well). After composer and director worked very closely together on Sánchez's improvising cues for individual scenes, Iñárritu played samples from over seventy demos they created to inspire the actors during the shooting (a commonly used silent film era technique).[10] Sánchez's improvisations closely tracked visual cues and trapped individual lines of dialogue. *Birdman* is the rare contemporary film score that uses a non-diegetically based jazz style for the underscore and also uses improvisation in a compositional context to create the final cues.

Jazz as an Improvisational Art Form

Jazz in its pure form is by nature an improvisational music that does not easily fit the strictures of the film score. Krin Gabbard writes that "the improvising jazz artist, who answers to a private sense of which sounds are right for which moment, is almost by definition incompatible with standard film music practice."[11] In sync-sound-era features, film music is almost always functioning in a supporting role to the image/narrative. However, in his groundbreaking article on improvised scores for silent film, Durant writes,

> The improvisers, as creative and spontaneous musicians, can respond musically to the overall narrative in unpredictable ways that may have a special connection to the understanding of a film's complexity; improvising musicians can "feel" and "remember" more impulsively what has happened in, say, a short segment of film, than a composer that perhaps composed the same segment over a few days or weeks. The musical comment at the end of that segment may be fresher and more truthful in a way, because there is a spontaneous reaction to it as it's being played.[12]

For the purposes of this discussion, it is necessary to separate jazz into two aspects:

1. The vernacular language of jazz: the harmony, the instrumentation, the expressive articulations, the syncopated rhythms, the triplet/swing feel, and the blues scale. This characterizes many of the aspects which identify jazz as a recognizable idiom and/or historical style.
2. The element of improvisation: the musician has "agency" to create their own invention, either within the framework of a composition or without. This notion of improvisation as "spontaneous composition" is not universally endorsed, but here it will be discussed in that context as a film scoring compositional tool.

In contemporary films, a rare example of these two coming together is Howard Shore's collaboration with Ornette Coleman for David Cronenberg's *Naked Lunch* (1991). For a number of the cues, Ornette Coleman improvised over Shore's precomposed orchestral music: an essential part of Shore's compositional process was the *choice* of Coleman as the soloist. In his opening Main Titles cue, Coleman's keening alto soars above an orchestral tone poem that is both dissonant and melancholy: the alto saxophone solo drifts in and out of the harmonic framework, occasionally adding a melancholy blues sound to Shore's more distanced and dissonant orchestration. Later in the film, Barre Phillips's frantic arco bass and Coleman's jabbering alto asynchronously underscore a mostly deadpan conversation between Bill Lee (Peter Weller) and his wife Joan (Judy Davis) about her intravenously injecting his insecticide in order to get high (he is mostly concerned about losing his day job as an exterminator; she calls it "a very literary high [. . .] a Kafka high: you feel like a bug"). The music contradicts everything about the scene (the tone, setting, and structure) but adds to the surreal context of the topic at hand.

Another example is Terje Rypdal's penultimate cue for Alan Rudolph's 1992 film *Equinox*. An ECM-style trio of guitar, bass, and drums goes on an improvised jazz/rock-based flight, expressing what? The terrifying expanse of the landscape? The unknown path ahead for the main character Henry (played by Matthew Modine)? The overwhelming emotions that Henry is experiencing, and the realization he has just had that he is one part of a set of twins? The capacity of improvised music for emotional ambiguity effectively expresses the intersection of powerful emotions and the indefinite outcome with which we (and Henry) are left at the end of the film. The music slowly unwinds and increases and then decreases in intensity over a lengthy helicopter shot which further and further dwarfs the diminishing figure of Henry in the ever-expanding Utah desert landscape.

Improvisation as a Strategy for Film Scoring

More often than not, film music cues are relatively short, and improvised solos occur within the tightly scripted framework of a surrounding composition. More stylized jazz scores such as *Streetcar Named Desire*, *The Man with the Golden Arm*, and *Odds Against Tomorrow* feature composed scores, using the jazz vernacular language, in which any solos are integrated into a tight compositional structure that functions in a traditional narrative film context as part of that language. That is not to diminish their significance, because they bring a unique, expressive element to the larger film scoring language. But the element of improvisation here figures as a relatively small adjunct to the larger compositional process.

Improvisation and improvised music as a form are two widely misunderstood topics. For the purposes of this discussion, I will use Derek Bailey's terms from his highly respected 1992 book *Improvisation*. He uses the terms "idiomatic" and "non-idiomatic" and defines them as follows:

> Idiomatic improvisation, much the most widely used, is mainly concerned with the expression of an idiom—such as jazz, flamenco or baroque—and takes its identity and motivation from that idiom. Non-idiomatic improvisation has other concerns and is most usually found in so-called "free" improvisations and, while it can be highly stylized, is not usually tied to representing an idiomatic identity.[13]

This distinction stands separate from the issue of form: whether a certain piece of music has a static structure or not, and form/structure is a central issue of the craft of film scoring. But a jazz trumpet solo which occurs as an element of a composed film cue, where the structure and even the dramatic arc of a given solo are predetermined but individual notes and phrases are not, falls within the definition of *idiomatic* improvisation. A scoring process wherein a group of musicians is asked to spontaneously respond to a scene from a film *could* potentially be an example of non-idiomatic improvisation. One can immediately see why free improvisation is not often used in contemporary narrative film scoring: it is too hard to control, too unlikely to conform exactly to the director's vision of the film and often unmoored to an idiom which has immediate semiotic or culturally coded associations. But improvisation of non- or less-idiomatic varieties has been used successfully in the film scoring process.

One application of this process was the Necks' score for Rowan Woods's 1998 Australian film *The Boys*. The director, being a fan of the Necks' edgy post-minimalist improvised music, felt that it would suit the mood he wanted to create in his film—not an obvious choice given that the film was based on a 1992 play by Gordon Graham about an Australian working-class criminal family. Rather than following a traditional process of scoring discrete cues locked-to-picture, the director showed the Necks some dailies and a rough cut of the film, and they went away and created a series of improvisations based on their response to the scenes, which were later refined, but without further recourse to the film. Woods then took those recordings and worked with his editor and music editor to conform them to the footage as he saw fit. The result was a chilling opening and other cues that heightened the drama, through the use of both acoustic and electronic elements, and evoked the despair and hopelessness of the main characters.[14] A-List Hollywood film music composer Cliff Martinez (*Sex, Lies and Videotape*, *The Driver*, *Contagion*) uses a different approach, as part of his process, to put the skills of talented improvisers to work in service of his scores. In creating some of the music for *Traffic* (Steven Soderbergh, 2000), he created "beds" of sound, over which he unleashed improvising musicians such as David Torn and Jeff Rona. He then took these various tracks and edited and remixed them to create the final cues for the film.[15]

In an interview with Michael Schelle, Elmer Berstein describes using free improvisation as an element to create an effective cue for one ultra-violent scene in Francis Ford Coppola's *The Rainmaker* (1997): "I composed the basic structure for it, and the solo instruments improvised wildly over that structure. I didn't care what they played, it just had to be wild and uncontrolled, bloodcurdling."[16]

A variety of different approaches, with a complex relationship to historical styles, come together in the film scoring work of John Zorn. His film music output (which he has documented on his own Tzadik label—his most recent is *Filmworks xxv: City of Slaughter / Schmatta / Beyond the Infinite*) falls into two different but sometimes related categories. The first is sync-sound film scores—including feature-length films (such as Raul Ruiz's 1990 *The Golden Boat*), shorts, and documentaries. The second is live performances to film, but rather than historical silent films, he prefers the avant-garde films of the 1940s–60s, such as the work of Harry Smith, Maya Deren, Joseph Cornell, and Kenneth Anger, removing the original soundtracks where they exist (which are rarely closely sync'd or involve significant dialogue) and adding his live improvised score. I say "related" because some of the documentaries he has scored have been *about* some of these 1960s filmmakers, such as *Notes on Marie Menken* (Martina Kudlácek, 2006) and *In the Mirror of Maya Deren* (Martina Kudlácek, 2001). He varies his approach depending on the film, but certain things are fairly consistent. Rather than work lock-to-picture in a traditional film composer workflow, he creates moods for scenes "with themes and vamps that are cued in and out, always while looking at the film." He uses hand signals to conduct the ensemble ("stop/start/ change/ imitate/vamp/sparse etc."). "Sometimes a player is given a particular character to relate to in advance, or spontaneously; sometimes themes for certain characters or moods or scenes are specified in advance, melodies, vamps etc.; but I conduct and cue spontaneously."[17] In each of these examples, the creator of the score uses some combination of improvisation and composition and chooses different points to exert authorial (compositional) control over the freedom of the improvisation.

Jazz and Improvised Music in Contemporary Scores for Silent Film

It is ironic that the most popular imagination of silent film music is that of a ragtime piano, inevitably performed on an out-of-tune spinet. Yet Marks,[18] Abel and Altman,[19] and other important writers about historical silent film practice do not cite any specific documented episodes of a ragtime score for a silent film.[20] Even from what little is definitively documented of impromptu scores of the time, they seem to have drawn mostly from elements of classical music and popular song. Despite anecdotes of Fats Waller playing organ for silent films in Harlem as a teenager, there is no record of what music he may have played (or improvised).[21] Yet the tradition of the improvised piano score is kept alive today by many dedicated pianists such as Donald Sosin, Philip Carli, and Mauro Columbis[22] who accompany silent films at museums, cinematheques, and film festivals, though most of these are not primarily rooted in the jazz idiom.[23] For most contemporary moviegoers however, it is enough that the score sounds "old" for it to feel historically correct. Thus, using elements of early jazz, blues, and folk, regardless of their historical accuracy, feels to most audiences that it is "authentic."

The Club Foot Orchestra's score for Buster Keaton's *Sherlock Jr.* (1924) discussed in Chapter 4 takes advantage of the association of early jazz and silent film. While many other styles are also referenced throughout, the score is built on the kind of thematic/motif-based development that is associated with film scoring in general and Silent Film/Golden Age scoring in particular. And many of the main themes are based on an early jazz style. However, even the specifically 1920s jazz-based themes include the use of electric guitar (not invented until 1931) and elements of extended modern jazz techniques, jagged stop-and-go rhythms and moments of dissonance that were not at all a common practice in the jazz of 1924. Furthermore, they effortlessly segue in and out of this historical music to styles that include electric blues, country and western, Hawaiian music, rock, and avant-garde jazz. While they make copious use of trapping and close following of dramatic beats, the actual implementation of these techniques is often done with irony, humor, and comic juxtaposition in a way that is decidedly postmodern. They also use other techniques associated with silent film scoring, such as musical sound effects (often used in conjunction with trapping) and musical quotations (using the audience's knowledge of current popular song titles to communicate ideas). Early in *Sherlock Jr.*, as Keaton returns to the shop where he had intended to buy a more expensive present for the object of his affections and checks his wallet (of which he has failed to increase the contents in the previous scene), the main riff from the 1933 Dubin/Warren song "We're in the Money" is played on a chorus of what sounds like out-of-tune slide whistles. It is an ironic application of a classic silent film scoring technique, using a non-idiomatic orchestration, in a song that was not written in 1924 (and doubly ironically may no longer be known by much of their modern audience).

In their score for *Felix Woos Whoopie* (Otto Mesmer, 1928), composed by Richard Marriott, they again return to an early jazz style, particularly as Felix enters the Whoopie Club, and later as other elements are underscored by jazz-style swinging with brushes on high hat. But the majority of the score combines very close trapping and musical sound effects with avant-garde extended techniques, musical abstraction, and free jazz—all very closely scored to the visuals. The CFO uses both jazz as an idiomatic style (particularly early jazz) to suggest time, place, and context and improvisation as a compositional technique (both in creating musical effects and as part of a free jazz musical language).

One approach used by jazz composers in creating contemporary scores for silent films has been to write a number of themes connected to different characters, moods, or narrative arcs (a time-tested compositional approach since the late silent film era), and then direct the band on the spot in improvising from one theme to another throughout the film.[24] The silent film scores of the Walter Thompson Orchestra go a step further. Thompson's completely improvised scores rely on his "conduction technique" (also practiced in different forms by Butch Morris and John Zorn): a language of elaborate memorized hand gestures which direct the musicians, individually or in groups, in their free improvisations. Thompson watches the film, reacts to it, and directs the musicians to express his reactions through their own improvisations, with no themes or motifs prepared in advance. The most extreme example of this approach is practiced by Chicago tenor saxophonist Ken Vandermark, who leads a group in improvising to silent films—but with their backs turned to the films. He relies on accidental juxtapositions with the film for any synchronicity, which Vandermark says occurs more often than he had expected or so he is told.[25] As discussed in Chapter 4, guitarist Gary Lucas takes yet a different approach in his silent film scores: he uses solo guitar with multiple pedals and effects (a mostly analog affair) to create a soundscape that moves gradually through the film. While he does make some use of larger thematic zones, he makes little attempt either to sound contemporaneous or to follow common film scoring practices like narrative cueing or continuity. Rather, he establishes a mood within which he develops musical ideas at his own pace until he is ready to move on.

Creating scores for historical silent films currently forms a small proportion of John Zorn's film scoring work, for which he often improvises solo at the organ[26]—much as a silent film era organist would, except using much more modern compositional material combining post-Schoenbergian dissonance, minimalism, and beyond. He says, "[I]mprovising with silent film for me comes out of the format of a single pianist watching the film and improvising—one person's vision. Even when there is a band, the other players function as an extension of the pianist's vision" who then becomes a conductor.[27] So, despite the modernism of the content, it functions here in a somewhat historical context for silent film accompaniment—an individual artist making improvised decisions, responding to the film based on their own intuitive response to the visual images and narrative. But according to silent film music improviser Petter Frost Fadnes, "by using Zorn's technique of sonorities open to visual interpretation, as well as playing music which often is unobvious (within Hollywood aesthetics) to the agenda of either a particular scene or the movie as a whole, the viewer is forced to make sense of the immediate chaos which is visually and aurally presented."[28]

In his experiments with approaches to improvising with silent films beginning in 2011, Durant defines five methodologies which reflect a range of levels of engagement with the film.

Method 1: Look first at the film in its entirety, with or without sound (preferable, as it doesn't then imply simple musical mimicking) then improvise and talk about the outcome.
Method 2: Look first at the film in its entirety, with or without sound, create and study preparatory material together, such as a simple cue sheet or graphic score. Then talk about how it will be played and establish limitations ahead of the first attempt. Then play and talk about the outcome.
Method 3: Go ahead and play from the beginning with the film, without any cue sheet or background, then talk about the outcome.
Method 4: Don't rehearse at all and play at first sight in the performance.
Method 5: The most extreme way—don't look at the film at all before, during or after the performance and simply improvise.[29]

Composition/Improvisation in My Own Work

In my own work, many of my scores use the first approach (a solo over a closely controlled structure or a structured improvisation over a prescribed segment of the film), with a few significant exceptions. In my first score for silent film, Tod Browning's *The Unknown* (1927), commissioned by the American Museum of the Moving Image in 1992, I took a fairly conventional approach (development of themes and motifs, following dramatic beats): my main innovation was using the powers of "narrative cueing"[30] to reverse the roles of the villain and the romantic duo of hero and heroine as discussed in Chapter 5. There is liberal use made of improvising for all instruments, but always within a prescribed structure, often with precomposed accompaniment. A variety of musical styles and genres are used, but the improvisations, while sometimes in a very modernist style, function either over chord changes, some sort of composed accompaniment, or within a prescribed length with instructions. The soloists add creative elements but do not largely alter the overall composition. Their improvisations function as compositional elements themselves, largely as they did in the 1950s jazz scores (albeit with modern improvising styles).

In my second program of contemporary music with silent film, which included eight short films by the early French film pioneer Georges Méliès, I approached different films differently and used the eight films as a laboratory to explore different relationships between music and film. Some of the scores were completely notated, but most used some combination of improvisation and composition. Some of the improvisations function in the same way as in *The Unknown*, and some were in some form of jazz style, but a number of them were only constricted by the boundaries of a particular scene, and within that scene, the soloist(s) was/were only given a single instruction, and within that time period were completely free as to what to play. For example, in *Voyage dans la lune* (Méliès, 1902), a scene in which a group of scientists changes from their scientific robes into traveling suits, the music is played by the double bass solo, with the instruction: "improvise, col legno" (literally "with wood"—playing percussively with the reverse side of the bow on the strings), evoking the feverish mood of the participants. My intention was that the music provide a musical sound effect of scrambling insects, like ants in an ant colony, because this was suggested to me by the visual. But within that period of time (which is surprisingly long), the bass can choose whatever particular notes or rhythms they wish to achieve this effect, and there is no attempt at trapping or following dramatic beats. In another film—*Le voyage à travers l'impossible* (Méliès, 1904)—a group improvisation is used to create musical sound effects to represent the disintegration of a submersible craft, the only instruction being to increase from sparse to dense throughout the scene. Later, a scene in which the party of adventurers is frozen is accompanied by another group improvisation with only the instructions "blowing sounds" and it lasts the length of the scene. Each of these interludes are surrounded by conventionally notated material, with the improvised sections functioning as interludes, always with some use of extended techniques, to create musical sound effects. Both of these examples use "extended techniques" such as slap tonguing, flutter tonguing, col legno, and hitting/slapping the instrument.

But after writing several primarily through-composed scores, I felt I wanted to use improvisation in a silent film score in a more integral way. When I was commissioned in 1998 by the Film Society of Lincoln Center to create a new score for Teinosuke Kinugasa's *Page of Madness* (1927), a Japanese Abstract Expressionist masterpiece with no title cards, shot entirely in an insane asylum, I decided that a greater use of improvisation would be appropriate, in order to create a more abstract score.

This excerpt from the first page of the score, a series of text instructions, shows that in a montage of very abstract short cuts early in the film, the only stipulation is what combination of instruments[31] are playing, leaving the other musical decisions to the musicians' choice. But the abstraction of the visuals renders what would be an avant-garde film cue *synchronous*, as the visuals are equally abstract as the music.

01 09	rain (streetlight)	soprano sax/piano/vibes/bass
01 17	windows (don't change)	bs
01 19	water tank, water spraying	pno/vbs
01 21	street, car driving	bs/sop
01 25	close-up of wheels	pno
01 27	dark, window	vbs
01 31	water flooding	sop
01 35	darkened figure	pno/bs
01 38	water flooding	sop/pno/vbs/bs
01 40	bright light through window, water flooding	vbs
01 44	steps, water, legs walking	pno/vbs/bs
01 49	bars with water	sop
01 51	dark, window	pno/sop
01 55	dark water on steps	vbs
01 57	rain (streetlight)	sop/pno/vbs/bs

While both the music and the film are relatively abstract by traditional film music/film standards, the music here fulfills Gorbman's principle of continuity[32] in following the editing structure of the film meticulously. All of the actual musical content of each section of this cue is freely improvised: the only thing that is composed is the structure (when to begin and end, dictated by visual cues) and the orchestration (what instruments are playing).

Other sections of the score combine composed material and a variety of improvising strategies, but large swathes of the film are scored only by visual cues for beginnings and endings, with either a brief verbal instruction or instruction to respond to the visual/narrative (the narrative in this case is fairly obscure).

Almost none of the music is in an idiomatic jazz style—much of it is polytonal or atonal—but the element of improvisation is used throughout to create both the content and the structure of music: the composition itself, while still dictated by the score overall, is much more influenced by the details of the improvisation. The improvisation is always closely scored to the film, but within many of the individual sections, it is almost completely free.

In my two subsequent silent film projects, I mostly use improvisation in a more controlled way and sometimes use the idiomatic jazz vernacular language. In my score for F.W. Murnau's *Faust* (1926), I use songs with lyrics written by librettist Hilary Bell (see Chapter 5), some of which are in a jazz style. But it also contains elements of free improvisation over a chromatic accompaniment (played on the ukulele), albeit within a carefully defined structure. In my score for Lotte Reiniger's *The Adventures of Prince Achmed* (1926), a German silent silhouette animation, I make wide use of styles based on the jazz/blues organ style of Jimmy Smith and other historical jazz styles, for example, a cutting contest in 5/4 time where the groove of funky organ jazz—coupled with the excitement of two "hot" jazz organ players trading solos—establishes the character of the Magician: wily, playful, potent, and slightly menacing. The structure and harmony are completely determined: only the details of the solos are improvised. This is a use of jazz and improvisation that goes back to the 1950s jazz film scores, albeit placed in an unexpected context.

Jazz and improvised music today contain multitudes. With its tradition of shape shifting and shamanism, jazz can combine with other music genres or stand on its own as an idiomatic "sound" for a given film score. The experienced improviser can respond to the film spontaneously, either within the composer's instructions or independently. This tool can be used to fulfill the film score's traditional functions, both synchronous to asynchronous (from narrative cueing to providing subtext), or it can work in service of more radical reinventions (changing the narrative, "Brechtian distanciation" or multimedia performativity). Gabbard writes that "the jazz film score . . . offers the viewer an opportunity to experience the film more critically as a modernist, even fragmented, work of art."[33] As David Butler, in part, connects the expansion of jazz into film music to its evolution from popular dance music to art music,[34] one can trace a continuation of this evolution into the art form of contemporary scores for silent film. In addition, as silent film scores originate in a practice of live performance (and as such, each performance is unique), there is nowhere better for the spontaneity of jazz and improvised music to flourish. The live performance of silent film with a jazz/improvised music score transforms a film screening into a kinetic performative event that combines the excitement of live music with the depth, emotion, and otherness of the rich body of work of the pre-sync-sound film era.

Notes

1. This chapter was previously published in a slightly edited form in Phillip Johnston, "Jazzin' the Silents: Jazz and Improvised Music in Contemporary Scores for Silent Film," in *Cinema Changes: Incorporations of Jazz in the Film Soundtrack #34*, ed. Emile Wennekes and Emilio Audissino (Turnhout: Brepols, Speculum Musicae, 2019), 19–32.
2. Prendergast, *Film Music: A Neglected Art*, 39.
3. Bernstein is quoted as writing, "my score was not a jazz score, but a score in which jazz elements were incorporated toward the end of creating [a] specific atmosphere for that particular film." In fact, all of the scores mentioned here incorporate different approaches to combining jazz and more traditional (read classical) film scoring practices. Julie Hibbert, *Celluloid Symphonies: Texts and Contexts in Film Music History* (Berkeley and Los Angeles: University of California Press, 2013), 262.
4. Prendergast, *Film Music: A Neglected Art*, 104–19.
5. Performed by an ensemble led by Shorty Rogers who also arranged them.
6. For an excellent discussion of this score, see Fred Steiner, "An Examination of Leith Stevens' Use of Jazz in *The Wild One*: Parts I & II," in *Film Music Notebook: A Complete Collection of the Quarterly Journal, 1974-1978*, ed. Elmer Bernstein (Sherwood Oaks: The Film Music Society, 2001), 240–52, 280–8.
7. Admittedly, Amram's score lost its jazz cues by the time it was released; but Amram had excellent credentials in both jazz and contemporary classical music, and the score is an excellent one in any case. Derrick Bang, *Crime and Spy Jazz on Screen, 1950-1970* (Jefferson, NC: McFarland & Company, 2020), 104.
8. Bang, *Crime and Spy Jazz on Screen, 1950-1970*.
9. Here is one of many examples: "In Damien Chazelle's new film 'Whiplash,' the very idea of jazz is turned into a grotesque and ludicrous caricature." Richard Brody, "Getting Jazz Right in the Movies," *The New Yorker*, October 13, 2014, https://www.newyorker.com/culture/richard-brody/whiplash-getting-jazz-right-movies.
10. Dian Panosian, "Awards 2015 Spotlight: Composer Antonio Sánchez Takes SSN into the Jam Sessions that Created Birdman's Dauntless Percussion Score," *SSN Insider*, December 3, 2014, https:// archive.li/9KIpr.

11 He adds that "jazz soundtracks seem to spin along on their own, seemingly oblivious to the action" (ibid). While I can't endorse this statement absolutely, which admittedly is taken a bit out of context, a wonderful example that supports it is Ralph Carmichael's big band jazz score for *4D Man* (Irvin Yeaworth, 1959), which seems to have very little to do with this low-budget 1950s sci-fi conglomeration of Dr. Jekyll and Mr. Hyde and Dracula, a follow up to *The Blob* (Irvin Yeaworth, 1958), which was made by the same director/composer team. Krin Gabbard, *Jammin' at the Margins: Jazz and the American Cinema* (Chicago: University of Chicago Press, 1996), 135.

12 Yati E. Durant, "Spontaneous Composition for Screen: linear and non-linear improvisation for instruments and electronics," *The New Soundtrack* 6.2 (2016): 173.

13 Derek Bailey, *Improvisation: Its Nature and Practice in Music* (Boston: Da Capo Press, 1992), xi–xii.

14 Conversation with the author, 2019.

15 Jason Foster, "Cliff Martinez' Traffic," *Film Score Monthly*, vi, no. 1 (2001): 15.

16 Michael Schelle, *The Score: Interviews with Film Composers* (Los Angeles: Silma-James Press, 1999), 54.

17 Conversation with the author, March 8, 2018.

18 Marks, *Music and the Silent Film*.

19 Richard Abel and Rick Altman, *The Sounds of Early Cinema* (Bloomington and Indianapolis: Indiana University Press, 2001).

20 There are occasional references to ragtime music, even in beautiful photo books like Peter Kobel's *Silent Movies* (which bears the imprimatur of Martin Scorsese, Kevin Brownlow and the Library Congress). "In the early nickelodeon days, when movies often changed every day, musicians sometimes just played ragtime regardless of what was on the screen." Unfortunately, there are no details of what they played or sources for this assertion. However, Kobel writes enthusiastically and insightfully about the work of Alloy, Einhorn, and Neil Brand, say, that their scores for Vertov's *Man with a Movie Camera* (1929, Alloy) and Einhorn's *Voices of Light* (see Chapter 4) "stand up as great works on their own, while enhancing the works that inspired them." Peter Kobel, *Silent Movies: The Birth of Film and the Triumph of Movie Culture* (New York: Little, Brown and Company, 2007), 259–61.

21 The closest we get is Russell Lack's hypothesis, in referring to silent films "charged with somehow capturing the essence of 'jazz life'"—he cites *The Girl with the Jazz Heart* (1921), *The House That Jazz Built* (1921), and others—that "although there are no surviving cue sheets from any of these rare films' exhibition tours, it seems highly probably that some sort of jazz-influenced textures would have found their way into the orchestra pit." Russell Lack, *Twenty Four Frames Under* (London: Quartet Books, 1997), 44–5.

22 This micro-niche of musicianship is celebrated in a master class in solo piano silent film accompaniment offered annually at the Pordenone Silent Film Festival since 2003. Ann-Kristin Wallengren, "To Be in Dialogue with the Film: With Neil Brand and Lillian Henley at the Masterclasses at Pordenone Silent Film Festival," in *Today's Sounds for Yesterday's Films: Making Music for Silent Cinema*, ed. K J Donnelly and Ann-Kristin Wallengren (London: Palgrave Macmillan, 2016), 192–215.

23 One of the few jazz-based pianists who has been accompanying silent films on a regular basis since the 1970s is "weird bop" pianist Joel Forrester, who has accompanied countless silent film programs at venues including the Louvre, the American Center, the Forum des Images, and the Musée d'Orsay in Paris and in New York, at the Film Forum, Brooklyn Museum, the Center for Photography, and Anthology Film Archives.

24 Similar to the "bridge" function described by Bellano in his "Silent Strategies," 58–61.

25 Peter Margasak, "Music Notes: Films Scored While You Watch," *The Chicago Reader*, September 21, 1995, https://www.chicagoreader.com/chicago/music-notes-films-scored-while-you-watch/Content?oid=888547.

26 For example, for *The Cabinet of Dr. Caligari* (Wiene 1920) on pipe organ for the premiere of the new restoration at the Berlin Film Festival in 2014 and at Mexico's Bestia Festival in 2015.

27 Conversation with the author, March 8, 2018.

28 Fadnes, *Improvising the Deluge*, 115.

29 Durant, Spontaneous Composition for Screen," 181.

30 In her "Classical Film Music: Principles of Composition, Mixing and Editing," Gorbman divides these into (i) referential narrative: music gives referential and narrative cues, for example, indicating point of view, supplying formal demarcations, and establishing setting and characters and (ii) connotative: music "interprets" and "illustrates" narrative events (Gorbman, *Unheard Melodies*, 73).

31 The original ensemble consists of soprano saxophone (sop), vibraphone (vb), piano (pno), and double bass (bs).

32 Continuity: music provides formal and rhythmic continuity—between shots, in transitions between scenes, by filling "gaps" (Gorbman, *Unheard Melodies*, 73).

33 Gabbard, *Jammin' At the Margins: Jazz and the American Cinema*, 135.

34 David Butler, *Jazz Noir: Listening to Music from Phantom Lady to the Last Seduction* (Westport: Praeger Publishers, 2002), 61.

7

Imaginary Authenticity
Scores for Modern Silent Films

In 2011, the French film *The Artist*, written and directed by Michel Hazanavicius, with a score composed by Ludovic Bource, seemingly came out of nowhere—a modern silent film!—to win broad audience and critical appreciation, and to be nominated for ten Academy Awards (winning five, including Best Picture, Best Director, and Best Score). While this high concept undertaking struck most filmgoers as audacious and unexpected, there has actually been a steady trickle across the globe of contemporary silent films over the last twenty or thirty years and beyond. These films—independent, quirky, original—are amazingly diverse, both in their style and subject matter and in their relationship to historical silent films. And when composers write for these films, they are faced with a dilemma: whether to score the film as a contemporary film (albeit one lacking in audible dialogue or other film sound) or as a historical "silent" film. Many choose a path somewhere between the two, but the way in which they negotiate that path sheds light on contemporary beliefs about silent film and silent film music, assumptions about film music more broadly, and ideas about modernity versus historicity. It speaks to the very heart of the relationship between music and film. Composers for contemporary silent films balance the need to suggest accurate depictions of silent film music with the musical expectations of contemporary film audiences and their own musical voices. Anahid Kassabian points out that the filmgoer has "a relationship of long-standing with the film music genre itself . . . a perceiver may derive pleasure from an instance of film music because it evokes an accumulation of meanings from previous film experiences."[1] This can be said to a lesser degree about the filmgoer's relationship with silent film, and both apply to a film director and composer as well as the audience. Thus, the questions asked here address the tension between expectations for "film music" and expectations for "silent film music."

The focus here will be primarily on three films: *The Artist* (2011/USA), *Dr Plonk* (2007/Australia), and *Blancanieves* (2012/Spain), in terms of both the films themselves and more closely, their scores—specifically at their relationship to their peculiar situation: balanced between today and yesterday. Or rather what they/we believe to be today and yesterday. I'll also look more briefly at a series of other contemporary silent films, mostly from the past twenty-five years or so. They include *Le Dernier Combat* (aka *The Last Battle*) (1983/France), *The Love Chariot* (aka *Pushpaka Vimanam*) (1987/India), *Sidewalk Stories* (1989/USA), *Begotten* (1991/USA), *Tuvalu* (1999/Bulgaria), *Juha* (1999/Finland), *Hukkle* (2002/Hungary), *Dracula: Pages from a Virgin's Diary* (2002/Canada), *Cowards Bend the Knee* (2003/Canada), *After the Apocalypse* (2004/Japan), *The Call of Cthulhu* (2005/USA), *Brand Upon the Brain! A Remembrance in 12 Chapters* (2006/Canada), *Claire* (2001/USA), *The Aerial (aka La Antena)* (2007/Argentina), and *La Tortue Rouge (The Red Turtle)* (2016/Japan/France/Holland). Mention will also be made of *Silent Movie* (1976/USA), *The Naked Island* (1960/Japan).

The specific issues discussed shed light upon what we think silent films are: the film techniques and the music composition techniques that are associated with the genre and thus are drawn upon in order to invoke it. The scores will be the focus here, with reference to the films as a whole for context. Note that I am looking specifically at narrative-driven feature films and not discussing more non-narrative, non-dialogue films done by filmmakers like Maya Deren, Kenneth Anger, Stan Brakhage, nor music-driven abstract animated film. Nor do I discuss silent (or non-dialogue) films which were still part of the early film era that were made during the early sync-sound era, such as Chaplin's *Modern Times* (1936) and the all-Balinese-cast *Legong: Dance of the Virgins* (Henri de la Falaise, 1935).

Background

For present purposes, it is useful to divide silent film era scoring techniques into two categories: (i) composition techniques that were established early on as general film scoring techniques and are still practiced today, and (ii) composition techniques that are specifically associated with the silent film era, and now considered anachronistic.

The first group includes following dramatic beats, synchronous scoring, the use of themes and motifs, and close adherence to the editing structure of the film. The second includes trapping (sometimes referred to as "Mickey-Mousing"), and *very* close following of dramatic beats, musical quotes, broad associative signaling (diminished chords for horror, major seventh chords for innocence), constant and sometimes literal use of motifs, and historical musical styles associated with the time: ragtime piano (mostly erroneously), organ music, lush Romantic era classical music, though a couple may cross the line a bit. Regarding the films themselves, popular associations with the silent film era include black-and-white film, a complete lack of synchronized sound (dialogue, sound effects, etc.), exaggerated makeup and acting styles, the use of title cards, the use of music more or less constantly throughout the film, and stylistic choices associated with German Expressionism (iris in/iris out, dramatic use of light and shadow, extreme acting styles associated with melodrama/Grand Guignol).

Reminder: Any discussion of music for historical silent films must acknowledge the fact that music for film before the era of synchronized sound recording was always by necessity performed live. The modern performance of new contemporary scores for silent film continues this convention and most practitioners acknowledge that live performances of music with film have a kinetic energy and performative excitement that cannot be reproduced by recordings: every performance, even that of a through-composed score, is unique.[2] In this context, any recorded score for a silent film can ultimately only be seen as a souvenir. However, in deference to all of the practicalities of production and distribution in the twenty-first century, while a few of the filmmakers here have flirted with live music performance as an adjunct to early releases, the ultimate vehicle must by necessity be a synchronized sound film, which mimics early film music practices. All of the films discussed here were viewed by the author on DVD.

It is the wide variety in the degree to which these individual films and scores adhere to techniques and tropes associated with the silent film era that makes contemporary silent films so fascinating: both because of the freedom with which they adopt or discard what are thought to be the requirements of a silent film and score, and also because of what their choices say about the nature and function of film music.

Questions

The following list of questions was chosen not as a strict measure of "silent film-ness" but, rather, as an invitation into the examination of each film:

1. Does it have any audio dialogue? If so, how much?
2. Is it in black and white or color?
3. Does it have production sound and sound effects? If so, how much?
4. Does it use Title Cards?
5. Is the film placed in a contemporary or historical setting? What is the style of the film?
6. Does the music invoke silent film techniques? If so, which ones?
7. What is the style of the music overall?
8. Is there music which is anachronistic to the silent film era? To the era in which the film is set (style, technique, instruments, technology)?
9. Is there any (implied) diegetic music? If so, how is it treated?
10. Is there music consistently throughout the film?

The Artist

Written and directed by Michel Hazanavicius, with a score composed by Ludovic Bource, *The Artist* is perhaps the most self-consciously postmodern of the main films looked at here (with the possible exception of *La Antena*). The director's background in genre parody laid a foundation for his tongue-in-cheek approach to *The Artist*. Before then he was most well known in France for a series of spy parodies: *OSS 117: Cairo, Nest of Spies* (2006) and *OSS 117: Lost in Rio* (2009), also scored by Bource.

Led by its charming and flawlessly mustachioed star Jean DuJardin, the film is both sincere and romantic, and witty and ironic. Clearly originating in a deep love of early film and early film music,[3] the film and score are both a passionate homage and a satirical commentary, full of in-jokes and film (and film music) references.

The film opens with a virtuosic seven-minute sequence that immediately establishes its postmodern, fourth-and-even-fifth-wall-busting credentials. The sequence begins (in black and white) with the tuxedoed hero (DuJardin) being tortured in an electric chair by enemy agents, accompanied by melodramatic orchestral music with requisite tremolo strings (signifying tension), diminished chords (signifying danger), and timpani (signifying conflict). There is no synchronized sound other than the orchestral music. The first "words" of the film are a title card expressing the words of the torturer: "Speak!"—already a pun on the fact that the unnamed hero is crying out in pain without making any audible (to the audience) sound. The music follows the dramatic beats very closely, but the camera soon cuts to a shot of a conductor conducting an orchestra, with a packed house of a large cinema audience behind him. The next shot is of the movie screen, but now from the point of view of an audience mid-theater, so we see the audience, the orchestra, and screen-within-a-screen. We have suddenly become an audience watching a silent film of an audience watching a silent film.[4]

Various erudite sight gags ensue. The audience in the film reacts in horror at a moment of danger in the film, then laughs and claps at his escape, but we hear no sound from them, only that of the orchestra playing—that is, playing the score of the film they are watching, which is simultaneously the score of *The Artist*. As DuJardin pulls off his escape, en masque, the adventure music invokes more of the Golden Age scores of Korngold and Rózsa, and via inheritance, the John Williams' scores for the *Indiana Jones* franchise (1981–2020). Bource's homage is historical, but not obsessively accurate; it annexes the entire history of film music of the first half of the twentieth century and mixes and matches freely. At one point the camera cuts to a sign (like a title card): "Please BE SILENT Behind the Screen"—this admonishing cinema workers not to distract the audience with bumps in the night but also makes a second pun on the situation of the film. The camera pans out to include the actor who plays George Valentin (DuJardin), the hero of this film, *A Russian Affair*, shaking hands with the backstage stagehands: this is the first time we have seen the "real" Valentin, the actor who is backstage at the premiere of his latest film. (He is also a hero because he is a "regular guy," not an aloof movie star.) He is accompanied by the same dog who is his best friend in the silent film being premiered—but also clearly is his "real" dog. We meet the other characters in the film *The Artist* backstage: his wife/costar Doris and the producer Al Zimmer, and then see Valentin from behind, watching himself on screen approvingly.

Accompanied by brass in a major key playing a triumphant fanfare,[5] the metafictional film ends with the hero proclaiming, "Long Live Free Georgia!" As we see on the screen "The End" printed in reverse (as we look at the film from behind, backstage), the audience and the studio executives backstage explode into wild applause—in utter silence, for the orchestra of course has stopped playing after the final triumphant chord. After a few moments of this pregnant silence, the second main music cue of the film begins, a jazzy two-beat number, which is ostensibly not played by the orchestra in the theatre (we see them in repose, applauding as well, as Valentin takes his bows), but is now part of the underscore for *The Artist*. The music has seamlessly moved from diegetic to non-diegetic.

But is the first music cue really diegetic? It is non-diegetic for *A Russian Affair*, the silent film that it is so expertly accompanying yet, at the same time, diegetic to the film *The Artist*. Yet we, as the audience for *The Artist*, are watching the film *Russian Affair* and enjoying it on its own terms, so the music is serving both diegetic and non-diegetic roles for us at the same time. And the second cue borders on the "meta-diegetic,"[6] serving not only as underscore but as Valentin's internal "theme music," reflecting his cool, Continental panache, as he views himself. This second cue, which is called "George Valentin," is essentially his theme music and is meant to express everything about George in a classically synchronous manner: it's bright, confident, charming, and oblivious. It accompanies his extended curtain calls and continues through the following scene outside at the stage door where he first meets Pepe Miller, his love interest, and ours. In doing so, it embodies virtually every one of Claudia Gorbman's Classical Film Music principles: it is a signifier of emotion, it gives narrative cueing (both referential and connotative), it creates continuity, and unity, as this theme is used again throughout the film.[7] The composer has gone from a cue that very specifically invokes techniques associated with the silent film era (with a postmodern twist) to a classic Golden Age-era style cue. But both are invoking historical film music styles.

While the film does use title cards, there are very few of them and the film is mostly told through images—and music. The rest of the film is a fictionalized retelling of the story of the transition between silent and sound film, a la *Singing in the Rain* (Kelly/Donen, 1952), replete with regular winking references to silence/sound and to classic silent and Golden Age films (and film music),[8] that falls into the rich body of films about film and Hollywood, from Keaton's silent *Sherlock Jr.* (1924) to Altman's *The Player* (1992) and Lynch's *Mulholland Drive* (2001), among many others. Of the films looked at here, both Sapir's *La Antena* and Brooks's *Silent Movie* make silence/sound the explicit topic of their narratives, and all of Guy Maddin's silent work makes more veiled reference to it.

Dr Plonk

Australian director Rolf De Heer's *Dr Plonk* takes a place in one of the most eclectic bodies of work in film history. From his "breakout" film, the outrageous *Bad Boy Bubbie* (1993) to the Aboriginal language film *Ten Canoes* (2008) (codirected with Peter Djigirr) and the more recent *Charlie's Country* (2013), his films have often provoked controversy or incomprehension. Composer Graham

Tardif has written the scores for many of his films, from *Bubbie* to *Charlie's Country*, and including *Dr Plonk*.

Dr Plonk immediately establishes itself as an homage to the classic silent film comedies of Charlie Chaplin, Harold Lloyd, and Buster Keaton (esp. Keaton). The making of the film was reputedly driven by De Heer's discovery of 20,000 feet of old unexposed film stock in his office refrigerator.[9] (Even this bit of promotional mythology invokes classic Hollywood style.) The film is shot in black and white and contains no sound except for the musical score, which is sync'd to the film, though the premiere in Adelaide featured a live performance of the score by the Stiletto Sisters, assisted by pianist Sam White, who perform Tardif's score.[10] A la Keaton, the film, while it has an elaborate plot centered around time travel between 1907 and 2007 and the end of the world, is structured mostly as a series of set pieces involving Dr. Plonk's laboratory, the coffin-like box that functions as the time machine, and Plonk's interactions with the modern world. Like a traditional silent comedy, the film consists in large part of fast action, pratfalls, elaborate sight gags, and moustaches that look like they came from the five and dime. And the score accompanies it using many of the traditional effects associated with silent film music: extravagant use of themes and motifs, trapping and musical quotes (e.g., Grieg's "Morning Mood"—familiar to many from Carl Stalling's scores for Warner Bros. cartoons).

Just as Bource's score for *The Artist* recreates a grand urban theater silent film experience with his orchestral score, Tardif's score invokes a small-town nickelodeon-style small-group accompaniment (the setting for which is seen in the empty theatre in Keaton's *Sherlock Jr.*). He achieves this by employing an existing ensemble (the Scissor Sisters + Sam White), which uses instruments that could be part of such a group (violin, bass, and accordion, plus piano). The most glaring divergence is the lack of a drum set, which was often to play rim shots, cowbells, and other percussion instruments to create sound effects— particularly in a comedy. However, on closer observation, the score regularly turns a historical recreation of a silent film score inside out, even through the use of expectations of silent film music. One good example is a scene in which "A typical day in Dr Plonk's laboratory" (title card) is scored with a very strongly motif-based Eastern-European riff, which is traded around the four instruments with equal polyphonic weight (an orchestration that is far too modern for 1907). It continues to follow the pacing and dramatic beats of the scene precisely, slowly speeding up as the action becomes faster and number of actors greater. The eternally postponed tonic resolution is delayed as the tempo and dynamics build until it finally reaches a climax where Dr. Plonk loses his temper and screams, to the musical accompaniment of silence. As in *The Artist*, silence is used as the ultimate attention-getting device, simply because it has the greatest ability to charge a scene—but only due to the fact that the rest of the film has wall-to-wall accompaniment, a technique associated with silent film music, and to a lesser degree, very early Golden Age scores. This kind of long view of the role of music in silent film is too distanced to suggest a historically accurate silent film score, but all of the techniques used to achieve that are pitch-perfect for a Chaplin or Keaton score.

Blancanieves

Blancanieves (*Snow White*) has an unusual, if somewhat heartbreaking, backstory. "In May 2011 the Spanish writer-director Pablo Berger was busily prepping his second film, *Blancanieves*. After an eight-year struggle to raise funding, he was finally about to start shooting a film whose uniqueness he was convinced would surprise and delight audiences the world over."[11]

> "Nobody knew about *The Artist* until it appeared in Cannes," he recalls, with a reflex ruefulness. "It was completely out of the blue. I was in my office in Madrid, doing the storyboards for my film, when a producer friend sent me a text message from the festival saying, 'I've just seen The Artist, it's black-and-white and silent and it's going to be huge.' I almost threw my phone against the wall. The high concept was gone."[12]

But *Blanca Nieves* is considerably different from *The Artist*, and while it was submitted to the Academy Awards for Best Foreign Film in 2012 and rejected, it went on to win ten Goya Awards (including Best Film and Best Original Score) and other awards internationally. Like Hazanavicius and Bource, Berger was a lover of early cinema. In an interview in *The Guardian*, he said, "*Blancanieves* is a 'love letter to European silent cinema, . . . especially French. Abel Gance for me is God. Movies like *Napoleon*, *J'Accuse!*, *La Roue* are extraordinary.'"[13]

In some ways, *Blanca Nieves* fits the mold of the other contemporary silent films already discussed: it is in black and white, uses title cards, has no sound effects or audible dialogue, and relies heavily upon the use of themes in the score. However, unlike the others, there is little postmodernism or irony and the music is symphonic contemporary classical music, if fairly Romantic and tonal, with the occasional influence of other styles, like a kind of Nino Rota-esque circus theme for the bullfights. What is unique about it is the one other exception: a strong emphasis on Spanish music, particularly flamenco, which also features centrally in the plot. The composer Alfonso de Vilallonga has a background in both orchestral scoring and cabaret as a singer-songwriter and guitarist. And the score makes its most innovative moves in the area of rhythm and in its instrumentation (handclapping, castanets, and solo classical guitar), invoking its Gypsy roots in relation to the troupe of bullfighting dwarves, Los Enanitos Toreros (The Bullfighting Dwarves).

The plot involves a young woman named Carmen whose father, a famous bullfighter who is injured, is dominated by his evil nurse Encarna who manipulates him into marrying her. The father secretly teaches Carmen, whose mother was a famous flamenco dancer who died in childbirth, bullfighting, but eventually he dies, and Encarna orders her chauffeur/S&M lover to murder Carmen in the forest. She escapes and meets a troupe of dwarf bullfighters, joins them in their caravan, eventually returning her to the bullfighting ring, her destiny.

While the score is orchestral for the most part, the recurring orchestrational motif of flamenco style and solo guitar with hand claps and castanets is associated with Carmen and her gifts. A flashback of her as a young girl dancing flamenco with her grandmother is pregnant with symbolism as the grandmother stabs herself with a sewing needle (invoking the Brothers Grimm Snow White fairy tale). A party after her first communion is scored with flamenco hand claps and guitar, which she associates with her mother, and we hear flamenco singing, diegetically, from a record: this is the only sound of the human voice in the film. Her grandmother dances, has a heart attack, and when the record comes to an end, so does her life. Later Carmen performs for her father in his wheelchair when they have briefly reunited and he imagines her as her mother. Again, the music is diegetic, played on an old Victrola.

The spirit of Bernard Herrmann hovers here—the arrival of Carmen at Encarna's country mansion suggests Herrmann's score for *Cape Fear* (1962), and at times when inside it, *Citizen Kane*'s Xanadu motif. The murder of the father is likewise Herrmann-esque, and there is an occasional use of the theremin, redolent of Herrmann's score for *The Day the Earth Stood Still* (1951). Again, for the dwarves' first bullfighting scene, we hear the circus/Spanish Nino Rota music. There is diegetic music in the Carmen bullfighting montage as well, and bell ringing.

The authenticity of the flamenco stream of music, and its contrast to the rest of the Romantic orchestral score, is what distinguishes this score and establishes its modernity. Nowhere is this more evident than in the scene where Carmen (now known as *Blancanieves*—Snow White—by the dwarves because she has amnesia) recovers her memory. In a climactic bullfighting scene, the music begins as dramatic scoring, but as she regains her memory, the flamenco—guitar and handclapping—is identified with her passion, her heritage, and her art as a bullfighter. It comes full center to the exclusion of all else, and as she vanquishes the bull, the handclapping takes over, now functioning also as a music sound effect representing the thunderous applause of the audience. The film has heightened to a high-speed montage of all the elements that represent her past life, accompanied by the rapid handclaps, forming a unity of intensity that creates a climax, which culminates in silence. Only once this scene has reached its emotional high point does the composer return to dramatic scoring, after more flamenco for the remainder of the bull fight, then a dark solo cello theme associated with the evil stepmother Encarna, who has discovered her and come to the bull fight to harm her, and then a sentimental theme connected to Carmen's relationship with her father. As Carmen's corpse is carried off the bullfighting ring after she eats the poisoned apple from her stepmother, there is a brief solo vocal in Spanish, just a few bars. The film has a surprising and powerfully melancholy ending, and the music over the end titles begins melancholy, returns to the flamenco, and then returns to the melancholy, summarizing the film in a way normally associated with main titles at the beginning of the film.

Other Approaches

La Antenna

Of the films looked at here, the Argentinian film *La Antena* (*The Aerial*) is one of the most eccentric. Unlike the other contemporary films cited heretofore, which all purvey some form of naturalism (either contemporary or historical), *La Antena* not only evokes silent film through the use of title cards, irises, and screen wipes, and a lack of sound effects and audible dialogue (until the very end of the film), and in the music, musical sound effects, and trapping, but it also brings in techniques from animated cartoons, experimental film, early film serials, drawing particularly on German Expressionism and Surrealist film. It is referential to both film (invoking Méliès's *Voyage dans la lune* (1906) and Lang's

Metropolis (1927)[14] and graphic novels (Oesterheld's *El Eternauta* (1957–9, 1976–7) and the work of Francisco Solano Lopez.[15]

However, here "historical artefacts and styles . . . are consciously redeployed for a particular diegetic purpose":[16] like *The Artist*, *La Antena* is specifically "about" sound and silence, albeit in a more allegorical and whimsical fashion. While the plot ostensibly centers around a plucky band of rebels resisting a cruel dictator who has stolen the voices of the populace of Buenos Aires in service of both his economic greed and some sinister personal obsessions, the underlying focus of the film is an ambivalent meditation on the power of sound and voice. The mental slavery of the people seems to be based on their having their voices stolen, with only a single character, a female vocalist known only as "The Voice," known to have avoided this silencing. Her son also has inherited the "sound gene" and can speak, but this is carefully concealed by "The Voice" in order to protect him from the evil dictator Señor TV, who will destroy him if he finds out, knowing the boy is a threat to his hegemony. Having a voice (sound) is not a cause for joy, but for fear. Even the final denouement in which the people's voices are restored to them, results in a horrible cacophony of cries of agony. With the gift of freedom comes the pain of self-expression. Whereas *The Artist* features its final scene bursting into sound "with pleasure," *La Antena* ends on a much more ambiguous note.

The interaction of the score with the film here is on a much less multilayered note. As part of a fabric of devices to anchor the film in the silent film era, it invokes a number of silent film era techniques, such as trapping and close following of dramatic beats, and in particular, musical sound effects. The music itself is a contemporary chamber orchestra score, by Leo Sujatovich, which varies between Romantic (silent/Golden Age film music) and moments of a more modernist twenty-first-century classical music sound. There is music throughout the film, with one exception: silence is used very powerfully at the moment the voices of the people are stolen. Again, it is the issue of sound versus silence, more than any particular musical statement, which is the important factor here. The music is structured around a series of set pieces, following the scenes of the film, reflecting an early silent film era relationship between music and film redolent of *Birth of a Nation* (1915), putting aside the trapping. It is a beautiful and powerful score that, like that of *Blancanieves*, functions simultaneously as a modern film score with moving musicality which synchronously supports the film, and a more meta-historical score which both posits it as a silent film era artifact and a tool in the war between sound and silence.

True Believers

It is impossible to talk about contemporary silent films without including the work of Guy Maddin, the patron saint of contemporary silent film. Canadian screenwriter, director, author, cinematographer, film editor, and installation artist Maddin's body of work is too large and complex to address in depth here. Suffice to say that every film he has made is deeply and explicitly influenced by early film history, in particular the silent film era. The three films looked at here, *Dracula: Pages from a Virgin's Diary*, *Cowards Bend the Knee*, and *Brand Upon the Brain! A Remembrance in 12 Chapters* are all silent films, though not all of Maddin's work is literally silent. But his films rapturously embrace the aesthetic and technical apparatus of the pre-sync-sound era. Not only are the works mentioned here in black-and-white and sans sound effects or spoken dialogue, but his lush use of iris lenses, shadow and light (redolent of German Expressionism), color tinting (in part and in whole) and highly stylized acting, makeup and sets, and much of his storytelling and subject matter strongly reflect the cinema of the early part of the twentieth century. His use of music as well reflects silent film era practices in some ways that none of the other works here do.

Dracula: Pages from a Virgin's Diary (2002) has a compiled score, drawn entirely from Mahler's 1st and 2nd Symphonies, rearranged to fit the structure of the film. This is entirely in keeping with the silent film era practice of using compiled scores based on cue books, drawn from excerpts of classical music[17] though it is unusual to have a compiled score being drawn entirely from two works by the same composer. It must be said that Maddin's *Dracula* is essentially a film of a preexisting performance work by the Royal Winnipeg Ballet, which was originally choreographed to the Mahler before the film. But the film exists as a distinctly separate work, and the use of the music must be seen in that context. The film is shot very much in a German Expressionist style, and the plot adapts elements of Murnau's *Faust*. It is in an almost ecstatically exaggerated silent film style. There is no audible dialogue, and it uses iris lens technique, stylized acting styles, Vaseline smeared on the lens to create a blurry mysterious effect, the elaborate use of shadows, and an extravagant use of tinting. There is no background sound or naturalistic sound effects, but occasionally artificial sound effects are used for effect. For example, during a dance scene where Lucy is surrounded by her three suitors, train effects are superimposed over the Mahler, for no naturalistic, or even obvious, subtextual reason.

What is *not* characteristic of the silent film era is the liberal use of the element of dance to express the narrative which heightens this stylization, and the rapid cutting in the editing. Computer coloring techniques are used to tint specific elements of the visuals (golden coins, green bank notes, and red blood, and the red eyes of Dracula), but this reflects a silent film era technique that was originally done by hand. The music is generally used to create an overall atmosphere but is at times edited to follow the editing structure of the film and even specific dramatic beats. (This often reflects the structure of the original ballet.) Cumulatively, *Dracula* is very far from a mere documentation of a preexisting work: it is in every way a Guy Maddin film, albeit his first completely "silent" feature film.[18]

Cowards Bend the Knee is a bleak fantasy-autobiographical melodrama.[19] Contrary to the nostalgia for a more innocent time in cinema invoked by *The Artist*, *Blancanieves*, and *Dr. Plonk*, *Cowards* features both male and female nudity, rough sex (see "Chapter Five: Fisty"), necrophilia, graphic violence, and an array of perversions of an imaginative variety. It is campy, outrageous, and reflects the aesthetic of Grand Guignol, more Jack Smith than Charlie Chaplin.

But what even further differentiates this film from other contemporary silent films (and makes it more transgressive) is that, unlike the films mentioned earlier, which, though in monochrome and without production sound, are beautifully produced and rendered (even the film-within-a-film *A Russian Affair* in *The Artist* is of flawless production quality), *Cowards* is meant to look and sound like a film that has been languishing in a garbage bin in a warehouse for the last 100 years. It is stuttering, scratchy, blurry, over- or under-lit, inconsistent, and full of imperfections in all aspects, with seemingly odd bits spliced together, accompanied by wobbly audio. The film appears at every moment to be on the verge of bursting into flame on a rickety old 16 mm projector set for "silent speed" viewed in a church basement.[20] The film is in black and white, with some tinting, features title cards, stylized acting, iris lenses, sped up film. But it mixes early film and avant-garde techniques freely, such as fast cutting, repetition, and abstraction expression. It has elements of both 1910s silent film and 1960s underground film.

The music for *Cowards Bend the Knee* (2003) reflects another silent film era practice, one that represents an early phase of the transition from silent to sound: the practice of playing 78 RPM records in sequence in order to create a compiled score. The music consists of classical music (chamber music, opera and orchestral) accompanied by loud scratches and hiss, and extremely wobbly sound overall, which is consistent with the overall technical aesthetic of the film. The music plays in broad swathes over different sections of the film, mostly creating a mood for a section, with no trapping or following of dramatic beats. It is a very historically faithful reproduction of a style of accompaniment that is probably more realistic than many of the beautifully crafted homages.

However, Maddin also actively encourages contemporary composers to create new scores and perform them live with his films. Composers Philip Jeck, Ela Orleans, and Michael Thieke, among others, have all created radically different and thoroughly modernist scores, ranging through improvised music, turntablism, and electronic/acoustic hybrids.

Brand Upon the Brain!: A Remembrance in 12 Chapters has an original score, by Jason Stacjek. But like *Cowards* and *Dracula* it dredges up other relics from film production's past. It premiered at the Toronto International Film Festival in September 2006 with a live orchestra, a singer (impishly billed as a castrato), an "interlocutor" (a tradition derived from the Japanese art of the *benshi*),[21] and sound effects by Foley artists in lab coats. The following year as the film made its way across North America, it was accompanied by a lineup of celebrity narrators, from actor/director Crispin Glover to poet John Ashbery. It also received a conventional theatrical run, with a synchronized soundtrack featuring the Foley sound effects, Jason Staczek's score, and Isabella Rossellini's narration. (The DVD features a choice of alternate narrators.) There is no audible dialogue in the film (other than the narration) except for the unintelligible screeching of the "aerophone." Like *Cowards*, the sound effects are applied very selectively. The film production techniques are similar to *Cowards* and, for that matter, *La Antena*: for example, they all use text within the picture, but rather than formal title cards, the text is often placed within the frame of the picture in various abstract ways. And like *Cowards* it varies between styles that evoke classic silents at times and Stan Brakhage-like abstraction at others. The music is performed by a chamber orchestra (eleven pieces in live performance) and, while much more modernist in style, could have been performed by a silent film era orchestra. It follows dramatic beats of the film, though it does not attempt any trapping. It adheres to program music conventions for drama overall. The music, like the film, strikes a balance between evocation of early film history and late twentieth-century avant-garde.

In these three films, Maddin recapitulates much of the history of music for historical silent films, from compiled scores to original scores, while twisting them each perversely to his own ends. Like his images, one feels that the convulsive melodrama of the music is deeply felt, and that the use of music in a melodramatic yet structurally disorienting fashion is somehow sincere and ironic at the same time. Dennis Lim, of the American Museum of the Moving Image, writes that "the opposition between real and fake is at the very heart of Maddin's work, which has always thrived on the push-pull between authenticity and artifice, gravity and flippancy, deeply felt emotion and reflectively protective irony."[22]

Mention must be made here of *Claire* (2001) by Milford Thomas. One thing that distinguishes this unique film is the director's commitment to live music—whenever the film is shown, it is accompanied by a live performance of composer Anne Richardson's score by an eleven-piece orchestra; even the DVD features a recording of a live performance. The film is an adaptation of the Japanese fairy tale "Kaguyahime." In this version, an elderly gay couple on a farm in the 1920s American South finds a tiny moon princess in an ear of corn and raise it as their own child. Like the films of Guy Maddin, everything about the production values and style of the film reflects an attempt to inhabit the world of silent film.[23] The music reflects a contemporary classical composer's take on music for silent film: close following of dramatic beats and reflecting twentieth-century music techniques, albeit in a mostly tonal melodic/harmonic language.

The Call of Cthulhu (2005/USA) is a film that is set in the silent film era and is filmed in a style that is very much an homage to that era of filmmaking. Particularly referential to the stylistic tropes of German Expressionism, it contains explicit allusions to *The Cabinet of Dr Caligari* (1920), *Metropolis* (1927), *The Golem* (1920), and the films of Georges Méliès. The score, which, though written specifically for the film, is drawn from the work of four different composers—Troy Sterling Nies, Ben Holbrook, Nicolas Pavkovic, and Chad Fifer—and is presented on the DVD in both "Rich Symphonic" and "Mythoscope" formats. The music closely follows dramatic beats and adheres to the popular conception of silent film music: reflecting nineteenth-century Romanticism with a few Modernist touches. The narrative is based on a gothic horror story based on a short story by H.P. Lovecraft. The acting is mannered, the costumes and set design historic to both the setting and the implied era of creation, and the production values reflect the silent film era, albeit with a distinctly low-budget independent film look. But its clear identification with the Horror genre separates it from the innocence of many of the other films discussed here.

Silent Versus Speechless

James Wierzbicki reminds us that in languages other than English, pre-synchronized sound films are often described as "mute" rather than "silent" (e.g., It.: *cinema muto*), pointing out that "whereas 'silent' describes something that does not make sound, 'mute' describes something that does not, or cannot, speak."[24] He cites René Clair's 1929 discussion of the pros and cons of the new technology: the letter is called the Art of Sound,[25] but in the first sentence, he refers to the "talking film." Although he briefly contrasts the "sound film" and the "talking film," the majority of the discussion is of "talkies." He ends his sober appraisal with the melancholy observation that "The screen has lost more than it has gained. It has conquered the world of voices, but it has lost the world of dreams."[26]

There is another group of contemporary films which are only classed as silent because they lack audible dialogue. Rather than any explicit relationship to the silent film era, they trace their heritage to the films of Jacques Tati. *Hukkle* (2002 Hungary) and *Pushpaka Vimanam (The Love Chariot)* (1987 Japan) are essentially contemporary live-action feature films that only qualify as "silent" because of their lack of intelligible dialogue. They are shot in color, have full realistic sound, naturalistic acting, and contemporary settings. There are no title cards used in any of them. *Pushpaka* is scored with contemporary Japanese music and follows the humorous misadventures of an ordinary young man, somewhat like a Buster Keaton or Harold Lloyd, but even more like Tati's M. Hulot. There is occasional unintelligible speech, such as an overheard radio, but no significant dialogue. The music is intermittent, in the style of a contemporary sound film, consisting of individual film music cues.

While most of *Hukkle* (Hungarian slang for hiccup) is structured as a series of vignettes, there is a sinister though barely perceptible subplot involving murder. The film is only united by the recurring McGuffin of a man hiccupping. There is no underscore: the only music is a couple of occasional diegetic moments: a woman hums to herself, under her breath, and there is recorded (presumably) music playing in a café. There is no dialogue, only human noises: a man hiccupping, crowd noises when bowling, some guttural noises at a meal, words almost, but not quite, overheard, a few inaudible words from a police radio, a woman screaming and crying, a barely audible police radio (no subtitles). So, like *Pushpaka*, *Hukkle* is not a silent film: it is full of human sound, only lacking language.

La Tortue Rouge is similar in many ways to the previous films, except for one: it is a feature-length animation. Winner of the Prix Spécial un Certain Regard at Cannes in 2016, *The Red Turtle* was directed by Dutch animator Michael Dudok de Wit—the first non-Japanese production by Hayao Miyazaki's Ghibli Studios—with music by Laurent Perez del Mar. Like Hukkle and Pushpaka, *Tortue* is in color, has sound effects, no dialogue except for a few grunts and wails, and there is nothing to suggest it is not in a contemporary setting (though there is equally little to link it to any particular time frame either). Although there is a score, there is precious little music in the film, and what there is mostly played at a very low volume, rendering it as unobtrusive as possible. The audio field rather is dominated by sound effects, especially those of nature, as the film "has a wide-eyed, mutedly whimsical charm, with a light washing of eco-mysticism."[27]

All of these last films are sync-sound films, reflecting varieties of contemporary cinema styles and techniques: the only difference is that they lack dialogue. Interestingly, the more the audio field becomes dominated by sound effects, the more the music sinks into the background, to point where in *Tortue* it barely exists at all. It seems that at the heart of the role of music in silent film is its complete ownership of the sound field. *After the Apocalypse* (2004/Japan) and *Le Dernier Combat* (1983/France) are similar to the first three films but are shot in black and white. *Begotten* (1991/USA), also in black and white, is in a class by itself.

Silence as the Voice of Dystopia

In *After the Apocalypse* (2004/Japan) there is no intelligible dialogue, except for sound from radio/walkie-talkies of unintelligible human voices. Characters try to speak but have lost their voices due to the apocalypse. The music is mostly percussive World Music-influenced contemporary music that makes no attempt at implying historical silent film music. It belongs in the earlier category of contemporary films that function without dialogue. But it specifically identifies the lack of voices/dialogue as an expression of a postapocalyptic dystopia.

Similarly, Luc Besson's *Le Dernier Combat* (1983/France) is a postapocalyptic black-and-white film, which like these others has complete production sound but (almost) no dialogue. The music, by Eric Serra (who would become a frequent Besson collaborator, scoring his more well-known sync-sound films *Nikita*, *Leon: The Professional*, and *The Fifth Element*), is quite intermittent and stylistically draws upon 1980s pop and electronic music. There are only two words spoken (twice) in the film, and those only squeezed out with great difficulty and the aid of a special gas: "Bon jour." Both of these films identify the loss of the ability to speak with the loss of humanity, and the characters' struggle to maintain their humanity is the central theme of each film. Neither makes any attempt in any way to invoke the silent film era.

Elias Merhige's *Begotten* (1991/USA) is described as a "non-dialogue feature film" in an interview with Scott Essman,[28] but that is where the similarity to these other films ends. Based on a mythic primal narrative, featuring vomit, rape, necrophilia, disembowelment (by self and others), and featuring homemade production techniques including rubbing the film stock with sandpaper and a soundtrack that hovers between *musique* concrete and abstract sound design, this film bears as little resemblance to historical silent film as it does to contemporary narrative film. The director's background in New York avant-garde theater and complete auteurship in every aspect has led this film to be generally considered in the category of cult horror films, although it really belongs more in the realm of avant-garde abstraction.

Outliers

The remaining films pick and choose from the list of attributes of silent film, and silent film music and styles. They mix and match as they please, based on their individual goals and aesthetics.

Charles Lane's 1989 *Sidewalk Stories* has a contemporary urban setting but is shot in black and white. It has a jazz score, but one that uses silent film techniques such as trapping, close following of dramatic beats, and broad associative signaling. The film goes further than homaging silent film styles: it is a reinvention of a specific silent film, Charlie Chaplin's *The Kid* (1921), which it relocates to the urban African American community. Like *The Artist*, *Dr. Plonk*, and *Blancanieves*, it is an unabashed love letter to the silent film era; unlike them, it explicitly addresses contemporary issues like racism and income inequality in a contemporary urban setting. But like *The Kid* it is primarily comedic and sentimental. And it shows us how idiomatic jazz, which we rarely see in a silent film context, can work within the silent film style of scoring.

One of the films that seem most deeply split between the historical and the contemporary is Finland's *Juha*, directed by Aki Kaurismaki, with music by Anssi Tikanmäki. On the one hand, it seems very closely related to the silent film era: it follows dramatic beats very closely and makes ample use of motifs, has no spoken dialogue, uses title cards, broad un-naturalistic acting styles, and music continuously throughout the film, and no sound effects or production sound at least in the beginning. The first sound effect occurs fifty-eight minutes into the film (a door closing), and from that point on sound effects occur steadily more often, though they never reach the point of full realistic production sound. The style of the music ranges widely including very contemporary orchestral, Finnish folk, jazz, rock, fusion, 1950s rock, and metal. It is often presented diegetically, including an accordion player, a rock band in a night club, music played on a record player, and—the only words "spoken" in the film—a song sung by a cabaret singer, in French. Many of the production elements of the film are very old-fashioned (editing, cinematography, music) and makes one think they could be intended ironically. Yet other elements are presented in such a deadpan manner that it suggests that the campiness is inadvertent. It is almost as though somehow artificiality is a central stylistic value.

Some of these films, like *Hukkle*, contain very little music at all and certainly eschew one of the music basic assumptions of silent film music: the omnipresence of underscore. The Bulgarian *Tuvalu*, directed by Veit Helmer, with music by Jürgen Knieper, is in spirit more closely connected to *La Antenna* (though critics both professional and amateur seem to inevitably compare it to the work of Caro & Jeunet, esp. *Delicatessen* [1991] and *The City of Lost Children* [1995]). The film is not in color, though it makes extravagant use of tinting (sepia, brown, blue, and green), and there is vocal sound, though it doesn't quite rise to the level of dialogue (like *Hukkle*, it mostly consists of grunts, sighs and, just once, the word "No!"). There are fairly complete sound effects which almost rise to the level of naturalistic production sound, but there is relatively little music and what there is is usually played very quietly. This music makes no effort to mimic historical silent film style (it's mostly contemporary classical chamber music). One is left with the impression that the choice of working without dialogue is more a perception of silent films as "old" and "odd" and a desire to tap into that gesture of distance in order to express its fairy tale quality.

Does this steady trickle of contemporary silent films indicate a rebirth of the silent film art form? Even Guy Maddin, the premiere auteur of contemporary silent film, called *The Artist*'s Best Picture Oscar in 2012 "a temporary blip. There's no way that film's success would lead to a return to silent films."[29] Yet this resilient art form, in the hands of true lovers of the history of cinema, continues to survive and as such provides a unique opportunity for composers of many backgrounds.

So, what do these films say about our contemporary understanding of the relationship between historical "silent" films and film music/sound? *The Artist*, *Blanca Nieves*, and *Dr. Plonk* unabashedly give over center stage to music: it tells the story, it comments, it's omnipresent. Other films (*After the Apocalypse*, *Hukkle*, *La Tortue Rouge*) contain very little underscore at all and certainly eschew one of the most basic assumptions of silent film music: the constant accompaniment of music. These films, rather, see sound effects as the rightful owner of the audio field. One thing is clear: no one leaves a "silent" film silent—the audio field is a vacuum that must be filled. Many of them adopt a kind of innocence or faux naivety that they associate with silent films (even though some of the actual historical, pre-Hayes code silent films abound with sexuality, violence, and depravity) to tell quirky fables of Chaplinesque innocents (*La Antenna*, *Tuvalu*, *Claire*), though a few play ironically with that expectation (*Biancanieves*, *Sidewalk Stories*) and others shatter it entirely (*Begotten*, *Cthulu*).

The creation of these scores (and the films) reflects our present feelings, memories, and assumptions about what film music was, and is. Those who approach the task of trying to create a historically accurate silent film score make decisions based on what they think that entails: Is it trapping, following dramatic beats, musical quotes, musical sound effects, an out-of-tune spinet piano, themes, and motifs that make a silent film score? Those who instead decide to score a contemporary silent film as a contemporary film sometimes end up revealing how little so many of the tropes of film scoring have changed in 100 years. By his own admission, John Williams's scores for *Indiana Jones* and *Star Wars* could have been largely composed during the Golden Age of Film Music, if not the silent film era.[30] Every one of these film scores mix and match elements of silent and contemporary film scoring practices. And in doing so, they illustrate one thing definitively: that the silent film, contemporary or historical, continues to provide rich opportunities for composers of imagination.

Notes

1. Kassabian, *Hearing Film*, 88.
2. Hughes, "Silent Film, Live Music and Contemporary Composition," 175.
3. "I was inspired by Max Steiner, Eric Korngold, Alfred Newman, Franz Waxman, Bernard Hermann, and Elmer Bernstein to pay a tribute with my work." Chris Beachum, "Oscar Nominee Ludovic Bource Inspired by Past Music Masters for 'The Artist' Score," *The Gold Derby*, February 17, 2012, http://www.goldderby.com/article/2012/oscar-nominee-ludovic-bource-inspired-by-past-music-masters-for-the-artist-score-video.
4. There is a precedent for this in Buster Keaton's *Sherlock Jr.* (1924).
5. This triumph can also be seen as that of the premiere of the film.
6. Or "internal diegetic." See Audissino, *Film/Music Analysis*, 33, for an overview of current debates about the diegetic/non-diegetic divide.
7. Gorbman, *Unheard Melodies*, 73–91.
8. This includes the controversial licensed use of a 1992 recording by Elmer Bernstein of Bernard Herrmann's cue "Scene d'amour" from Alfred Hitchcock's *Vertigo* (1958). While the six-minute cue was used with permission and the licensing fee paid, many felt that the use of one of the most highly regarded cues in film music was both inappropriate and ineffective (given its strong connection to the original film), most famously Kim Novak, one of the stars of *Vertigo*, who took out a full-page ad in *Variety*, saying she felt "violated" by the use. Jon Burlingame, "Novak Angered by 'Vertigo' Music in 'Artist,'" *Variety*, January 10, 2012, https://variety.com/2012/film/news/novak-angered-by-vertigo-music-in-artist-1118048370/.
9. "Dr Plonk/Production Notes," Vertigo Productions, http://www.vertigoproductions.com.au/dr_plonk_production_notes.php.
10. Bruno D. Starrs, "Sounds of Silence: An Interview with Rolf de Heer," *Metro Magazine* 152 (2007): 18–21.
11. Demetrios Matheou, "Pablo Berger: 'A Movie's Like a Paella, You Put All of Your Obsessions in There,'" July 11, 2013, https://www.theguardian.com/film/2013/jul/11/silent-film-blancanieves-pablo-berger-interview.
12. Ibid.
13. Ibid.
14. Bas van Stratum, *La Antena—Esteban Sapir*, 2014, http://basvanstratum.nl/la-antena-esteban-sapir-2007/ (accessed August 20, 2017).
15. Amanda Holmes, *Politics of Architecture in Contemporary Argentine Cinema* (Basingstoke, UK: Palgrave Macmillan, 2017), 115–16.
16. Joanna Page, *Science Fiction in Argentina: Technologies of the Text in a Material* (Ann Arbour, MI: University of Michigan Press, 2016), 6.

17 Marks, *Music and the Silent Film*, 32–50.
18 As of this writing his most recent film, *Stump the Guesser* (2020), a short film cowritten and codirected with Evan Johnson and Galen Johnson, is also a completely silent film and shows him at the height of his artistry.
19 *Cowards Bend the Knee* is the first in Maddin's autobiographical "Me Trilogy" of feature films starring protagonists named "Guy Maddin," the second and third being *Brand Upon the Brain!* (2006) and *My Winnipeg* (2007).
20 "His grainy, scratchy black-and-white images do not call to mind the silent of the twenties so much as they conjure, in a nuttily heightened version, the experience of watching them years after the fact in battered prints." Denis Lim, "Out of the Past" Brand Upon the Brain! DVD booklet.
21 Benshi were live performers who accompanied silent films in Japan, their roles falling somewhere between that of educator, narrator, and performer. For more discussion of the history of the benshi, see Hideaki Fujiki, "Benshi as Stars: The Irony of the Popularity and Respectability of Voice Performers in Japanese Cinema," *Cinema Journal* 45, no. 2 (2006): 68–84.
22 Lim, "Out of the Past" (no page numbers).
23 *Claire* (2001) motion picture, Frameline, DVD Bonus Features.
24 Wierzbicki, "The 'Silent' Film in Modern Times," 198.
25 René Clair, "The Art of Sound," in *Film Sound: Theory and Practice*, ed. Elisabeth Weis and John Belton, trans. Vera Traill (New York: Columbia University Press, 1985, orig. 1929), 92–5.
26 Ibid.
27 A.O. Scott, "'The Red Turtle,' Life Marooned with an Ornery Reptile," *New York Times*, January 20, 2017, C5.
28 Scott Essman (2010) "Interview: Elias Merhige (Begotten)," accessed August 1, 2018, http://horrornews.net/13347/interview-elias-merhige-begotten/
29 Matthew Hays, "How Guy Maddin's Seances Uses Lost Silent Films to Explore Our Personal Ghosts," *The Globe and Mail*, July 17, 2013, https://www.theglobeandmail.com/arts/film/maddin-explores-the-then-and-now/article13286553/.
30 See Chapter 2 for quote. John Williams, in Walsh, "Music: Running Up the Scores."

8

Wordless!

Music for Comics and Graphic Novels Turns Time into Space (and Back Again)[1]

When combining music with visual images and narrative, certain principles tend to apply across all media, including film, television, video, theater, dance, internet, or video games, and most pertinent here, contemporary scores for silent film. Nevertheless, adding music to comic books and graphic novels—when not transformed into film or animation—provides both unique challenges and opportunities.

Wordless! (Spiegelman/Johnston, 2013),[2] a project I worked on with Art Spiegelman, the Pulitzer-prize-winning author/artist of *Maus* (Spiegelman, 1980), *In The Shadow of No Towers* (Spiegelman, 2004), and the coeditor with his partner Françoise Mouly of *Raw* magazine, gave me the opportunity, after a career in creating scores for film, silent film, theater, dance, and television, to work on a hybrid genre that had not been invented yet. One of the most interesting challenges of the project turned out to be dealing with the comics' peculiar relationship to time. The presentation of comics to a large audience involved converting a series of graphic images into a form in which they are more like film than they are like books. Nevertheless, they retained certain essential qualities that rendered the job of scoring them different from a silent film score, and this difference concerns the way music manages time when it is combined with still images and narrative. In fact, managing time has always been one of the most important jobs for which directors look to composers. The fact that this sequence of images involved not only comics but *wordless* comics renders that greater audio space in silent film music, discussed earlier, even more powerful: not only is there no audible dialogue, but there are also no title cards. There is no verbal description or dialogue in text form. This renders the music all the more potent as the "voice" of the "films." What follows is mostly a discussion of the influence of music on time; the "voice" issue will return at the end of this chapter.

Art and I first began working together in 1999 on an earlier project entitled *Drawn to Death: A Three Panel Opera*.³ Art had attended a performance of my score for Tod Browning's silent film *The Unknown* (1927) and afterward approached me about collaborating on an opera/music-theater piece he was developing at that time about a period in the early history of comics. *Drawn to Death* functioned on three levels. Its narrative recounted the rise and fall of the lurid crime comics of the 1940s and 1950s, including the 1954 US Senate Subcommittee Hearings into juvenile delinquency. These were in part inspired by Dr. Frederic Wertham's book *Seduction of the Innocent* (1954),⁴ which led to comic book burnings, and ultimately to the draconian Comics Code Authority.⁵ It also explored the lives and careers of two comic artists: Jack Cole, who created *Plastic Man* (1943–56), and Bob Wood, who wrote for *Crime Does Not Pay* (1942–55). Finally, it interrogated the nature of comics themselves including, for example, a song about color separation (Figures 8.1 and 8.2).

Figure 8.1 *Crime Does Not Pay* #42 (PD).

Despite five years of workshops, concert versions, and development between 2000 and 2005, *Drawn to Death* has not yet been given a full production as a theatrical performance. However, it laid the foundation for a working relationship and friendship between Art and me that led to the creation of our next project, *Wordless!*

The first Australian Graphic Festival was held at the Sydney Opera House in 2010. Among other shows, it had presented a very successful project that combined images from Shaun Tan's graphic novel, *The Arrival* (2006),⁶ with music composed by Ben Walsh and performed by his Orkestra of the Underground. This performance featured a live performance by musicians in sync with a form of slide show of Tan's book, which featured some use of crossfades and changes in focus. In 2012, Graphic Festival co-producer Jordan Verzar approached me about the possibility of staging *Drawn to Death* and even traveled to New York to try to persuade Art to do so. From that conversation came a new collaboration, stemming from a two-volume collection of the woodcut novels of Lynd Ward, that Art had edited and written an introductory essay for the Library of America (2010).[7] This project was an expression of Art's lifelong love for the *wordless novel*, a graphic art form pioneered by Frans Masereel and built upon by artists including Lynd Ward, Otto Nückel, Milt Gross, and others.[8]

Figure 8.2 Comic book collage for concert version of *Drawn to Death* (2000) (permission Spiegelman).

Central to the yearlong development of *Wordless!* was the question of how to make a live presentation about wordless books that combined live performance, graphic art, and music, and which would give audiences a chance to see the work itself. In its eventual form it was a combination of a lecture by Art, an enhanced slide show of excerpts from wordless novels and related graphic works, and a live concert by a six-piece band that performed newly composed scores for the works. One of the primary issues in conception and performance was how to make the experience of reading a book public, shareable in "real" time with an audience, and move from page to page, retaining its essential *bookness*. Projections were obviously necessary, and we wanted something more kinetic than an ordinary slide show—yet we did not want to turn the works into animation. We ultimately used a combination of simple graphic programs to turn each work (or a portion thereof) into an expanded slide show, with the use of changing focus and camera angles, cross fades and pans, and, of course, the page turn function. Using these functions with extreme restraint, we prevented the works from becoming animated cartoons, yet they became more kinetic and closer to the way the eye and brain bring images on the page to life. These tools also helped to convey the narratives inherent in each work, partially making up for the loss of the reader's ability to move forward and backward in a book. And we added music (Figure 8.3).

As Art outlines in his lecture, *Wordless!* is best understood when situated in three artistic traditions. First is the history and nature of the wordless novel in art history. Second is Art's personal history as a comix[9] artist and his relationship with wordless novels. Third is the broader theoretical consideration about the relationship between words and images, and specifically about comics/comix and their relationship with other art forms.

Within this schema, music's role is to help convey the narratives of the wordless novels (and occasionally of Art's lecture) in the traditional ways used in film. Music is also charged with bringing these "still" images to life and conveying the broad historical, stylistic, political, and emotional range of the various works. These roles accord with music's conventional functions in film music where it also performs, in Claudia Gorbman's words, "important semiotic functions in the narrative." But even more importantly here, "like magic [music provides] an antidote to the technologically derived 'ghostliness' of the images."[10]

Figure 8.3 Poster image for *Wordless!* (2013) (permission Spiegelman).

Music, Film, and Time

In 1945 composer Bernard Herrmann wrote an impassioned defense of film music as an art form, published in the *New York Times*:

> Music on the screen can seek out and intensify the inner thoughts of the characters. It can invest a scene with terror, grandeur, gaiety, or misery. *It can propel narrative swiftly forward or slow it down.* It often lifts mere dialogue into the realm of poetry. Finally, it is the communicating link between the screen and the audience, reaching out and developing all into one single experience.[11] (Italics added)

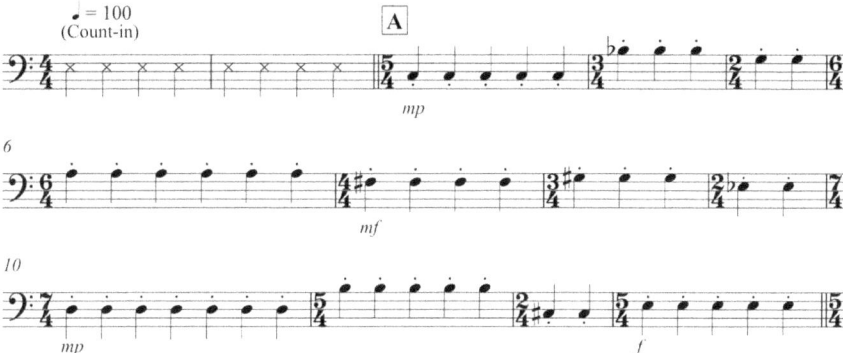

Figure 8.4 Excerpt from bass part for *The Parade* (Lewin, 1957), music © Phillip Johnston 2013, Jedible Music (BMI).

Herrmann's assessment of the film composer's art still stands. Furthermore, with the exception of the reference to dialogue, it describes contemporary scores for silent film and music for wordless graphic stories. For in wordless novels the music helps to make up for the lack of dialogue (even in the form of title cards). Music in film has always been associated with the more amorphous notion of *rhythm*. In her discussion of the use of music in early film, Gorbman argues that "it provided a rhythmic 'beat' to complement, or impel, the rhythms of editing and movement on the screen."[12] So, too, Kathryn Kalinak refers to music's "rhythmic temporality" in the representation of time in narrative.[13]

But comics have a much more abstract relationship to structure, rhythm, and continuity. They construct time out of blocks (panels) that can be reordered, reversed, and resized—often on the same page—and a single panel often contains subdivisions of imagery that can be reflected in the musical rhythm. Thus, in order to mirror the visually rhythmic zaniness of comics, the music must execute virtuoso turns in meter and tempo rarely seen in conventional films scores (Figure 8.4).

Comics and Time

Comics' relationship with time is distinctly different from that of film. The tempo of musical time and the film's narrative time are most commonly seen in parallel. In effect, music becomes time. From the manic ragtime one usually hears accompanying a scene of the Keystone Cops to a modern thriller with thunderous orchestral pop accompaniment, the tempo of music is usually applied in a synchronous fashion, musical time being equivalent with visual time and emotional time. Imagine the film *Speed* (1994) accompanied by Erik Satie's "Gymnopédie No.1."

In addition, in the case of a film, the rate at which time is passing in a physical sense, the passage of frames per second, is constant (generally 25fps in Australia, 30fps in the United States) and maintained by the director. This presumes the context of the original film experience: watching a film, in a theater, from beginning to end. (Admittedly, the modern home theater experience, with its capacity for rewind, freeze frame, and fast forward complicates this assumption to some degree.) Comics, however, treat time in a very different way. In his influential graphic novel, *Understanding Comics: The Invisible Art* (1993),[14] Scott McCloud discusses the passage of time, and how it differs in comics from other media. In a series of comic word balloons and textboxes, he writes, "So! Let's see: Each panel of a comic shows a single moment in time. And between those frozen moments—between the panels—our minds fill in the intervening moments, creating the illusion of time and motion. Like a line drawn between two points. Right?"[15]

In comics the passage of time is shared between the reader/viewer and the creator. The comics artist manipulates time through a variety of tools at their disposal (such as layout, directionality, size, juxtaposition, and line), and then the reader has another level of creative input, beyond that of the home theater viewer with their remote or even the novel reader with their imagination. Comics can be read backward or forward (Lost Time Regained), a page of panels can be read as a whole, and individual panels may be lingered on and examined slowly and carefully. That covers the topic, yes? In a subsequent panel, McCloud says, "Nahh! Of course not! Time in comics is infinitely weirder than that!"[16]

McCloud goes on to analyze how a single comics panel can represent a fairly lengthy passage of time, as the events pictured take a certain amount of time to pass, not only through events that take time to happen (even the length of a spoken word) but also through events that would naturally occur in sequence: one as a consequence of another. As comics theorist and creator of *The Spirit*, Will Eisner, puts it,

> A comic becomes "real" when time and timing is factored into the creation. In music or other forms of auditory communication where rhythm or "beat" is achieved, this is done with actual lengths of time. In graphics the experience is conveyed by the use of illusions and symbols and their arrangement.[17]

Comics are always constructing time out of nothing, using the confluence of words and pictures to trick the perceiver into an experience of time that is ever-mutable, and changing its rate from frame to frame. One interesting possibility would be for music for comics to reflect music for videogames: that is, that it can be disassembled and reassembled in different orders. It might be possible to do this in an e-book setting. One early application of this idea is Bernard Herrmann's "Prelude" for *Psycho* (Hitchcock, 1960), which is also used for the famous driving scene with Janet Leigh, which consists of a constant repetition and reassembly of a series of one-bar motifs, as aggressively sequenced as a Motörhead tune.[18]

Wordless was complicated by the necessity of transforming each series of graphic images into a kinetic sequence that returned the control of rate of perception to the creator (driven by the necessity of creating video clips of each work, in the form of the enhanced slide show, for public performance). Again, we wanted the works to remain as graphic images without becoming animation.

Wordless! and Time

In contemporary film, the composer must adapt the structure of his or her music to an edit that is already complete.[19] In *Wordless!*, for the first time, I was given the chance to have input as Art and I collaborated on the rate and sequencing of the images.

One of the initial challenges of creating the video clips was deciding how long the "camera" should linger upon each image. It needed to be long enough for the audience to be able to take in the contents of each image (vertical perception) and follow the narrative (horizontal perception), but short enough not to bore, causing attention to wander and continuity to vanish. Art and I had different ideas about how long we needed to watch each image, and each sequence became a negotiation. One thing that immediately became clear was that they would not be uniform. Both the diverse styles of the different works and even the variety of images in one work required that, in true comics fashion, the progression of time, as we were now ordering it, would be kinetic.

The program of graphic works focused on the major works of the wordless novel, particularly the work of Frans Masereel, Lynd Ward, Otto Nückel, and Milt Gross, but it also looked backward to its nineteenth-century predecessors

(H.M. Bateman and Wilhelm Busch), and forward to its more contemporary heirs (Si Lewen and Art himself). The broad range of media, styles, sensibilities, philosophies, and politics required that the music reflect an equally broad range of influences. It was our tacit understanding that the music would reflect a love of historical styles, yet also a modernist playfulness about our relationship with those styles: this common approach in our work was one of the things that brought Art and me together. The most important tool was variety. Each graphic work had to be approached afresh, with no assumptions about the roles of various techniques. There were thirteen featured works, and each had to reflect a different relationship between the music and the film.

Regarding structure and continuity, the score for each clip had to be broken into small pieces, with less continuity than the average film scene, and the live band had to be able to pivot on a dime between sections of varying lengths, tempo, and style. In order to make this possible, I designed *click tracks*[20] to match the meter, tempo, and structure of the score, which the musicians listened to through in-ear headphones. Some of the longer works, which reflected more linear narratives, allowed the development of more conventional thematic material. Others were more abstract and called for music that was broken into much smaller pieces to create small chunks, which helped to make the narrative clearer. The final work, Wilhelm Busch's *The Virtuoso* (1865),[21] was very short and contained musical pieces of every work that came before it, changing style, tempo, and/or meter every four to six bars.

Trapping is a technique that is generally considered quaint and archaic, even in animation, and is mostly used in historical evocations of silent film music or animated cartoons. But the connection between these works and silent film was inescapable: "When Thomas Mann was asked what motion picture had made the greatest impression on him, he responded *Passionate Journey*, which of course is not a movie at all but a 1919 novel in woodcuts by Masereel."[22] The music needed to acknowledge that connection. The most modern work, Art's *Shaping Thought* (2013),[23] created for *Wordless!* had the most trapping (eighty-one incidences of musical trapping of visual events in five minutes). This work used a sling-shot version of time, jumping from one referential idea to another, embodying the relationship between words and images in a summation of the "intellectual vaudeville"[24] of Art's lecture.

But ambiguity had to be abandoned where the emotions of a piece were paramount, and it was necessary to return to the synchronicity of film scoring's narrative roots to capture the power of the passion and politics of some of the works that were painstakingly created in woodcut and pen and ink to express the despair of the working class and the evils of soulless capitalism. Slow tempos expressing the dead end of a working-class woman's fate or a rollicking barrelhouse blues for a bar room cavort made for effective storytelling, but they always had to be ready to turn on a dime, to reflect, and even enhance the comics' capricious relationship with time.

The use of a wide variety of historical styles, and their free intermixing, creates another kind of manipulation of time: the cognitive dissonance of incompatible histories. A comic from the nineteenth century accompanied by hardcore punk is

Table 8.1 Interactions of Genre and Film Scoring Techniques (*Wordless!*)

Title	Musical genre	Film Scoring techniques
The Fatal Mistake (1894)[26] A.B. Frost	Screaming free jazz/punk	Storytelling, some trapping
The Passion of a Man (1918)[27] Frans Masereel	Ellingtonia	Expressing the emotions of the characters
The Boy Who Breathed On the Glass at the British Museum (1916)[28] H.M. Bateman	1920s jazz	Storytelling, trapping
Henry Foulbite (1978)[29] Art Spiegelman	Klezmer	Trapping, storytelling
Shaggy Dog Story (1979)[30] Art Spiegelman	Tango	Humorous effect, some visual trapping
The City (1925)[31] Frans Masereel	5/4 funky groove	Storytelling, providing subtext, delineating structure
God's Man (1929)[32] Lynd Ward	Nuevo Tango	Storytelling, expressing emotion and inner thoughts of characters, subtext
Destiny (1930)[33] Otto Nückel	Blues/slow drag	Storytelling, expressing emotion and inner thoughts of characters, commentary
He Done Her Wrong (1930)[34] Milt Gross	1930s jazz/ rhythm and blues	Storytelling, expressing emotion and inner thoughts of characters, referencing cartoon music and jazz
The Parade (1957)[35] Si Lewen	New music/ avant jazz	Storytelling, expressing emotion of artist, political commentary
Shaping Thought (2013) Art Spiegelman	Jazz/film noir/funk	Historical and postmodern references, genre references (film noir) extreme trapping
The Virtuoso (1865) Wilhelm Busch	All of the above	Following visual beats, humorous effect, structure and continuity

placed next to a San Francisco underground comic featuring charming bestiality accompanied by a traditional tango. But it once more brings to mind Gorman's final Classical Principle: "A given film score may violate any of the principles above, providing the violation is at the service of the other principles."²⁵ Table 8.1 illustrates some of the "violations" regarding musical styles and film scoring techniques used in the various works.

The most polysynchronous scores were applied to the earliest and most contemporary works. A.B. Frost's 1894 comic *The Fatal Mistake* (titled "Our Cat Eats Rat Poison" in an earlier version) is accompanied by a combination of screaming free jazz and punk, which qualifies as upending traditional styles of silent film music, especially when paired with nineteenth-century illustration, but also clearly expresses "referential narrative" as it follows the manic death sprint of a poisoned feline. The Noir-ish rendezvous in Spiegelman's 1979 *Shaggy Dog Story* is treated with a dignified tango, despite being centered on cheerful bestiality.

Here we return to the idea of the music as the "voice" of the film, because the style/genre is inherently a large part of defining that voice, in the same way that LA hardcore defines the "voice" of *Repo Man* and grand opera defines the voice of *The Godfather (Part 3)*. The use of bluesy jazz to support the Film Noir referencing in the visuals of *Shaping Thought* is ironic, as is the use of tango to support the dog/human sex in *Shaggy Dog Story*. But the use of slow blues in *Destiny* is completely unironic: it expresses the pure emotion of the situation. Yet there is an element of irony in using a bar room blues to underpin a tale of German working-class tragedy. Emotionally it is synchronous; stylistically it is polysynchronous.

Music for graphic novels and comics needs to be as rubbery, as versatile, and as unpredictable as the medium of comics itself. It must combine the invention of the film score composer with the shape shifting of the comics/graphic artist.

One of the final graphic sequences, created by Art specifically for the

Figure 8.5 *Plastic Man* #18 (PD).

show, is *Shaping Thought*, a comix work embedding the ideas expressed in the show about the relationship between words and pictures, and the possibilities of wordless graphic stories, into a classic Film Noir comic, referencing many of the ideas and works by other artists in the show. The score for this work combines stylistic historical reference and postmodernity, classic sound and silent film tropes, and a variety of music styles, and, as a playful examination of the relationship between music and pictures, ramps them up to the extreme. As Art Spiegelman says in *Wordless!*, "Comics turn time into space." I would add that music turns space into time (Figure 8.5).

Notes

1 This chapter was originally published as Phillip Johnston, "Wordless! Music for Comics and Graphic Novels Turns Time into Space (and back again)," *Southerly* 76, no. 1 (2016): 95–110.
2 *Wordless!* book and lyrics by Art Spiegelman, music by Phillip Johnston, Sydney Opera House, Sydney, Australia, October 5, 2013.
3 *Drawn to Death: A Three Panel Opera* (Concert Presentation), book and lyrics by Art Spiegelman, music by Phillip Johnston, Arts at St. Anne's, New York, USA, May 18, 2000.
4 Frederic Wertham, *The Seduction of the Innocent* (New York: Rinehart & Company, 1954).
5 David Hajdu, *The Ten-Cent Plague: The Great Comic-Book Scare and How It Changed America* (New York: Farrar, Straus and Giroux, 2008), 97–304.
6 Shaun Tan, *The Arrival* (London: Hodder & Stoughton, 2006).
7 Art Spiegelman, ed., *Lynd Ward: Six Novels in Woodcuts* (New York: Penguin Group, 2010).
8 For more on the subject of wordless novels, see David Beronä's *Wordless Books: The Original Graphic Novels*.
9 The term "commix" is generally used to describe underground and alternative comics.
10 Gorbman, *Unheard Melodies*, 53.
11 Bernard Herrmann, "Music in Films–A Rebuttal," *New York Times*, June 24, 1945, 27.
12 Gorbman, *Unheard Melodies*, 53.
13 Kalinak, *Settling the Score*, 82.
14 Scott McCloud, *Understanding Comics: The Invisible Art* (New York: HarperCollins, 1993), 94–5.

15 Ibid.
16 Ibid. This looks much better with the graphic part of the graphic novel.
17 Will Eisner, *Comics and Sequential Art* (Tamarac, FL: Poorhouse Press, 1985), 6.
18 Phillip Johnston, "Bernard Herrmann: Pioneer of Loops and Sequencing," *Music and the Moving Image*, May 28, 2016, New York, University, New York, NY. Conference Presentation.
19 Or rather a series of subsequent edits. At any rate, the composer usually has no input here.
20 A *click track* is a series of beats, similar to a metronome, that the musicians can follow to stay in sync with the film. With contemporary technology they can be designed with great precision, changing meter, and tempo as needed.
21 Wilhelm Busch, *Der Virtuo* (Berlin: Braun Schneider, 1865).
22 Beronä, *Wordless Books*, 10.
23 Art Spiegelman, *Shaping Thought*, premiered at Graphic Festival, Sydney Opera House, Sydney, Australia, 2013.
24 Art's description of *Wordless!*
25 Gorbman, *Unheard Melodies*, 73.
26 A.B. Frost, *Stuff & Nonsense* (New York: Scribner's, 1884), 20–7.
27 Frans Masereel, "Passionate Journey," in *Graphic Witness: Four Wordless Graphic Novels by Frans Masereel, Lynd Ward, Giacomo Patri. and Laurence Hyde*. Selected and introduced by George A. Walter (Richmond Hill, ON: Firefly Books, 2007), 33–60.
28 H.M. Bateman, "The Boy Who Breathed on the Glass at the British Museum," London: *Punch Magazine*, 1916.
29 Art Spiegelman, "Henry Foulbite—His Fine Day," in *Mondo Snarfo* (Milwaukee: Kitchen Sink Press, 1978).
30 Art Spiegelman, "Shaggy Dog Story" (originally printed in *Playboy Magazine*, 1979; reprinted in *Co-Mix: Art Spiegelman: A Retrospective of Comics, Graphics and Scraps*. Montreal: Drawn + Quarterly, 2013), 23.
31 Frans Masereel, *The City* (New York: Dover, 1972).
32 Lynd Ward, *God's Man: A Novel in Woodcuts* (New York: St. Martin's Press, 1978).
33 Otto Nückel, *Destiny: A Novel in Pictures* (New York: Dover, 2007).
34 Milt Gross, *He Done Her Wrong: The Great American Novel and Not a Word in It—No Music, Too* (Seattle: Fantagraphics Press, 2005).
35 Si Lewin, *The Parade: An Artist's Odyssey* (New York: Abrams, 2016).

9

Silent Film Composers Speak!

Generally, the work of a composer, like that of a novelist, poet, or painter, is done in solitary. Filmmakers, theater artists, and dancer/choreographers practice more social art forms in their creation. But although performing musicians spend a great deal of their time waiting around to play, and thus discuss their process and lives, composers rarely have regular opportunities to talk to each other about their craft. With the increase of interest in film scores, and their composers, over the last few years, there are now books, articles, and half a dozen podcasts discussing their work, and even some that interview them. But to date any kind of serious discussion of contemporary silent film score composition as a craft, beyond reviews of performances, is rare.

Here I interview a few of the creative, dedicated, and inventive composers of silent film scores about how they practice their craft and what they think about it.[1] The majority here spend from all to a large part of their professional time creating and performing silent film scores. The one exception here is Richard Einhorn, who has only created one major work in the field, and one that can be performed without the film at that; however, I felt that his work *Voices of Light* (1994), which is inspired by and performed with Dreyer's *The Passion of Joan of Arc* (1928), was so significant and unusual that I wanted to discuss it with him. Interestingly, three of the composers interviewed here sometimes/often/always create their scores collectively, something that is rare in contemporary film composition, though sound film composers, especially in Hollywood, sometimes work with a small army of collaborators in the form of music editors, music supervisors, orchestrators, conductors, musicians, and contractors, and sometimes maintain production houses where some work is delegated. But silent film scoring is a less lucrative and more obsession-driven craft and sometimes realized by a performing ensemble which composes and performs its music collectively. This describes the work of the Alloy Orchestra, the Blue Grassy Knoll, and some of the scores of the Club Foot Orchestra. I have interviewed the leaders of these groups, but they all stress the importance of the creative and practical collaboration with their collaborative ensembles.

Richard Einhorn is an orchestral composer who also has a background in film, concert music, and electronic music. He has only composed this single work of silent film music but has scored at least twenty sound features and several hundred short films and documentaries. Richard Marriott (Club Foot Orchestra) has written operas, electronic music, dance scores, and jazz tunes. He also has a significant background in film scoring and, either solo or with the CFO, has scored at least fifteen silent films, including many of the acknowledged classics (*Caligari*, *Nosferatu*, *Metropolis*, and *Potemkin*). The Club Foot Orchestra began as an avant jazz band in San Francisco and originally brought in silent films to enhance their music, rather than the other way around. The Alloy Orchestra, of whom Ken Winokur is interviewed here, had a background in scoring animation, and segments of Sesame Street. They are probably the ensemble most single-mindedly dedicated to silent film scoring: they have scored countless silent films and have earned their living composing and performing scores internationally for decades. The Blue Grassy Knoll, of whom Gus Macmillan is interviewed here, is an Australian performing ensemble, sometimes described as a bluegrass band, and focuses primarily on the work of Buster Keaton. The following "conversation," organized into some big topic areas, draws upon interviews I did with all of them in 2015,[2] and includes some thoughts of my own. They were incredibly generous in sharing their thoughts, techniques, and philosophies about their practice. One thing I loved was that when I asked them to name their favorite other silent film score composers, several of them named each other.

Methodology

The first question is "How do you do it?"[3] One of the issues I was wondering about is whether silent film composers' workflow is similar to that of sound film composers, and if composers who have a greater background in contemporary film scoring, or art music, or live ensemble performance, approach the process differently. I was also interested in how the answer to these questions would correlate to broader questions about their attitudes toward this kind of writing.

Richard Einhorn was the outlier here.

> I began at the beginning, wrote a few movements, then skipped ahead to the torture sequence and wrote from there to the end of the film. Then I filled in the rest of the movements. The last orchestral movement to be completed was the interrogation of Joan that begins with her recitation of Pater Noster. The last piece to be completed was the a capella performance of the chant Deus Aeterne, which is heard before the credit sequence during live performances, in darkness, before the film begins.
>
> I watched the movie several times. I broke the film down into 15 sections. Now I knew I had 15 movements. I titled each section, timed each section, and composed without checking in too much with the film.

I think you will have to look far to find a film music composer who gets this far from the film while composing. But Einhorn was not following either silent or sound film scoring conventions with reference to trapping, following dramatic beats on a micro level or other traditional film scoring techniques. He *was*, however, conforming the music to the overall editing/narrative structure of the film in his fifteen sections.

Ken Winokur aligns with Einhorn about watching the film a number of times before beginning. When he says, "some kind of structure starts to take root," this reinforces the collective nature of the intuitive modus operandi that Alloy has developed over the years. He also cites the use of "character themes"—a classic film scoring trope, both silent and sound.

> Even though we do start at the beginning of the film and start writing, we have all seen the film (sometimes a number of times). Some form of structure starts to take root from those early viewings. We'll know for instance, that there might be a number of characters in the film that will require their own theme. We'll know the arc of the film and where the subtle parts will need to be developed. Or where, for instance, we feel that the film's own momentum is flagging and we're going to be challenged to try to bring the energy and interest up in our composition. We have tried a couple of times, early in our career, to start composing without watching the whole film through. This really didn't work. The composition seems to just wander off into unknown territory. It's important to start the composition with some idea where it's going and how it's going to get there.

It's also interesting that he mentions the technical function of the music to try to "fix" any weak areas of the film. All contemporary film composers will recognize, from every spotting session, the instructions from a film's director to try to solve specific problems in the film that they were unable to solve during earlier production stages,[4] be it acting, structuring, or storytelling. In Alloy's case, they make their own assessments and try to support the film as they interpret that.

Richard Marriott's process mirrors aspects of Einhorn's and Winokur's, with his emphasis on watching the whole film before beginning and on mapping out structure ahead of time.

> I usually watch a film numerous times before I "start." I let my ideas and emotions flow over me, and I'll get some creative ideas on how to approach a particular sequence. Sometimes I'll get an inspiration for the dramatic arc of the film, maybe a concept for orchestration. It might be a small thing, like a particular clarinet flourish to match a gesture. Sometimes I hear a fully orchestrated cue and I write it down.
>
> Next, I may divide up the movie into cues. I believe this is almost intuitive, humans have an innate respect for narrative and group together events in a way to engage the listener. When the subject character falls asleep is almost always a division point—unless he has a dream or a nightmare that has been elicited from a recent waking action. Change of character, environment, time, action or mood are often the dividing points.

His description of techniques reveals the collaborative nature of his process. He also refers to the use of themes and the connection to contemporary and historic film scoring approaches.

> If this is to be a collaborative score, I may assign sections to composers at this point. As was said before, I'm likely to assign a section to a composer who will relish it. (a pitch down the middle, in baseball terms).
>
> Often the film will have sequences that represent an evolution of a theme. I would be likely to establish an identifiable theme, tempo, or timbre to these sequences and show a musical development which corresponded with the thematic development. I'm also likely to score scenes that share a location in an identifiably similar way. This is a common technique, a kind of leitmotiv, used by countless composers in opera and sound films.
>
> Rehearsals may start before all the cues are finished, sometimes even before all the cues have been assigned. Frequently composers will do a rewrite after they hear their work in rehearsal.

Gus Macmillan's description of process goes the furthest in the direction of collectivity.

> We write in a collaborative fashion. After viewing the film together several times (as well as on our own) we analyze what kind of film we are dealing with. Major themes—emotional, physical etc.—are discussed, as well as characters and scenes that are memorable or perhaps confusing—plot structures are mapped out, and timing of scenes is noted. Often, we clarify where obvious and less obvious shifts in the film may benefit different shifts of music. This initial viewing is always done in silence and at no time do we listen to any other scores that exist.
>
> We then go away and write bits and pieces of music as individuals. Some is specifically for scenes, or characters, or themes (love theme, chase theme, etc.) others might simply be pieces of music that have been written spontaneously without any part of the film in mind. These are then brought to rehearsal and played through by the band. Other times it may be a melody and some chords, a scrap of something scrawled on the back of an envelope, or even something recorded on a phone late at night. Once they are offered up in rehearsal they are surrendered to the band—people can suggest alterations, improvements, changes, from key signatures to time signatures, structures, variations of melodies, additional sections. Sometimes two pieces will be merged, or one piece will be split in two. Pieces that may have been written for a specific scene might end up being used for a completely different section. Often, we find ways of re-using a particularly satisfying piece of music many times by re-arranging it, altering themes slightly, using the same chords but finding different melodies, or combining two pieces together. Changing tempo and time signature can help keep a theme going without becoming repetitive or transposing it to its relative minor.

He describes the development through rehearsal process that follows, which is completely wedded to film's images/narrative—the exact opposite of Einhorn's.

> We often find ourselves learning the music and arranging it at the same time—trying out structures as we play along to the film, seeing if they fit and how to keep the variety within the score. This, I suspect, lends a very organic feel to the scores, so that they are very wedded to the pictures—by doing this we learn each edit of the film, and take cues from gestures and motions of the actors and movements and angles of the camera. We get to know the film as we get to know the music—and often find inspiration from the pictures. By the end of the process we have memorised the entire score (with some help from cheat notes) but need the pictures to prompt us as to what happens next musically.

You can see one difference between Einhorn's conservatory training and the BGK's band aesthetic: what Einhorn would call a score and parts, Macmillan calls "cheat notes."

My own process reflects bits and pieces of all of these, some more or less than others: I watch the film, map out structure, make use of themes and motifs. But individual scores have different requirements, depending upon what overall concept I have chosen for that score. For *Faust*, which I had decided would contain songs, I worked with the librettist Hilary Bell[5] to make a list of topics that we wanted to address with songs, based upon the themes of the film as a whole. Then we started writing entire songs that we knew would address certain scenes. Once we had a song, it became my job to structure it in such a way that matched the dramatic beats and scene structure of the film. We then found places where that thematic content was developed and then wrote variations of the songs to express that development. Finally, instrumental music was filled in between the songs, but even much of that would sometimes draw upon thematic material from the songs.

But sometimes my approach to structure is more arbitrary. *The Adventures of Prince Achmed* was already divided up into parts, and those could often be fairly easily divided into scenes. But in my first analysis of the film (which took a week of working on it full time), I also made more arbitrary divisions. I wrote down the dialogue or narration in every title card in the film and also wrote out another structure based on colors, as the film was tinted different colors (red, blue, green) for different settings. There were also a number of different stories from the original Arabian Nights that needed to be tracked as well as the usual characters. Some of these ideas I later discarded when I actually began writing, but the opening of the film became a particularly obscure practical joke. After the opening credits, the film begins with a series of short set pieces introducing the main characters. For each of these characters I wrote a short theme, based upon a simple motif that could be repeated and associated with that character for the rest of the film. However, once I introduced those themes, I never used them again, and indeed never used any "character themes/motifs" for the rest of the film.[6] Instead, I developed thematic material based on either broader thematic ideas or purely musical ideas that related to the composition as a whole but were then wrapped around the dramatic structure of the film. I began the score with a *toolbox*: a list of musical materials that I intended to apply globally to the score, and as I progressed, I returned to that list periodically to make sure I was making full use of them. For this film, the list included (i) the jazz organ blues style of Jimmy Smith and Shirley Scott, (ii) ideas drawn from early minimalism or process music (Philip Glass/Steve Reich/Terry Riley/LaMonte Young), (iii) repeated use of polymeter, polyrhythm, and polytonality, (iv) a score that, in live performance, would combine a prerecorded audio track (including both a studio recording of live jazz drummer Nic Cecire and the use of electronic loops and samples, including a sample library of John Cage prepared piano sounds) and a live musical performance featuring a notated score that included elements of improvisation. I then created a large-form structure for the entire film that alternated between developing the musical materials on a purely musical basis (i.e., not strictly mirroring the narrative structure) and more traditional film music structures, following scene changes, narrative, and even sometimes including trapping and close following of dramatic beats. The score thus combined a single investigation of a single musical idea, remaining in the same key and repeatedly returning to a single chord (Dm6), yet regularly departing from this for completely unrelated "episodes" which related to the content of the film. The back-and-forth between these form and content areas underlies the overall structure of the score.

One of the fundamental differences between silent films and sound films is that silent films are usually accompanied with more or less constant music throughout, whereas contemporary sound films use music mostly intermittently.[7] This has profound implications for the structure of the score and offers a composer the opportunity to think more explicitly in terms of a large-scale work. Thus, thinking about, and being aware of, the structure of this work at some point in the process (at the beginning or during) is going to be important. Structure is paramount to both the screenwriting and film editing process in film, and thus significant structural elements will already exist. A traditional approach for a composer of both silent and sound film scores is to help define, reinforce, and support these preexisting structures. Whether a composer follows this path or decides to take a different (possibly more polysynchronous) approach is a central decision in the creation of the score.

The application of established film scoring techniques—for example, the use of themes and motifs (for characters, locations, or narrative ideas) and their development, the close or loose following of dramatic beats and the use of tempo, timbre, orchestration, and genre will be at the composer's disposal and of use. The way these are applied depends not only on the composer's art and craft but on their *intent*. All applications of these techniques will need to serve the composer's choice of a relationship of the music to the film and need not be uniform throughout the entire score. All of these are *choices* and as such can be thought about and examined, not taken for granted.

Intent

As discussed in previous chapters, one of the most controversial issues for academics and some creators of historically based silent film scores is the issue of "being faithful to the director's intent." Here there is some disagreement among composers, and I think this derives from each composer's idea of what they are creating. Richard Einhorn, who is utterly unconcerned with the director's intent, says, "I look at these as two parallel works of art which, combined, create a third." His relationship is with Joan of Arc, not so much with Dreyer, the film's director. Yet, he still concedes that "the trick is to contradict the narrative in a meaningful way!" The other composers still view their music as underscore for the film. They all are willing to contradict the putative "original intent" but only under certain circumstances. For Winokur and Macmillan, it is something to do only rarely and for a very good reason, whereas Marriott is much more playful with this idea. He gives one example from his score for Murnau's *Nosferatu* (1922).

> A typical reading of the film would require the viewer's sympathy lie with the headstrong naive Harker and be at one with his horror as the vampire strikes. I decided to instead follow the vampire and the compulsions which drives this amazing 400-year-old creature, a juxtaposition of sex and repulsion as described in the Bram Stoker novel.[8]

Both Macmillan and Winokur refer to extended band discussion before a decision to contradict is made. Macmillan gives examples of small additions they sometimes make and invoking "historical perspective" as motivating the decision. Winokur likewise gives an example of a score for Dziga Vertov's *Man with a Movie Camera* (1929) in which they contradicted the director's notes, which asked for music that was "relentlessly happy and upbeat." He adds that "we felt that as Americans from our time period, we had a different attitude about the success of the Soviet state. We added in music that had more tension and was less 'merry' than the notes suggested." A more dramatic expression of contradiction drives DJ Spooky's multimedia performance of his score for Griffith's *Birth of a Nation* (1915).[9] Griffith's film (based on the 1905 novel and play *The Clansman* by Thomas Dixon Jr.) was immediately indicted as both an absurd revisionist distortion of history and a racist white supremacist tract. DJ Spooky's performance involves an actual reedit of the film, with voice-over commentary, which focuses on an indictment of the racial/political content of the film.

My own attitude is a little different: when I look for a new silent film to score, I specifically go *looking* for an opportunity to reinvent the film with the music. For me, that is part of the interest. Whether it involves swapping heroes and villains (another case of this is our transformation of *Faust* from a Christian allegory to an indictment of societal hypocrisy) or a chance to add significant parallel narratives or just a chance to do the unexpected, I always try to find ways, small and large, to interrogate the relationship between image/narrative and music. But like the other composers here, my doing this comes from a deep love of the silent film art form and an equally deep respect for the practitioners who created these works, so my motivation is not to undermine them but to create a new and surprising experience for audience, always with the goal of inspiring deep enjoyment of the experience. And the majority of any of my scores support the film in more or less traditional ways—I find that my use of polysynchronicity is most effective when it is applied selectively.

All of the composers say that they write with an awareness that they and the audience are viewing the film with a twenty-first-century (non-contemporaneous) perspective. Some cite the difference between sincerity and irony; others mention the greater tolerance for/exposure to dissonance. All say it influences their work, with the exception of Einhorn, whose composition is influenced by medieval music, but certainly not limited to it. But do they use the actual *language* of silent film scoring (as described in Chapter 2) in their work? Marriott says, generally, no, but with some use of musical quotes and sound effects in particular cases for effect, advising their use in small doses. And he makes no attempt to use music that is historically accurate, except, again, for effect in particular situations. This illustrates the point made earlier that traditional film scoring tropes can be used to create different effects by the knowledgeable practitioner, for example, ironically when CFO uses "We're in the Money" in *Sherlock Jr.* precisely when Buster Keaton goes to buy a gift for his girl while lacking the amount of money he needs. But both Marriott and Winokur refer to the issue of "competence": the shared (with the audience) knowledge of a lifetime of watching films and absorbing the tropes of their film music language.

But Winokur and the Alloy Orchestra generally eschew the use of historical-silent-film-style music—with one exception: diegetic music. When there is a band or musician playing in a film, they try to simulate what they might actually be playing. Otherwise, they score a silent film with the same tool box a contemporary film music composer would use to score a sound film, which means using contemporary styles of music based on associations held by contemporary audiences, within their own style, skill set, and predilections, as does the Blue Grassy Knoll, and, in a different way, does Richard Einhorn. They both use the word "intuitive" to describe their approach. The word "intuitive" is here understood to imply shared bits of meaning with the audience. One difference here is that rather than an upright piano, organ, or small symphonic orchestra, their palettes are quite unique to their own genre: a bluegrass band (BGK), a junk percussion trio, with sampling synthesizer, accordion, and clarinet (AO), a mixed ensemble with conductor: half jazz band and half chamber music ensemble (CFO) and a full orchestra with chorus and four vocal soloists (Einhorn). They all bring original creative musical identities, both individually and collectively, to the craft of film scoring, linked only by a great love of the medium with which they are collaborating.[10]

I promised in the Prelude not to take a deep dive into the issue of live performance of music for silent films. While it runs deeply as a presence throughout the book, I have focused on the issues around composition and theory. But when I interviewed these composers, I didn't know yet that that would be the case, and they all spoke passionately about both the pleasures and challenges of live performance, so I'd like to share some of their thoughts. For me, playing a composed score live for a silent film is one of the most challenging things that a musician can do. Aside from musical skill and collaborative suppleness, it requires concentration that can't lapse even for a few seconds, for 60–120 minutes without a break, with music that is often changing tempo, meter, instrumentation, and style on a regular basis, with few conventional transitions. I began my career as a silent film musician in the era of celluloid: challenges included unexpectedly different prints, incorrect projections speeds and aspect ratios, mechanical breakdowns (in one case, a film burst into flame in the middle of a screening); today in the digital world the potential hazards are different, but no less numerous.

Richard Marriott enumerates the challenges: "sound is often compromised, hearing within the ensemble is often compromised, difficulties of reading the score or following the conductor in the less-than-optimal light, difficult setups into a small space, no ability to doubletrack, clean up mistakes or 'fix it in the mix.'" Gus Macmillan says,

> The challenge is getting tempos right so that pieces sync up naturally to the actions and editing of the film and making a transition between two sometimes very different styles of music feel natural and unforced. There is also the challenge of learning and memorising 75 minutes of music so that the band can be watching the film rather than reading music and listening to each other so the whole process feels organic rather than composed.

Ken Winokur cites the challenge of memorizing and performing multiple scores while on tour, and the broader rigors of travelling and performing.

However, all are very enthusiastic about the rewards as well. Winokur finds it "enormously satisfying" and goes on to say, "I make music to be heard and enjoyed by others. It's great to actually see an audience respond to the performance." Marriott calls it "just plain more exciting!" Macmillan cites communication with the audience in a unique way and bringing silent films to life for an audience.

> There is a three-way interaction of energy that happens when performing a live film score—between the band and the film, the audience and the film, and band and the audience. Each reacts to and draws energy from the other. On good nights, there is also an interaction between the audience and the band—we react to their reactions and vice versa and spur us on and we all go on the film's journey together. We can lead them through the story, showing them how best to absorb and respond to the material they are witnessing.

And Richard Einhorn adds, "The satisfaction is that it adds to the sense of the evening being an important event—and there is always something different and exciting with each performance. I've seen over 75 live performances of Voices of Light with PJOA and in each case, I've learned something new."

Clearly, there is a kinetic energy that combines the spontaneity and excitement of a live music performance, the drama, pathos and humor of a silent film, the thrill of time travel, the daredevil feat of an ensemble staying in sync with the film, and, where present, the virtuosic invention of improvised music. When I finish performing and conducting my own music to a silent film, it's with great satisfaction, but I also feel like I've been run over by a truck. It's impossible to separate the pleasure of the live performance from the identity of the art form: the video recording is ultimately just "evidence." But, like audio recordings of great film music without the film, we are still grateful to have them.

When a modern composer approaches a silent film, they must confront the notion of anachronism. The sooner they acknowledge that it is impossible for either the composer or the audience to experience the films the way they were experienced at the time of their first release, the freer they are to consider this issue without prejudice. There is a joy in the historically oriented compiled musical accompaniments of Rick Altman and the Mont Alto Orchestra. These practitioners allow us to time travel to another era and invoke and celebrate the practitioners of that time. The original orchestral scores restored and conducted by Gillian Anderson similarly showcase the work of now-neglected composers who bring us into the world of film music of the last century. The virtuosity and imagination of solo piano accompanists express their love, skill, and knowledge of that very specific tradition that has continued in different forms since the beginning of film. And composers who create new music for silent film, reinventing and reimagining the very relationship between music and film that we have taken for granted for so many years, create new multimedia, which, like these other approaches, celebrates the work of the silent film era practitioners, even while making something new which stands alongside these more traditional approaches. And hopefully, all bring attention to this incredibly rich and resonant body of work.

Ultimately, *polysynchronicity* is a way of thinking about things, rather than a category with strictly defined boundaries. My intention is not to indulge in debate about whether a given film music cue or score is polysynchronous or not: it is to expand the consideration of film music beyond pure functionality in relation to the images and narrative of the film with which it is collaborating. Ideally, thinking about these ideas will lead to both the continuing evolution of a young art form and the enrichment of contemporary synchronized sound film music as a whole.

Notes

1. To avoid a blizzard of footnotes around individual quotes, direct and indirect: all of these interviews were conducted via email in 2012, based on a quite lengthy questionnaire that I sent to each of them, unless otherwise noted. They were incredibly generous with their time, candor, and thoughtfulness in their replies, for which I will be eternally grateful.
2. See Appendix 2 to see the questionnaire I used to gather data.
3. The exact questions were: (2) Can you give a rough breakdown of your own work process on the film, from first draft to final version? and (3) If you haven't already discussed this, do you begin with a complete structural analysis of the film and proceed with composition with that in mind, or do you just begin at the beginning of the film and start writing?
4. Adding music is usually the final stage of postproduction before the final sound mix that is the last phase of production.
5. Hilary Bell is an Australian playwright, screenwriter, and children's book author, best known for her plays *Wolf Lullaby* (1997) and *The Splinter* (2012/2019), and *Alphabetical Sydney* (2013), with illustrator Antonia Pesenti.

6 In fact, I don't think I've ever made much use of any themes or motifs attached to particular characters in any of my silent film scores. I personally prefer to attach themes and motifs to ideas, subtext, emotions, or elements of purely musical development.
7 The film *Pi* (Aronofsky, 1998) is a rare example.
8 This is in harmony with my own approach to Tod Browning's *The Unknown* (1927) in which I used the music to portray the villain as the hero and vice versa (see Chapter 5).
9 DJ Spooky That Subliminal Kid, John Hyde, Anthony James, Stephen J. Cohen, Stacey Jade Smart, and Gary Breslin, *DJ Spooky's Rebirth of a Nation*. Burbank, CA: Distributed by Anchor Bay Entertainment, 2008.
10 My own silent film scores are written for various ensembles, among them: soprano saxophone, vibraphone, piano, and bass (*Page of Madness/Méliès*), cello, accordion, saxophone, piano, ukulele, and voice (*Faust*), or trombone, soprano saxophone, two organs, prerecorded samples, digital loops, and drum kit (*The Adventures of Prince Achmed*).

Appendix 1

Scores

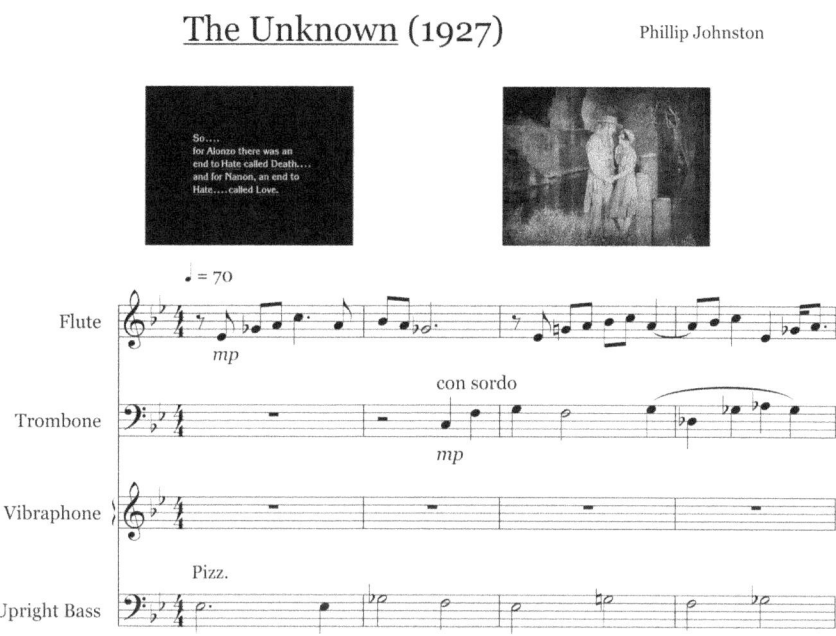

Figure A.1 *The Unknown* (Browning, 1927), music composed by Phillip Johnston ©1993 Jedible Music (BMI). This is the music at the end of the film, as described in the Chapter 5.

Appendix 1

Dance of Fire

Master Score (2012 revision) — Phillip Johnston (1998)

Figure A.2 *Danse du feu* (Méliès, 1899), music composed by Phillip Johnston ©1997 Jedible Music (BMI). The change described in the text occurs at Letter B, with the appearance of the dancer. This is the full orchestration performed by The Transparent Quartet.

Appendix 1

Hydrothèrapie Fantastique

Master Score

Phillip Johnston

Figure A.3 *Hydrothérapie Fantastique* (*The Doctor's Secret*) (1909), music composed by Phillip Johnston ©1997 Jedible Music (BMI). This score contains a reduction of some of the thematic material from the score, beginning with a reduction of the original Chopin theme, followed by a new jazz theme, written over the Chopin harmony, and then shows some of the more chromatic original contrapuntal thematic material. All of this material is developed further throughout the length of the score.

Appendix 1 193

Page of Madness

PART 0 Prelude

Phillip Johnston

fade with film

Page of Madness

PARTING THE WATERS (Part 5)
Phillip Johnston

Page of Madness

THE MASKS (Part 11)

Phillip Johnston

Figure A.4 *Page of Madness* (Kinugasa, 1926), music composed by Phillip Johnston ©1998 Jedible Music (BMI). This is an example of the development of thematic material used in this score, a traditional film scoring technique. The theme attached to the "mad dancer" occurs three times over the course of the film, which runs sixty to eighty minutes (depending upon projection speed). In its first incarnation near the beginning of the film, the melody is presented over a pedal and is essentially modal (Phrygian). When it returns about halfway through the film, (modal) harmony has been added, superimposed upon the original melody. When it returns a final time near the end of the film, the melody and harmony have been substantially developed, based on the original material, finally returning to the original theme at the very end, ending on the flat second (no resolution). Note in Part 11, bar 20, the shocking appearance of the single measure of chromatic material in the entire piece (except for a brief move to a related key at bar 29) (piano reduction).

Figure A.5 *Faust* (Murnau, 1926), music composed by Phillip Johnston ©2002 Jedible Music (BMI). This is a lead sheet for the short art song which occurs early in the score, introducing the idea of a meta-commentary, as discussed in Chapter 5.

Appendix 2

Contemporary Composer for Silent Film Interview

Name of Composer:
Name of Ensemble:
City/Country of Residence:
List of Works, with dates:

I Background

1) How did you originally get interested in composing original scores for silent film? When did you compose your first silent film score, and how did it come about?
2) Did you have a background in composing music for contemporary films before you wrote your first silent film score?
3) What generally is your background in music composition?
4) What types of compositions have you written in addition to composing original scores for silent film (if any)?
5) Are your scores performed live, or are they recorded in a studio to be synched with the film? If both, do you consider one form more important than the other?
6) If applicable, can you speak about the challenges and satisfactions of performing the score live with the film in front of an audience?

II Methodology

1) Are you the sole composer, or do you work in a collaborative fashion with co-composers and/or members of your ensemble? If the second, can you talk a little bit about how this process works?

2) Can you give a rough breakdown of your own work process on the film, from first draft to final version?
3) If you haven't already discussed this, do you begin with a complete structural analysis of the film and proceed with composition with that in mind, or do you just begin at the beginning of the film and start writing?
4) Do you consider the issue of whether the score will be faithful to the director's original intention (either for the entire film or for individual scenes)? Do think it is acceptable to directly contradict the clear/apparent narrative intent of the film?
5) Do you ever intentionally attempt to change the meaning of scenes, characters, plot, or any other aspects of the film with your musical underscore?
6) Do you ever intentionally reference what is conventionally thought of as "silent film music" in your scores? If so, how much? Is this an issue that is much on your mind as you compose?
7) Does knowledge of the history of film music (both silent and sound) inform your scores for silent film, or do you proceed intuitively as a composer?
8) Do you consider the issue of musical anachronism at all? By "musical anachronism" I mean the use of musical instruments, styles, or historical references that are from a time period later than that of the film.
9) Do you ever use techniques that are associated particularly with the silent film era, such as using the presumed audience knowledge of songs (and in particular their titles) to express something very specific (as in, for example, Joseph Breil's use of "Old Folks at Home" in his score for *Birth of a Nation*, or Carl Stalling's use of "The Lady In Red" in Bugs Bunny cartoons), or using musical "sound effects"? If so, do you use them because they are traditional silent film techniques, or just because they work (or for some other reason)?
10) Do you make a conscious attempt to make your scores for individual films different from one another, or do you work intuitively in this respect (i.e., do you approach each score from the same starting point)?
11) Do you ever begin a score with an overarching concept in mind, specific to that film? If so, can you give an example?
12) In what way do you think that the unique aspects of the silent film art form (the acting style, the lack of audible dialogue, the use of title cards, the narrative structure, etc.) affect the way you write music for it?

13) Do you have a particular way of interacting with title cards and/or dialogue?
14) Do you think it is ever acceptable to intentionally mock or make fun of the film or elements of it?
15) Do you attempt to draw attention to or divert attention from the musicians who are playing the live score, or neither? Why or why not?

III Philosophy

1) Do you think it is morally acceptable for an artist to take another artist's work and change the original meaning of it—to in effect use it for his or her own ends? (We are not engaging here with the legal issues of copyright—that is a separate issue)
2) Do you think about whether the original director would have appreciated or approved of your work on their film? Do you think they would have? Does it matter?
3) Do you consider the fact that twenty-first-century audiences are viewing the film in completely different way than twentieth-century (or even nineteenth-century) audiences (i.e., contemporaneous with the film—the "original" audiences) would have? Does this have an impact on your writing?
4) Do you think that it is important that every piece of music in a film must "mean something" (i.e., have a particular narrative function in the score)?
5) What, for you, is unique about the silent film art form?
6) Do you think that the craft of contemporary scores for silent film is a unique art form, or do you see it as a subset of the overall craft of film scoring?
7) Do you have plans for future scores for silent films?

IV Auteurship

1) Can you choose one or two scenes from a silent film that you've scored in which you engage with the film in an unexpected or unconventional way, and talk a little bit about it/them?

2) Do you think you have a recognizable style in silent film scoring, or that your work is chameleon-like (like some composers for contemporary film)? If so, how would you characterize that style?
3) Do you make an attempt to see/hear the work of other contemporary composers for silent film? If so, can you mention a couple that you admire, and why?
4) Do you identify yourself as a practitioner of this particular art form—that is, do you consider yourself, not necessarily primarily but importantly, as a "composer of original scores for silent film"?

Note that not all topics from the interviews are included in Chapter 9.

References

Abel, Richard, and Rick Altman. *The Sounds of Early Cinema*. Bloomington, IN: Indiana University Press, 2001.

Alloy Orchestra. "Alloy Orchestra: The New Sounds of Silent Films." Accessed April 3, 2014. http://www.alloyorchestra.com/.

Altman, Rick. *Silent Film Sound*. New York: Columbia University Press, 2004.

Anderson, Gillian. "Gillian Anderson: Conductor." http://www.gilliananderson.it.

Anderson, Gillian. *Music for Silent Films 1894–1929: A Guide*. Washington, DC: Library of Congress, 1988.

Anderson, Tim. "Reforming 'Jackass Music': The Problematic Aesthetics of Early American Film Music Accompaniment." In *Movie Music: The Film Reader*, edited by Kay Dickinson, 49–60. New York and London: Routledge, 2003.

Audissino, Emilio. *Film/Music Analysis: A Film Studies Approach*. Southampton, UK: Palgrave Macmillan, 2017.

Baily, Derek. *Improvisation: Its Nature and Practice in Music*. Boston: Da Capo Press, 1992.

Bang, Derrick. *Crime and Spy Jazz on Screen, 1950–1970*. Jefferson, NC: McFarland & Company, 2020.

Barthes, Roland. *Image/Text/Music*. New York: Hill & Wang, 1977.

Barton, Ruth, and Simon Trezise, eds. *Music and Sound in Silent Film: From the Nickelodeon to the Artist*. New York and London: Routledge, 2019.

Bateman, H.M. "The Boy Who Breathed on the Glass at the British Museum." London: *Punch Magazine*, 1916.

Beachum, Chris. "Oscar Nominee Ludovic Bource Inspired by Past Music Masters for 'The Artist' Score." *The Gold Derby*, February 17, 2012. http://www.goldderby.com/article/2012/oscar-nominee-ludovic-bource-inspired-by-past-music-masters-for-the-artist-score-video

Bellano, Marco. "Silent Strategies: Audiovisual Functions of the Music for Silent Cinema." *Kieler Beiträge zur Filmmusikforschung* 9 (January 2013): 46–76.

Bellano, Marco. "The Tradition of Novelty – Comparative Studies of Silent Film Scores: Perspectives, Challenges, Proposals." In *The Sounds of Silent Films: New Perspectives on History, Theory and Practice*, edited by Claus Tieber and Anna Katharina Windisch, 208–20. New York and Hampshire: Palgrave Macmillan, 2014.

Bernstein, Elmer. *Elmer Bernstein's Film Music Notebook: A Complete Collection of the Quarterly Journal, 1974–1978*. Sherman Oaks, CA: Film Music Society, 2004.

Berona, David. *Wordless Books: The Original Graphic Novels.* New York: Harry N. Abrams, 2008.
Blue Grassy Knoll. "The Blue Grassy Knoll: Live Film Scores to Silent Movies." Accessed April 3, 2014. http://bluegrassyknoll.com.
Brecht, Bertolt. *Brecht on Theatre.* Edited by Marc Silberman, Steve Giles, and Tom Kuhn. London: Bloomsbury Methuen Drama, 2014.
Brody, Richard. "Getting Jazz Right in the Movies." *The New Yorker*, October 13, 2014. https://www.newyorker.com/culture/richard-brody/whiplash-getting-jazz-right-movies.
Brown, Royal S. *Overtones and Undertones: Reading Film Music.* Berkeley and Los Angeles: University of California Press, 1994.
Bruce, Graham. *Bernard Herrmann: Film Music and Narrative.* Ann Arbor, MI: UMI Research Press, 1985.
Buhler, James. "Analytical and Interpretive Approaches to Film Music (II): Analysing Interactions of Music and Film." In *Film Music: Critical Approaches*, edited by K.J. Donnelly, 39–61. New York: Continuum, 2001.
Burlingame, John. "Novak Angered by 'Vertigo' Music in 'Artist.'" *Variety*, January 10, 2012. https://variety.com/2012/film/news/novak-angered-by-vertigo-music-in-artist-1118048370/.
Burt, George. *The Art of Film Music.* Boston: Northeastern University Press, 1994.
Busch, Wilhelm. *Der Virtuos.* Berlin: Braun and Schneider, 1865.
Butler, David. *Jazz Noir: Listening to Music from Phantom Lady to the Last Seduction.* Westport: Praeger Publishers, 2002.
Carli, Philip C. "Musicology and the Presentation of Silent Film." In *Film History* 7, no. 3, edited by Gregory A. Waller, 315. Bloomington: Indiana University Press, 1995.
Chion, Michel. *Audio-Vision: Sound on Screen.* New York: Columbia University Press, 1994.
Chion, Michel. *Film, A Sound Art.* New York: Columbia University Press, 2003.
Clair, René. "The Art of Sound." In *Film Sound: Theory and Practice*, edited by Elisabeth Weis and John Belton, trans. Vera Traill, 92–5. New York: Columbia University Press, 1985 (Orig. 1929).
Club Foot Orchestra. "Club Foot Orchestra: Pioneers of Modern Music for Silent Film." Accessed April 3, 2014. http://www.clubfootorchestra.com/.
Cohen, Annabel J. "How Music Influences The Interpretation of Film and Video: Approaches from Experimental Psychology." In *Perspectives in Systematic Musicology*, edited by Roger Allen Kendall and Roger W. H. Savage, 15–36. Los Angeles, CA: Dept. of Ethnomusicology, University of California, 2005.
Cohen, Annabel J. "Music as a Source of Emotion in Film." In *Music and Emotion: Theory and Research*, edited by Patrick Juslin and John Sloboda, 249–71. Oxford and New York: Oxford University Press, 2001.

Cook, Nicholas. *Analysing Musical Multimedia*. New York: Oxford University Press, 1998.
Cooke, Mervyn. *A History of Film Music*. London: Cambridge University Press, 2008.
Cooper, David. *Bernard Herrmann's Vertigo: A Film Music Handbook*. Westport, CT and London: Greenwood Press, 2001.
Davis, Blair. "Old Films, New Sounds: Screening Silent Cinema with Electronic Music." *Canadian Journal of Film Studies* 17, no. 2 (Fall 2008): 77–98.
Davison, Annette. *Hollywood Theory, Non-Hollywood Practice: Cinema Soundtracks in the 1980s and 1990s*. Leeds: University of Leeds, 2004.
Donnelly, K.J., ed. *Film Music: Critical Approaches*. New York and London: Continuum, 2001.
Donnelly, K.J. *Occult Aesthetics: Synchronization in Sound Film*. Oxford, UK: Oxford University Press, 2014.
Donnelly, K.J. and Ann-Kristin Wallengren, eds. *Today's Sounds for Yesterday's Films: Making Music for Silent Cinema*. UK: Palgrave Macmillan, 2016.
Durant, Yati E. "Spontaneous Composition for Screen: Linear and Non-Linear Improvisation for Instruments and Electronics." *The New Soundtrack* 6, no. 2 (2016): 171–89.
Einhorn, Richard. "Richard Einhorn: Composer." Accessed April 3, 2014. http://www.richardeinhorn.com/.
Eisenstein, Sergei. *The Film Sense*. London: Faber & Faber Ltd., 1943.
Eisler, Hanns and Theodor Adorno. *Composing for the Films*. New York: New York University Press, 1947.
Eisner, Will. *Comics and Sequential Art*. Tamarac, FL: Poorhouse Press, 1985.
Essman, Scott. "Interview: Elias Merhige (Begotten)," 2010. Accessed August 1, 2018. http://horrornews.net/13347/interview-elias-merhige-begotten/ (originally: Essman, Scott. "Begotten." Interview with Elias Merhige. January 31, 2009).
Ezra, Elizabeth. *Georges Méliès: The Birth of the Auteur*. Manchester, UK: Manchester University Press, 2000.
Fadnes, Petter Frost. "Improvising the Deluge: Live Film Scoring and Improvisational Practices." *Jazz-Hitz*, 01 (2018): 107–23.
Flaig, Paul. "The Living Nickelodeon and Silent Film Today." In *New Silent Cinema*, edited by Katherine Groo and Paul Flaig, 130–7. New York: Routledge, 2015.
Foster, Jason. "Cliff Martinez's *Traffic*." *Film Score Monthly* 6, no. 1 (2001): 15.
Frazer, John. *Artificially Arranged Scenes: The Films of Georges Méliès*. Boston: G.K. Hall & Co., 1979.
Frost, Arthur Burnett. *Stuff & Nonsense*. New York: Scribner's, 1884.
Fujiki, Hideaki. "Benshi as Stars: The Irony of the Popularity and Respectability of Voice Performers in Japanese Cinema." *Cinema Journal* 45, no. 2 (2006): 68–84.
Gabbard, Krin. *Jammin' at the Margins: Jazz and the American Cinema*. Chicago: University of Chicago Press, 1996.

Gorbman, Claudia. *Unheard Melodies: Narrative Film Music*. Bloomington, IN: Indiana University Press, 1987.

Gross, Milt. *He Done Her Wrong: The Great American Novel and Not a Word in It–No Music, Too*. Seattle: Fantagraphics Press, 2005.

Gunning, Tom. "'Now You See It, Now You Don't': The Temporality of the Cinema of Attractions." In *The Silent Cinema Reader*, edited by Lee Grieveson and Peter Krämer, 41–50. London: Routledge, 2004.

Hagen, Earl. *Scoring For Films*. Van Nuys, CA: Alfred Publishing Co. Inc., 1971.

Hajdu, David. *The Ten-Cent Plague: The Great Comic-Book Scare and How It Changed America*. New York: Farrar, Straus and Giroux, 2008.

Hammond, Paul. *Marvelous Méliès*. London and Bedford: Gordon Fraser Gallery Ltd., 1974.

Harrison, Louis Reeves. "Jackass Music." *Moving Picture World* 8, no. 3 (January 21, 1911): 124–5, reprinted in *The Routledge Film Music Sourcebook*. Edited by James Wierzbicki, Nathan Platte, and Colin Roust. New York and London: Routledge, 2012.

Hays, Matthew. "How Guy Maddin's Seances Uses Lost Silent Films to Explore Our Personal Ghosts." *The Globe and Mail*, July 17, 2013. https://www.theglobeandmail.com/arts/film/maddin-explores-the-then-and-now/article13286553/.

Herrmann, Bernard. "Music in Films–A Rebuttal." In *The Routledge Film Music Sourcebook*, edited by James Wierzbicki, Nathan Platte and Colin Roust, 119–21. New York and London: Routledge, 2012.

Hibbert, Julie. *Celluloid Symphonies: Texts and Contexts in Film Music History*. Berkeley and Los Angeles: University of California Press, 2013.

Holmes, Amanda. *Politics of Architecture in Contemporary Argentine Cinema*. Basingstoke, UK: Palgrave Macmillan, 2017.

Hughes, Ed. "Silent Film, Live Music and Contemporary Composition." In *Today's Sounds for Yesterday's Films: Making Music for Silent Cinema*, edited by K.J. Donnely and Ann-Kristin Wallengren, 175–91. UK: Palgrave Macmillan, 2016.

Johnston, Phillip. "Bernard Herrmann: Pioneer of Loops and Sequencing." Conference Presentation, *Music and the Moving Image, New York*, May 28, 2016.

Johnston, Phillip. "The Polysynchronous Film Score: Songs for a Contemporary Score for F.W. Murnau's Faust (1926)." *Screen Sound Journal*, no. 3 (2012): 89–105.

Johnston, Phillip. "Jazzin' the Silents: Jazz and Improvised Music in Contemporary Scores for Silent Film." In *Cinema Changes: Incorporations of Jazz in the Film Soundtrack no.34*, edited by Emile Wennekes and Emilio Audissino, 19–32. Turnhout: Brepols, 2019.

Johnston, Phillip. "Wordless! Music for Comics and Graphic Novels Turns Time into Space (and back again)." *Southerly* 76, no. 1 (2016): 95–113.

Kalinak, Kathryn. *Settling The Score: Music and the Classic Hollywood Film*. Madison: University of Wisconsin Press, 1992.

Kardish, Laurence. *Weimar Cinema, 1919-1933: Daydreams and Nightmares*. New York: The Museum of Modern Art, 2010.
Karlin, Fred and Ray Wright. *On The Track: A Guide to Contemporary Film Scoring*. New York: Schirmer/MacMillan, 1990.
Kassabian, Anahid. *Hearing Film: Tracking Identifications in Contemporary Hollywood Film Music*. New York and London: Routledge, 2001.
Kittler, Friedrich. *Optical Media*. Cambridge: Polity Press, 2010.
Kobel, Peter. *Silent Movies: The Birth of Film and the Triumph of Movie Culture*. New York: Little, Brown and Company, 2007.
Lack, Russell. *Twenty Four Frames Under*. London: Quartet Books, 1997.
Larsen, Peter. *Film Music*. London: Reaktion Books, 2005.
Lewin, Si. *The Parade: An Artist's Odyssey*. New York: Abrams, 2016.
Lim, Denis. "Out of the Past." In *On Film / Essays*. The Criterion Collection, 2008.
Lipscomb, Scott and D.E. Tolchinsky. "The Role of Music COMMUNICATIOD. N in cinema." In *Music Communication*, edited by D. Miell, R.A.R.Macdonald, and D.J. Hargreaves, 383–404. London: Oxford University Press, 2005.
Lipscomb, Scott and Roger A. Kendall. "Perceptual Judgment of the Relationship Between Musical and Visual Elements in Film." *Psychomusicology* 13 (1994): 60–98.
Manvell, Roger. "Psychological Intensity in the Passion of Joan of Arc." In *The Classic Cinema: Essays in Criticism*, edited by Stanley Solomon, 111–14. New York: Harcourt Brace Jovanovich, New York, 1973.
Manvell, Roger, and John Huntley. *The Technique of Film Music*. New York: Communications Arts Books, 1967.
Margasak, Peter. "Music Notes: films scored while you watch." *The Chicago Reader*, September 21, 1995. https://www.chicagoreader.com/chicago/music-notes-films-scored-while-you-watch/Content?oid=888547.
Marks, Martin M. *Music and the Silent Film: Contexts and Case Studies 1895–1924*. New York: Oxford University Press, 1997.
Masereel, Frans. *The City*. New York: Dover, 1972.
Masereel, Frans. "Passionate Journey." In *Graphic Witness: Four Wordless Graphic Novels by Frans Masereel, Lynd Ward, Giacomo Patri, and Laurence Hyde*. Selected and introduced by George A. Walter, 33–60. Richmond Hill, ON: Firefly Books, 2007.
Masereel, Frans. *The Sun, The Idea & Story Without Words*. New York: Dover, 2009.
Matheou, Demetrios. "Pablo Berger: 'A Movie's Like a Paella, You Put All of Your Obsessions in There.'" *The Guardian*, July 11, 2013. https://www.theguardian.com/film/2013/jul/11/silent-film-blancanieves-pablo-berger-interview.
McCloud, Scott. *Understanding Comics: The Invisible Art*. New York: HarperCollins, 1993.
Meyer, Leonard B. *Emotion and Meaning In Music*. Chicago: University of Chicago Press, 1956.
Milne, Tom. *The Cinema of Carl Dreyer*. New York: A.S. Barnes, 1970.

Mont Alto Motion Picture Orchestra. "The Mont Alto Motion Picture Orchestra." Accessed May 10, 2014. http://www.mont-alto.com.
Neumeyer, David, and James Buhler. "Analytical and Interpretive Approaches to Film Music (I): Analyzing the Music." In *Film Music: Critical Approaches*, edited by K.J. Donnelly, 16–38. New York: Continuum, 2001.
Nückel, Otto. *Destiny: A Novel in Pictures*. New York: Dover, 2007.
Page, Joanna. *Science Fiction in Argentina: Technologies of the Text in a Material*. Ann Arbour, MI: University of Michigan Press, 2016.
Panosian, Dian. "Awards 2015 Spotlight: Composer Antonio Sanchez Takes SSN into the Jam Sessions That Created Birdman's Dauntless Percussion Score." *SSN Inside*, December 3, 2014. https://archive.li/9Klpr.
The Passion of Joan of Arc. 1928. DVD. Directed by Carl Theodor Dreyer. New York: Criterion, 1999.
Prendergast, Roy M. *Film Music - A Neglected Art*. 2nd ed. New York: W. W. Norton, 1991.
Rapée, Ernö. *Encyclopedia of Music for Pictures*. New York: Belmont, 1925.
Redner, Gregg. *Deleuze and Film Music: Building a Methodological Bridge between Film Theory and Music*. Chicago: Intellect Ltd. University of Chicago Press, 2011.
Richard Einhorn. "Richard Einhorn: Composer." Accessed April 3, 2014. http://www.richardeinhorn.com/.
Riesenfeld, Hugo. "Music and Motion Pictures." *The ANNALS of the American Academy of Political and Social Science* 128, no. 1 (November 1926): 58–62.
Rona, Jeff. *The Reel World: Scoring for Pictures*. Milwaukee, WI: Hal Leonard Books, 2009.
Schelle, Michael. *The Score: Interviews with Film Composers*. Los Angeles: Silman-James Press, 1999.
Scott, A.O. "'The Red Turtle,' Life Marooned With an Ornery Reptile." *New York Times*, January 20, 2017.
Silva, Manuel Deniz. "'The Sounds of Silent Films': An Interview with Claus Tieber and Anna K. Windisch." *Aniki: Portuguese Journal of the Moving Image* 5, no. 1 (2018): 166–75.
Smith, Jeff. "Unheard Melodies? A Critique of Psychoanalytic Theories of Film Music." In *Post-Theory: Reconstructing Film Studies*, edited by David Bordwell and Noel Carroll, 230–46. Wisconsin: Wisconsin University Press, 1996.
Spiegelman, Art. "Henry Foulbite–His Fine Day." *Mondo Snarfo*. Milwaukee: Kitchen Sink Press, 1978.
Spiegelman, Art, ed. *Lynd Ward: Six Novels in Woodcuts*. New York: Penguin Group, 2010.
Spiegelman, Art. "Shaggy Dog Story." Originally printed in *Playboy Magazine*, 1979, reprinted in *Co-Mix: Art Spiegelman: A Retrospective of Comics, Graphics and Scraps*. Montreal: Drawn + Quarterly, 2013.

Starrs, D. Bruno. "Sounds of Silence: An Interview with Rolf de Heer." *Metro Magazine* 152 (2007): 18–21.
Steiner, Fred. "An Examination of Leith Stevens' Use of Jazz in *The Wild One*: Parts I & II." In *Film Music Notebook: A Complete Collection of the Quarterly Journal, 1974–1978*, edited by Elmer Bernstein, 240–52, 280–8. Sherwood Oaks: The Film Music Society, 2001.
Stewart, Garrett. "Keaton Through the Looking-Glass." *The Georgia Review* 33, no. 2 (Summer 1979): 348–67.
Tan, Shaun. *The Arrival*. London: Hodder & Stoughton, 2006.
Thorp, J. and McPhee, E. "Alternate Soundtracks: Silent Film Music for Contemporary Audiences." *Screen Sound: The Australasian Journal of Soundtrack Studies* 2, (2010): 64–74.
Tieber, Claus and Anna Windisch. *The Sounds of Silent Films: New Perspectives on History, Theory and Practice*. New York and Hampshire: Palgrave Macmillan, 2014.
Trezise, Simon. "Carl Davis Interview." In *Music and Sound in Silent Film: From the Nickelodeon to The Artist*, edited by Ruth Barton and Simon Trezise, 149–59. New York and London: Routledge, 2019.
van Stratum, Bas. "La Antena – Esteban Sapit –2007" (2014). Accessed August 20, 2017. http://basvanstratum.nl/la-antena-esteban-sapir-2007/
Vertigo Productions. "Dr Plonk/Production Notes." Accessed August 20, 2017. http://www.vertigoproductions.com.au/dr_plonk_production_notes.php
Wallengren, Ann-Kristin. "To Be in Dialogue with the Film: With Neil Brand and Lillian Henley at the Masterclasses at Pordenone Silent Film Festival." In *Today's Sounds for Yesterday's Films: Making Music for Silent Cinema*, edited by K J Donnelly and Ann-Kristin Wallengren, 192–215. London: Palgrave Macmillan, 2016.
Walsh, Michael. "Music: Running Up the Scores." *Time Magazine*, September 5, 1995.
Ward, Lynd. *God's Man: A Novel in Woodcuts*. New York: St. Martin's Press, 1978.
Weiss, Jason. *Always In Trouble: An Oral History of ESP-Disk: The Most Outrageous Record Label in America*. Middletown, CT: Wesleyan University Press, 2012.
Wertham, Frederic. *The Seduction of the Innocent*. New York: Rinehart & Company, 1954.
Weschler, Lawrence. *Boggs, a Comedy of Values*. Chicago, IL: University of Chicago Press, 1999.
Whiteoak, John. *Playing Ad Lib: Improvisatory Music in Australia 1836–1970*. Sydney, Australia: Currency Press, 1999.
Wierzbicki, James. *Film Music: A History*. New York: Routledge, 2009.
Wierzbicki, James. "The 'Silent' Film in Modern Times." In *Music and Sound in Silent Film: from the Nickelodeon to* The Artist," edited by Ruth Barton and Simon Trezise, 198–208. New York and London: Routledge, 2019.
Wierzbicki, James, Nathan Platte and Colin Roust, eds. *The Routledge Film Music Sourcebook*. New York and London: Routledge, 2012.

Winters, Ben. "Musical Wallpaper? Towards an Appreciation of Non-narrating Music in Film." In *Music Sound and the Moving Image* 6, no. 1 (2012): 39–54.

Wood, Nancy. "Text and Spectator in the Period of the Transition to Sound." PhD diss., University of Kent, 1983.

Zimmer, Hans. "Hans Zimmer Teaches Film Scoring." *Masterclass.com*. Accessed May 5, 2019. https://www.masterclass.com/classes/hans-zimmer-teaches-film-scoring.com

Index

20th Century Fox   81

A-1 Video   57, 58
Abel, Richard   129
abstraction   83, 114, 131, 134, 151, 152, 156
Academy Awards   125, 146
Academy of Music   90
"Adagio for Strings" (Barber)   2
Adorno, Theodore   9, 10
Adventures of Prince Achmed, The (1926)   96, 135, 178
Aerial, The (*La Antena*, 2007)   140, 144, 148–50, 152, 157, 158
affiliating identifications   42, 63, 91, 105, 108, 111
After the Apocalypse (2004)   140, 155, 158
Air   62
Alexandrov, G. V.   9
alienation effect   10
Alix, Victor   33, 90
Alloy Orchestra   54, 55, 63, 64, 84–91, 173, 175, 176, 181, 182
Alloy Orchestra Plays Wild and Weird: 14 Fascinating and Innovative Films (1902-1965), The (Flicker Alley)   58, 61–2
"Alternate Soundtracks: Silent Film Music for Contemporary Audiences," (Thorp and McPhee)   44
alternative film music thought
   in contemporary sound film era   11–12
   in early film   8–11
Altman, Rick   1, 12, 25 n.75, 129, 183
Altman, Robert   12, 23, 115, 144
Ambrose, Stan   51
"America (My Country 'Tis of Thee)"   33
American Museum of the Moving Image   xiv, 132, 153
American music   32
Amram, David   124

anachronism   43, 79, 140, 183
Analysing Musical Multimedia (Cook)   3
Anatomy of a Murder (1959)   123
anchorage   13
Anderson, Gillian   33, 55, 183
Anderson, Paul Thomas   11, 12
Anderson, Tim   xvi, 28, 29, 42
anempathetic music   14
Anger, Kenneth   6, 129, 140
Animaniacs (1993–1998)   38
Anonymous 4   90
Antheil, George   6
Apocalypse Now (1979)   54, 82
Arcadia Players   90
Arrival, The (2006)   162
Arte Video   57–60
art form   xiv–xv, xix, 1, 2, 15, 16, 19, 34, 45, 51–5, 63, 96, 135, 164, 173, 181
Artist, The (2011)   139, 140, 142–6, 149, 151, 156, 158
art music   12, 135, 174
Art of Sound   154
Ascenseur pour l'échafaud (1958)   123
Ashbery, John   152
assimilating identifications   42
Astralwerks   58, 62
asynchronicity   xvii, xviii, 2–3, 5, 7–9, 15, 16, 18, 105, 107, 108, 115, 118, 120, 135
Audissino, Emilio   7, 43
"Auld Lange Syne"   33
Auster, Paul   xiv
Australian Graphic Festival   162
Australian Silent Film Orchestra   71
avant-garde   1, 4, 6, 7, 11, 55, 125, 130, 151, 152, 156
   filmmakers   6
   films   6, 7, 129, 134
   style   11
Axt, William   33
Ayler, Albert   6

Baczewska, Christine   xiv
Bad Boy Bubbie (1993)   144, 145
Bailey, Derek   127
*Ballerinas from Hell: A Georges
   Méliès Album* (Unknown
   Video)   58, 59
Ballet Mécanique (1924)   6, 43
Bang, Derrick   124
Barber, Samuel   2
Barfoot, Simon   71
Barrett, Dave   71
Barthes, Roland   13, 17, 25, 111
Barton, Ruth   45
Bateman, H. M.   168
Battleship Potemkin (1925)   9, 80, 174
BBC   105, 106
bebop   125
Begotten (1991)   140, 155, 156, 158
Bell, Hilary   79, 115, 135, 178
Bellano, Marco   xvi, 19–20, 28, 45
Bellini, Vincenzo   33
Benedek, László   123, 124
Bennett, Samm   xiv
Berger, Pablo   146
Berlin, Irving   44
Bernstein, Elmer   123–5, 128
Besson, Luc   155, 156
Beynon, George W.   30
BFI   51
Bird (1988)   125
Birdman (2014)   125
Birth of a Nation, The (1915)   8, 14, 32,
   33, 89, 149, 180
black-and-white film   44, 141, 145, 146,
   151, 155
Black Francis   44, 76–80, 90, 97 n.6
Blancanieves (*Snow White*, 2012)   140,
   146–8, 151, 156, 158
Blessed Angela of Foligno   92
Blessed Margarita   92
Blue Grassy Knoll (BGK)   63, 64, 70–5,
   85, 89, 91, 99 n.46, 173, 174,
   177, 181, 182
Blue Hungarian Band   27
blues   53, 80, 82, 115, 120, 126, 130, 135,
   169, 170, 178
Boese, Carl   44
Boggs, J. S. G.   106–8

Boisen, Myles   71
Bonapart, Napoleon   54
"The Bonnie Blue Flag"   33
Bordwell, David   4, 43
Boulanger, Nadia   124
Bource, Ludovic   139, 142, 143, 145, 146
Bowman, Euday   44
Boys, The (1998)   128
Brakhage, Stan   6, 140
Brando, Marlon   124
*Brand Upon the Brain! A Remembrance
   in 12 Chapters* (2006)   140,
   150, 152–3
Breakfast At Tiffany's (1961)   124
Brecht, Bertolt   10, 23, 25, 135
Brecht on Theatre (Brecht)   10
Breil, Joseph Carl   14, 32, 33, 89
Bride of Frankenstein, The (1935)   52
Brock, Timothy   51
Brody, Raoul   71
Broken Blossoms (1919)   33
Brooklyn Academy of Music Next Wave
   Festival (1989)   77
Brooks, Richard   124
Brown, Royal S.   32
Brown, Sheldon   71
Browning, Tod   xiv, 44, 108–10, 132, 162
Brownlow, Kevin   54
Brubeck, Matt   71
Buckley, Jeff   76
Bugsy Malone (1976)   39
Buhler, James   5, 13
Busch, Wilhelm   168
Butler, David   135
Bye, Matti   51
Byrd, Rob   90
Byron, Don   xiv, 80

Cabinet of Dr. Caligari, The (1920)   xiv,
   43, 44, 55, 71, 153, 174
Cage, John   179
Call of Cthulhu, The (2005)   140, 153, 158
Cape Fear (1962)   147
Captain Beefheart   76
Captain Blood (1935)   52
Carli, Philip   130
Carney, Ralph   76
Caro, Marc   157

Carter, Jason 76
Cat Power 90
"Cavalleria Rusticana" (Mascagni) 2
Cecire, Nic 179
Chaney, Lon xiv
Chaplin, Charlie 33, 140, 145, 146, 151, 156
Charlie's Country (2013) 144, 145
Chazelle, Damien 125
Chinatown (1974) 40
Chion, Michel 14
Chopin, Frédéric 112
Christensen, Benjamin 43
chromaticism 72, 75, 82, 110–13, 135, 192, 196
"cinema of attractions" xvi, 29, 51, 64
Cinematic Orchestra 44
Cinématographe 57
Citizen Kane (1941) 147
City of Lost Children, The (1995) 157
"City of Stars" (song) 125
Clair, René 6, 154
Claire (2001) 140, 153, 158
Clansman, The (Dixon) 180
classical film
    Hollywood 4, 11
    music 2, 5, 42, 130
classical music 27, 44, 54, 60, 113, 123, 129, 141, 149, 150, 152, 171
    European 13, 32
    film 42
"Classical Principles" (Gorbman) 2, 4, 5, 38, 39, 66, 114, 120, 138, 144, 170
Clayton, Jack 44
click tracks 168, 172 n.20
Club Foot Orchestra (CFO) xiv, 54, 55, 63, 64, 70–5, 90, 130, 131, 173, 174, 181, 182
Cohen, Annabel J. 4, 14
Cole, Jack 162
Coleman, Ornette 125, 126
Columbis, Mauro 130
comics xx, 161, 162, 164–7, 169, 170
Comics Code Authority 162
"Comin' Thru the Rye" 33
Committed (1984) xiv
commodification 6

compiled scores xvi, xxii n.11, 28, 29, 31–2, 34, 44, 54, 55, 85, 150, 153
complimentary 3
Composing for the Films (Eisler and Adorno) 9
computer coloring techniques 151
conduction technique 131
connotative music 3–4, 27, 144
Conrad, Tony 6
Contagion (2011) 128
contemporary film(s) 125, 126, 128, 173
    culture 36
    music 42, 43, 118, 158, 174, 176
contemporary music composers 2, 63, 64, 90, 105, 139, 167, 175
contemporary silent film music xix, xx, xxi, 15–20, 36, 43–5, 51, 54–6, 63, 64, 65 n.16, 80, 83, 84, 96, 115, 120, 123, 129–32, 135, 139, 161
    Aerial, The (La Antena, 2007) 140, 144, 148–50
    Artist, The (2011) 139, 140, 142–4
    Blancanieves (Snow White, 2012) 140, 146–8
    Brand Upon the Brain! A Remembrance in 12 Chapters (2006) 140, 150, 152–3
    Call of Cthulhu, The (2005) 153
    Claire (2001) 153
    Cowards Bend the Knee (2003) 140, 150–2
    Dracula: Pages from a Virgin's Diary (2002) 140, 150–1
    Dr Plonk (2007) 140, 144–6
    silence as voice of dystopia 155–6
    silent vs. speechless 154–5
    techniques 140–1
continuity music 4, 131, 134, 144, 165, 168
Cook, Nicholas 3
Cooke, Mervyn 14
Coolidge Corner Theater 55, 84
Cooper, Merian 13, 52
Coppola, Carmine 53, 82
Coppola, Francis Ford 2, 53–4, 128
Cora, Tom xiv, 80
Cornell, Joseph 129

counterpoint   3, 5, 7, 9, 11, 16
Cowards Bend the Knee
    (2003)   140, 150–2
Crawford, Joan   xiv
Crime and Spy Jazz on Screen, 1950-1970
    (Bang)   124
Crime Does Not Pay (1942–55)   162
Criterion Collection   51, 90
critical writing   5–7, 16, 40, 42, 52
Cronenberg, David   126
cue books   xvi, xxii n.11, 28–31, 34,
    85, 150
Cuff, Paul   54
Curtiz, Michael   52, 124
Custer, Beth   71
"Custom All the Way" (song)   79

Da Camera Singers   90
Danse du feu (*The Dance of Fire*,
    1899)   111
Dariau, Matt   80
Darth Vegas   42
Davis, Blair   43, 44, 54, 79
Davis, Carl   53
Davis, Judy   126
Davis, Miles   123
Davison, Annette   6, 11, 37
Day the Earth Stood Still, The (1951)   147
De Heer, Rolf   144, 145
Delerue, Georges   11
Deleuze and Film Music (Redner)   3
Delicatessen (1991)   157
Delteil, Joseph   89
Denio, Amy   xiv
Deren, Maya   129, 140
Der Golem, wie er in die Welt kam (*The
    Golem, How He Came into the
    World*, 1920)   75–82, 92,
    97 n.6
Deserter (1933)   9
Desired Woman, The (1927)   31
Destiny (1921)   170
Détective (1985)   11
diegetic music   11, 12, 37, 53, 84, 124,
    125, 143, 181
Die Walküre (Wagner)   82, 83
Dirty 3   90
dissonance   83, 112, 113, 130, 131, 169

Divers at Work on the Wreck of the "Maine"
    (1898)   57
Dixieland jazz   124, 125
Dixon, Thomas, Jr.   180
Djigirr, Peter   144
DJ Spooky   44, 180
dodecaphonic music   10
Donahue, Terry   84
Donen, Stanley   48, 124
Don Juan (1926)   33
Donnelly, K. J.   8, 25, 41, 45, 121
Dorf, Michael   xiv
Dörrie, Doris   xiv
Dracula (1931)   44
Dracula: Pages from a Virgin's Diary
    (2002)   140, 150–2
dramatic beats   9, 38, 56, 74, 81, 83, 85,
    86, 89, 112, 115, 130, 132, 133,
    140, 141, 143, 145, 149, 152,
    153, 156–8, 175, 178, 179
Drawn to Death: A Three Panel Opera
    (1999)   162, 163
Dreyer, Carl   89–92, 96, 173, 180
Dreyfus affair   57
Driver, The (2011)   128
Dr Plonk (2007)   140, 144–6, 151,
    156, 158
Dubin, Al   130
Dudok de Wit, Michael   155
DuJardin, Jean   142, 143
DuPont, E. A.   75
Durant, Yati E.   125, 132
DVD   51, 56, 57, 59, 60, 63, 77, 90,
    99 n.46, 153

early film music literature (1909–26)   6
Eastwood, Clint   125
Edison, Thomas   27
Edwards, Blake   124
Egner, Dick Deluxe   71
Eight Girls in a Barrel (1900)   57
Einhorn, Richard   63, 64, 89–92, 95, 96,
    173–7, 180–3
Eisenstein, Sergei   8, 9, 12, 17
Eisler, Hanns   9, 10
Eisner, Will   166
electronic music   xv, xvii, 4, 43, 44, 81,
    123, 156, 174, 179

electronic synthesizers   84
El Eternauta (Oesterheld)   149
Elgin Theater   xiv
Ellington, Duke   123
Elton, Mark   71
Emotion and Meaning in Music (Meyer)   41
empathetic music   14
Ende, Josh   71
Entr'acte (1924)   6
Equinox (1992)   126–7
Erdmann, Hans   33
Essman, Scott   156
Eureka!/Transit Film   51
experimental filmmakers   6, 56
experimental music   12, 51
experimentation   xviii, 63
"extended techniques"   133

Fadnes, Petter Frost   132
Fairy Tales: Early Colour Stencil Films from Pathé (1901–8)   51
Falconetti, Renée Jeanne   90
Farrar, Geraldine   30
Fatal Mistake, The (1894)   170
Faust (1926)   51, 53, 79, 92, 115–20, 135, 150, 178, 181
feature films   54, 84, 129, 140, 154
Feldman, Eric Drew   71, 76
Felix Woos Whoopie (1928)   130
Fellini, Federico   12
Fifer, Chad   153
Fifth Element, The (1997)   156
Film Acting (Pudovkin)   9
film festivals   xv, 45, 55, 130
film history   14, 36, 58, 70, 144, 150, 152
film music   139
  accompaniment   28–9
  analysis   3–8, 41–3
  conventions   12, 16, 19
  criticism   11
  evolution   6, 27, 28
  history   11, 14, 40
  as music for film   13–15
  practices   1, 6, 29
  styles   13
Film Music (Larsen)   42
Film/Music Analysis (Audissino)   7, 43

film music literature (1987–98)   6
film-music relationship   xvi, xix, xx, 2, 5, 6, 10–12, 17, 19, 20, 139, 149
Film Noir   106, 170, 171
Film Sense, The (Eisenstein)   8
Film Society of Lincoln Center   133
Film Technique (Pudovkin)   9
Filmworks xxv: City of Slaughter/Schmatta/Beyond the Infinite (album)   129
Flame, Opter   71
Flicker Alley   57, 58, 60–2
Foley sound effects   152
folk music   32, 54, 123
Forbidden Planet (1956)   4
Forest, Lee De   36
Forrester, Joel   xix
Four Troublesome Heads, The (1898)   57
Fox   36
Frampton, Hollis   6
Frankenheimer, John   124
Frankenstein (1931)   75
free improvisations   127, 128
French Société Générale des Films   89
Freund, Karl   75
Friedhofer, Hugo   39, 40
From the Earth to the Moon (1998)   57
Frost, A. B.   170

Gabbard, Krin   125, 135
Gance, Abel   53
Geld (1989)   xiv
General, The (1926)   71, 85–7, 89
genre   xvi, xvii, 1, 8, 13, 16, 20, 55–62, 83, 90, 110, 124–5, 132, 135, 139–40, 142, 154, 161, 169–70, 179, 182
Georges Méliès: First Wizard of Cinema (1896-1913) (Flicker Alley)   58, 60
Georges Méliès Project, The (1899–1909)   110–13, 120
German Expressionism   75, 81, 141, 148, 150, 153
Ghibli Studios   155
Gig, The (1985)   125
Glass, Philip   44, 178
Glover, Crispin   152

Godard, Jean Luc   11, 14
Goddess, The (1934)   77
Godfather (1972, 1974, 1990)   54
Godfather, Part III, The (1990)   2–3, 170
"God Save the King/Queen" (song)   112
Golden Age composers   13, 38, 40
Golden Age films   144
Golden Age of Film Music   123, 143, 144, 146, 158
Golden Boat, The (1990)   129
Goldsmith, Jerry   39, 40
Golem, The (1915)   75
Golem, The (1920)   44, 153
Golem and the Dancing Girl, The (1917)   75
Gorbman, Claudia   3, 5, 7, 10, 14, 30, 37–9, 42, 52, 114, 120, 134, 144, 164, 165, 170
Gottschalk, Louis Moreau   33
Gould, Elliott   12
Go West (1925)   71
Goya Awards   146
Graham, Gordon   128
Grand Guignol   151
graphic novels   xx, 161, 170
graphic works   163, 167, 168
Great Gatsby, The (1974)   44
Greenwood, Jonny   11, 12, 14
Grieg, Edvard   33
Griffith, D. W.   14, 32, 33, 89, 180
Gross, Milt   163, 167
Guardian, The   146
Guen, Eric Le   60
Gunning, Tom   xvi, 29, 51
"Gymnopédie No.1." (song)   166

Haas, Philip   xiv, 105–8
Hagen, Earl   39
Hancock, Herbie   125
Hands of Orlac, The (1924)   71
Hangover Square (1945)   4
hardcore   55, 123, 169
Haxan: Witchcraft Through the Ages (1922)   43
Hazanavicius, Michel   139, 142, 146
Hearing Film: Tracking Identifications in Contemporary Hollywood Film Music (Kassabian)   5

Helmer, Veit   157
Hendrix, Jimi   82
Hepworth, Cecil   27
Herrmann, Bernard   xiv, 3, 12, 16, 83, 147, 164, 165, 167
"The Hidden Heritage of Film Music: History and Scholarship" (Donnelly)   41
Hill, Andy   39, 40
historical silent film(s)   xix, xx, 1, 20, 42, 54, 129, 131, 139, 141, 144, 153, 156, 176
   era   89
   music   27–8, 55, 56, 113, 123, 155, 181
   practice   129
historical style   126, 128, 168, 169
historicity   39, 139
Hitchcock, Alfred   12, 167
Holbrook, Ben   153
Hollywood   2, 11, 39, 144, 173
Horn, Walter   77
How the Landlord Collected His Rents (1909)   31
Hughes, Ed   xix
Hugo (2011)   57
Hukkle (2002)   140, 154–5, 157, 158
humorous music   29
Huppertz, Gottfried   33
Huron, David   40
Hurwitz, Justin   125
Hydrothérapie Fantastique (*The Doctor's Secret*, 1909)   112–13

idiomatic improvisation   127, 128, 131, 135
Image/Music/Text (Barthes)   17
improvisation   27, 28, 45, 53, 80, 83, 112, 114, 115, 123, 125–9, 131–6, 179
Improvisation (Bailey)   127
improvised scores   xvi, xx, 27, 80, 120, 123, 125–32, 134–6, 152, 183
improvising musicians   126, 128, 132
Iñárritu, Alejandro   125
inaudibility   3, 5, 121
In Cold Blood (1967)   40, 124
incongruous music   29
independent films   2

Indiana Jones franchise (1981–2020)   143, 158
indie rock genre   xvii, 83
Inherent Vice (2014)   12
instrumental music   xiv, 12, 63, 76, 77, 80, 83, 178
instrumentation   4, 16, 55–7, 69, 80, 82–4, 126, 147, 182
intent   xvii, xviii, 3, 13, 15, 17, 18, 20, 29, 44, 56, 64, 65, 97, 107, 111, 118, 133, 179, 180, 184, 199, 200
In the Mirror of Maya Deren (2001)   129
In The Nursery   90
In The Shadow of No Towers (2004)   161
Intolerance (1916)   33
intra-diegetic music   7
Intrator, Jerald   124
Intersection Theater   xiv
invisibility   3, 17, 65 n.5
Irwin-Brandon, Margaret   90
"I Wish I Was in Dixie"   33

"jackass music"   xix, 28, 29
Jarvis, Duane   76
jazz   xiv, xv, xix, xx, 1, 4, 6, 12, 13, 16, 27, 39, 53, 55, 65, 73, 80, 106, 112, 114, 115, 120, 123–7, 129–31, 133, 135, 136, 143, 156, 157, 169, 170, 174, 178, 179, 182, 192
  in contemporary scores for silent film   123–7, 129–33, 135–6
  history in film   123–5
  as improvisational art form   125–7
Jazz Singer, The (1927)   1, 36
Jeck, Philip   152
Jeunet, Jean-Pierre   157
Joan of Arc   91
Joan of Arc (band)   90
Johnston, Phillip   161
Jones, Quincy   39, 40, 124
Juha (1999)   140, 157
junk percussion   84, 85, 182

Kalinak, Kathryn   3, 7, 43, 165
Kardish, Laurence   75
Karlin, Fred   39, 40
Kassabian, Anahid   5, 11, 16, 20, 25, 42, 63, 91, 111, 139

Kaurismaki, Aki   157
Kavee, Elliot   71
Kazan, Elia   124
Keaton, Buster   xiv, 63, 69–74, 86–7, 130, 144–6, 154, 174, 181
Kelly, Gene   48 n.44, 144
Kid, The (1921)   156–7
King, Clydie   12
King Kong (1933)   13, 37, 52, 53
Kino International   51, 76
Kinugasa, Teinosuke   113–15, 134
Kirk, Steve   71, 130
Knieper, Jürgen   157
Knife in the Water (1962)   123
Knitting Factory   xiv
Komeda, Krzysztof   123
Kopplin, Dave   71
Korngold, Erich   38, 52, 123, 143
Kõrvits, Tõnu   90
KTL   51
Kubrick, Stanley   38
Kudláček, Martina   129
Kutavičius, Bronius   90

Labourer's Love (1922)   71
la Falaise, Henri de   140
La La Land (2016)   125
La Marseillaise   54
Landsberger, Hans   76
Lane, Charles   156
Lang, Fritz   33, 44, 53, 75, 84, 148
La Passion of Joan of Arc (*The Passion of Joan of Arc*, 1928)   33, 89–92, 94–6, 173
Larsen, Peter   42
L'Assassinat du duc de Guise (1908)   32
Last Laugh, The (1924)   75
La Tortue Rouge (*The Red Turtle*, 2016)   140, 155, 158
Le Dernier Combat (*The Last Battle*, 1983)   140, 155
Lee, Bill   125
Léger, Fernand   6, 43
Legong: Dance of the Virgins (1935)   140
Leigh, Janet   167
Leigh, Vivien   124
leitmotifs and themes   1, 4, 35, 38, 45, 82
Le Mepris (1963)   11

lengthy close-ups   53
Leone, Sergio   12
Levi, Louis   29
Le voyage à travers l'impossible
   (1904)   133
Le Voyage Dans La Lune
   (Astralwerks)   58, 62
Lewen, Si   168
Lewis, John   124
Library of America   163
licensed music   3, 11, 20 n.5, 38, 49 n.69,
   76, 125
Ligeti, György   11, 12
"Light Cavalry Overture" (von
   Suppé)   44
Lim, Dennis   153
"Little Stars Theme"   81
live performance   xiv, xviii, xxi, 8, 13, 14,
   17, 34, 36, 37, 52, 56, 77, 97 n.6,
   129, 135, 136, 141, 145, 153,
   162, 163, 174, 179, 182, 183
"The Living Nickelodeon"
   (Altman)   25 n.75
Lloyd, Harold   44, 145, 154
Long Goodbye, The (1973)   12
Lost Weekend, The (1945)   4
Love Chariot, The (*Pushpaka Vimanam*,
   1987)   140, 154, 155
Lovecraft, H. P.   153
Lowe, Mundell   124
Lucas, Gary   44, 76–7, 80–2, 131
Lumière Brothers   27, 57
Lynch, David   124

McCloud, Scott   166
McGill University   43
McLaughlin, Shelia   xiv
McLeod, Phil   71
Macmillan, Gus   71, 174, 176, 177, 180,
   182, 183
McPhee, Eleanor   44
Maddin, Guy   84, 144, 150–3, 158
Mahler, Gustav   150, 151
Mainstream jazz   125
Malle, Louis   123
Manchurian Candidate, The (1962)   124
Mancini, Henry   123, 124
Mandel, Johnny   12

Mann, Thomas   168
Manvell, Roger   90
Man with a Movie Camera (1929)   43,
   44, 80, 180
Man with the Golden Arm, The (1955)   4,
   123, 124, 127
Maraval, Emile   27
Marguerite d'Oingt   92
Marie Menken (2006)   129
Marks, Martin   27, 32, 33, 129
Marriott, Richard   54, 71, 174,
   176, 180–3
Martinez, Cliff   128
Marvelous Méliès (A-1 Video)   58
Marxist ideology   9
Mascagni, Pietro   2
Masereel, Frans   163, 167, 168
Master, The (2012)   11, 12
Maté, Rudolph   91
Maus (1980)   161
Meisel, Edmund   9
Melbourne Recital Centre   71
Méliès, Georges   27, 56, 59, 60, 110–13,
   133, 148, 153
Méliès the Magician (Arte Video)   58–60
melodic/harmonic conventions   35, 39
melodrama   1, 29, 35, 57, 69, 70, 141,
   142, 151, 153
Melomaniac, The (1903)   111–12
Merhige, Elias   156
Merry Frolics of Satan, The (1906)   57
Mesmer, Otto   130
Messiaen, Olivier   12
meta-diegetic music   144
meter   32, 111, 135, 165, 168, 169, 172,
   179, 182
Metropolis (1927)   33, 44, 53, 55, 75, 84,
   149, 153, 174
Meyer, Leonard B.   41
"Mickey-Mousing"   38
Milland, Ray   4
Miller, Roger   84
Mill Valley Film Festival (1987)   55
mimetic music   34, 38, 83
minimalism   16, 44, 53, 58, 128, 131, 178
"Miriam and Florian" (song)   77–8
Miyazaki, Hayao   155
Mo Better Blues (1990)   125

modernity   43, 56, 69, 139, 147
Modern Jazz Quartet   124
modern silent films music. *See*
    contemporary silent film music
Modern Times (1936)   140
Modine, Matthew   127
monaural sound age (1927–56)   6
Money Man (1992)   105–8, 120
Monk, Thelonious   xiv
montage   9, 111, 113, 114, 134, 148
Mont Alto Motion Picture Orchestra   51, 55, 183
Moroder, Giorgio   44
Morricone, Ennio   xiv, 12
Morris, Butch   131
Mostow, Jonathan   57
Motion Picture Company   44
Mouly, Françoise   161
Movietone   36
Moving Pictures Show   55
Mozart, Wolfgang   33
Mr. Hulot's Holiday (1953)   154
Mulholland Drive (2001)   144
Murnau, F. W.   xix, 33, 42, 51, 53, 75, 115–20, 135, 150, 180
Murphy, Dudley   43
music
    and narrative/image   xv, xviii, xxi, 1, 2, 7, 11, 13, 16, 17, 29, 43, 45, 96, 111, 113, 125, 177, 181
    performances   1, 29, 42, 54, 141
    sound effects   29, 34, 36, 38, 52, 56, 74, 130, 133, 145, 149, 158
    structure of   35, 38, 168
Music and Sound in Silent Film (Barton and Trezise)   45
Music as a Source of Emotion in Film (Cohen)   4
Music of Chance The (novel) (Auster)   xiv
Music of Chance (film, 1993)   xiv
musicology   41, 42

Naked Island, The (1960)   140
Naked Lunch (1981)   125
Naked Lunch (1991)   126
Napoléon (1927)   53
Na Prous Boneta   92

narrative cueing/referential narrative   3, 131, 132, 135, 144, 170
narrative films   xvi, 7, 18, 36, 127, 128, 156
Necks, The   128
neoformalism   7, 43
Netherlands Radio Choir and Orchestra   90
Neumeyer, David   5, 13
New Babylon, The (1929)   9
Newman, Alfred   39, 40, 81, 123
New York Eye and Ear Control (1964)   6
New York Film Festival   84
New York Times   164
Nick Cave   90
Niehaus, Lennie   125
Nies, Troy Sterling   153
Nikita (1990), *Leon: The Professional* (1994)   156
Nina (Paisiello)   54
non-diegetic music. *See* underscore music
non-idiomatic improvisation   127, 128, 130
non-parallel approach   9
North, Alex   123, 124
Nosferatu (1922)   xix, 33, 42, 71, 174, 180
"Now You See It, Now You Don't: The Temporality of the Cinema of Attractions" (Gunning)   51
Nückel, Otto   163, 167

"Obedient Servant" (song)   77
obtuse meaning   17
Odds Against Tomorrow (1959)   124, 127
Oesterheld, Héctor Germán   149
O'Hara, Steph   71
Ondes Martinot   12
On The Track: A Guide to Contemporary Film Scoring (Karlin and Wright)   39
orchestral music   11, 12, 14, 32, 39, 41, 43, 51, 53–5, 60, 76, 80, 81, 84, 90, 124, 126, 145, 147, 149, 152
orchestration   35, 39, 51, 56, 179
organ music   35, 43, 59, 62, 129, 131, 135, 141
original scores   32–4, 84, 85, 153
Orkestra of the Underground   162

Orleans, Ela   152
OSS 117: Cairo, Nest of Spies (2006)   142
OSS 117: Lost in Rio (2009)   142
Our Hospitality (1923)   71

Page of Madness (1926)   113–15, 120, 134
Paisiello, Giovanni   54
Pandora's Box (1929)   71
Paradox Trio   80
parallelism   2, 3, 5, 7, 9, 11, 16, 21
Parker, Alan   39
parody   142
Passionate Journey (Masereel)   168
Pavkovic, Nicolas   153
Pavlenko, Piotr   8
Pawnbroker, The (1964)   40, 124
Penderecki, Krzysztof   12
Pérez de Azpeitia, Javier   51
Perez del Mar, Laurent   155
Perry, Katy   57
Pete Kelly's Blues (1955)   124
Peters, William Frederick   33
Phantom Carriage, The (1921)   51
Phantom Thread (2017)   11, 12
Phelps, Nik   71
Phillips, Barre   126
Phonophone   36
Pink Panther, The (1963)   124
The Pixies   44, 76
Planet of the Apes (1968)   40
Plastic Man (1943–56)   162
Platoon (1986)   2
Player, The (1992)   144
Poelzig, Hans   75
Polanski, Roman   123
polysynchronicity   ix, xviii, xix, xx, 24 n.63, 56, 69, 82, 83, 86, 96, 170, 181, 184
  application of   105–20
  contemporary scores for silent film   15–18
  criteria for   18–20
Pope, Joseph   76
pop music   39, 90, 156
popular music   44, 123
popular songs   13, 27, 31, 32, 129
postapocalyptic dystopia   155

postmodernism   28, 70, 75, 130, 142, 146, 171
Pouget, Leo   33, 90
precomposed music   27, 31, 32, 54, 80, 126
Preminger, Otto   123
Pré-Nom: Carmen (1983)   11
prerecorded music   14, 179
pre-sync-sound era (1896–1927)   xvi, 27, 136
"Principals of Composition: Classical Film Music: Principles of Composition, Mixing and Editing" (Gorbman)   3, 7, 38, 114, 144
Prix Spécial un Certain Regard, Cannes (2016)   155
professionalism   xvii, xx, 5, 14, 29, 89
Psycho (1960)   3, 167
psychoanalytic theory   7
Puccini, Giacomo   123
Pudovkin, V. I.   9, 10
punk   35, 169, 170
Pursuit Theme   87

Queen   57

Radiohead   11, 12
ragtime   39, 60, 83, 129, 141, 165
Rainmaker, The (1997)   128
Rapée, Ernö   30
Raw   161
"Recognisable Music" (Thorp and McPhee)   44
recorded music   57, 77
Redner, Gregg   3, 5, 41
Red Planes Fly East (1938)   8
Reel World: Scoring For Pictures, The (Rona)   40
"Reforming "Jackass Music"" (Anderson)   28–9
Reich, Steve   178
Reineger, Lotte   96, 135
Reinhardt, Max   75
Reisenfeld, Hugo   30
Ren and Stimpy Show, The (1991–1996)   38
Repo Man (1984)   170

rhythm   4, 7, 9, 13, 14, 34, 35, 38, 52, 86, 87, 111, 126, 130, 133, 147, 165
Ribot, Marc   8
Richardson, Anne   153
Ride of the Valkyries (Wagner)   33, 82, 83
Riley, Terry   178
RKO orchestra   37
Robair, Gino   71
Robert-Houdin, Jean-Eugène   56
rock   xv, xvii, 13, 16, 55, 73, 76, 79, 82, 123, 130
rock and roll   53, 107
Rogers, Shorty   123
Rona, Jeff   128
Rosenman, Leonard   39
Rossellini, Isabella   152
Rossini, Gioachino   44
Rota, Nino   xiv, 12
Round Midnight (1986)   125
Royal Winnipeg Ballet   150
Rózsa, Miklós   38, 123, 143
Rubinstein, Anton   29
Rudolph, Alan   126
Ruiz, Raul   129
Rypdal, Terje   126

Saint Saëns, Camille   32
Sampson, Caleb   84
Sánchez, Antonio   125
San Francisco International Film Festival   97 n.6
San Francisco Silent Film Festival   76, 84
Sapir, Estaban   124
Satan in High Heels (1962)   124
Satie, Erik   6, 166
Scar of Shame (1927)   80
"scene change sequence"   71–4
Schelle, Michael   128
Schifrin, Lalo   39, 40
Schoedsack, Ernest   13, 52
Schwartz, David   xiv
Science   40
Scoring for Films (Hagen)   39
Scorsese, Martin   38, 57
Scott, Shirley   178
Seduction of the Innocent (Wertham)   162
semiotics   15, 39, 41, 42, 44, 128

Serra, Eric   156
Sesame Street (TV show)   174
Sex, Lies and Videotape (1989)   128
"A Shaft of Light" (song)   117–19
Shaggy Dog Story (1979)   170
Shaping Thought (2013)   168, 170, 171
Shaporin, Yuri   9
Sheldon, Jack   12
Sherlock Jr. (1924)   69–71, 130, 144, 145, 181
Shore, Howard   125, 126
Shostakovich, Dmitri   9
Sidewalk Stories (1989)   140, 156, 158
signifier of emotion   3, 144
silence   9, 17, 29, 62, 65, 88, 113–14, 143, 144, 146, 148–50, 155, 159, 177
silent film era (1895–1927)   1, 5, 9, 14, 15, 35, 39, 51, 52, 54, 57, 64, 83, 90, 131, 144, 149–52, 154, 157, 158
silent film festivals   xiv, xv, 45, 50, 55, 65, 76, 77, 84, 97, 138
silent film music composers   173–84
silent film music conventions   34–9
Silent Movie (1976)   140, 144
Silent Movies/Loud Music (1993)   xiv
Silvers, Louis   33
Simpsons and *Futurama, The* (TV show)   57
Singing in the Rain (1952)   144
Sjöström, Victor   51
Smashing Pumpkins   57
Smedley, Julian   71
Smith, Harry   129
Smith, Jack   6, 151
Smith, Jeff   7
Smith, Jimmy   135, 178
Smulovitz, Stefan   90
Snakefinger   71
Snow, Michael   6
Snow White and the Seven Dwarfs (1937)   60
Soderbergh, Steven   128
Solano Lopez, Francisco   149
Sommer, Leo   27
"Songs of a Dead Dreamer" (DJ Spooky)   44
Sosin, Donald   130

sound film(s)   xvi, xx, 8, 15, 20, 37, 43, 144, 179
  composers   173, 174
  contemporary   xviii, 2, 11–12, 42, 154
  era   36, 39, 52, 57
  music   36–9, 105, 123, 175
  practitioners   39–41
Speed (1994)   166
Spiegelman, Art   161-4, 167, 168, 170, 171
Spirit, The (1939–2005)   166
Stacjek, Jason   152
Stalling, Carl   38
"The Star-Spangled Banner"   82
Star Wars (1977–2019)   158
"Statement on Sound" (Pudovkin, Eisenstein and Alexandrov)   9
state-of-the-art electronics   84
Steiner, Max   13, 37, 38, 52, 123
stereo sound age (1927–56)   6
Stevens, Leith   123–5
Stiletto Sisters   145
Sting, The (1973)   39
Stone, Oliver   2
Strauss, Johann   123
Streetcar Named Desire, A (1951)   124, 127
Sujatovich, Leo   149
Surrealist film   148
suspense music   16
Sweet Smell of Success, The (1957)   125
Sydney Opera House   162
symbolic music   34–5, 38, 83
"A Symposium on the Composer's Views Towards Psychology"   39
synchronicity   xvii, xviii, 2–3, 5, 7–10, 15, 16, 18, 34, 43, 56, 81, 86, 90, 105, 107, 108, 115, 118, 120, 131, 134, 135, 140, 141, 168, 184
synchronization   xxii, 9, 10, 20, 34, 66, 90
sync sound   35, 37, 52, 54, 125, 129, 155, 156

Tan, Shaun   162
Tarantino, Quentin   38
Tardif, Graham   144–5
Tati, Jacques   154

Tavernier, Bertrand   125
Tchaikovsky, Pyotr Ilyich   29, 33
Telluride Film Festival   84
tempo   xi, 2, 25, 32, 35, 38, 57, 60, 86–9, 98, 110–12, 145, 165, 168, 169, 172, 176, 177, 179, 182
  as melody   86–7
  and rhythm matching   35, 38
Ten Canoes (2008)   144
themes and motifs   64, 73, 80, 81, 83, 87, 115, 124, 130, 131, 140, 141, 146, 176, 178, 179
There Will Be Blood (2007)   11, 12
Thief of Baghdad, The (1924)   32, 33
Thieke, Michael   152
third meaning   18
Thomas, Milford   153
Thompson, Kristin   43
Thompson, Walter   131
Thorp, Jan   44
Tieber, Claus   20
Tikanmäki, Anssi   157
Tillman, Lynne   xiv
Time   40
Tiny Toon Adventures (1990–1992)   38
Today's Sounds for Yesterday's Films (Donnelly and Wallengren)   45
Torn, David   128
Toronto International Film Festival (2006)   152
"The Torture Chamber" (scene)   92, 94–6
Touch   51
Touch of Evil (1958)   124
traditional film music   80, 134, 175, 179, 181
"The Tradition of Novelty-Comparative Studies of Silent Film Scores: Perspectives, Challenges, Proposals" (Bellano)   19
Traffic (2000)   128
trapping   56, 62, 66 n.22, 74, 81, 83, 85, 86, 89, 112, 130, 133, 141, 145, 148, 149, 152, 156, 158, 168, 175, 179
Trezise, Simon   45
Tuvalu (1999)   140, 157, 158
"Twelfth Street Rag"   44
Tzadik   129

Ugress   90
underscore music   7, 11, 21 n.11, 37, 53, 84, 124, 125, 143, 158
Understanding Comics: The Invisible Art (1993)   166
"Unheard melodies? A Critique of Psychoanalytic Theories of Film Music" (Smith)   7
Unholy Three, The (1925)   77
unity music   4, 144
Unknown, The (1927)   xiv, 108–10, 120, 132, 133, 162
Unknown Video   57–9
US Library of Congress   33
US Senate Subcommittee Hearings (1954)   162

Vaché, Warren   125
Valse in Ab   112
Vampyr (1932)   77
van de Booren, Jon   90
Vandermark, Ken   131
van Vliet, Don   xiv
Variety (1925)   75
Vaughn, Bob   59
vernacular jazz   123, 124, 126, 127, 135
Vertigo (1958)   83
Vertov, Dziga   43, 180
Verzar, Jordan   162
Vilallonga, Alfonso de   147
Virtuoso, The (1865)   168
visual cues   111, 125, 134
Vitaphone   36
Vitascope   27
Voices of Light (album)   90, 91, 173, 183
von Suppé, Franz   33, 44
Voyage dans la lune (*Trip to the Moon*, 1902)   27, 56–62, 133, 148

Wagner, Richard   33, 35, 82, 83, 123
Wallengren, Ann-Kristin   45
Waller, Fats   129
Walsh, Ben   162
Walsh, Michael   54
Walsh, Raoul   32

waltz   9, 87, 112
Ward, Lynd   163, 167
Warner Bros.   31, 36, 38
Warren, Harry   130
Waxman, Franz   52, 123
Way Down East (1920)   33
Webb, Jack   124
Weber, Carl Maria von   33
Wegener, Paul   44, 75
Weill, Kurt   xiv
Weller, Peter   126
Welles, Orson   124
"We're in the Money" (song)   130
Wertham, Frederic   162
West Coast "cool-school"   125
Whale, James   52, 75
"What'll I Do" (Berlin)   44
Whiplash (2014)   125
White, Sam   145
Wiene, Robert   xiv, 43
Wierzbicki, James   154
Wild One, The (1953)   123–5
Williams, John   12, 14, 38, 40, 143, 158
"William Tell Overture" (Rossini)   29, 44
Wilson, Mortimer   32, 33
Windisch, Anna   20
Winokur, Ken   55, 84, 85, 91, 174–6, 180, 181, 183
Winters, Ben   7
Wizard, the Prince and the Fairy, The (1900)   57
Wood, Bob   162
Woods, Rowan   128
Wordless! (2013)   161–4, 167–71
wordless novel   163–5, 167
Wright, Ray   39, 40

Young, Arny   71
Young, LaMonte   178
Young Man with a Horn (1950)   124
"You're Gonna Pay" (song)   78

Zimmer, Hans   xv, 40
Zimmermann, Alijoscha   76
Zorn, John   14, 128, 131, 132

www.ingramcontent.com/pod-product-compliance
Lightning Source LLC
Chambersburg PA
CBHW062143300426
44115CB00012BA/2021